# The Gay Mystique

# The Gay Mystique

## THE MYTH AND REALITY OF MALE HOMOSEXUALITY

**PETER FISHER**

STEIN & DAY/*Publishers*/New York

First published in 1972
Copyright © 1972 by Peter Fisher
Library of Congress Catalog Card No. 73-186149
All rights reserved
Published simultaneously in Canada by Saunders of Toronto, Ltd.
Designed by David Miller
Manufactured in the United States of America
Stein and Day/*Publishers*/7 East 48 Street, New York, N.Y. 10017
ISBN: 0-8128-1431-2

*For Marc, who is everything*

*with thanks to my brothers and sisters*

# Contents

# The Gay Mystique

# How Do You Know You're Not Gay?

People tend to assume that either one is a homosexual or one is not and knows it. For some people this is true, but for most homosexuals, finding out is a slow and often perplexing process.

Many people avoid identifying themselves as homosexuals as long as possible, even when their homosexual preference is clear. When I got my notice to report for a preinduction physical, I knew that I would be expected to commit myself one way or the other. When I was finally confronted with the medical-history form, which included "homosexual tendencies" along with venereal disease, drug addiction, alcoholism, and bed-wetting, the moment of truth had come: should I check the box or not?

Looking back, there is some humor in the situation, but at the time it made me very anxious, even frightened. I had had a great deal more homosexual than heterosexual experience and knew perfectly well that I preferred men to women, but did this have to mean that I had homosexual tendencies? Actually, what I had was a lot more than tendencies, and I knew it, but I desperately tried to rationalize about the matter.

I had dated women throughout high school, and had just been through a very deep heterosexual affair that might have led to marriage (I convinced myself). I had not slept with a man in several months. Perhaps I had not really been homosexual, perhaps I would never have another homosexual experience, perhaps it had all been an adolescent phase. Why not?

Still, it would be more honest to check the box and admit to tendencies— I certainly qualified for that. But if I did so, I would be on record as a homosexual, people would want to know how I had gotten a deferral, the truth might come out to haunt me years later and cost me my job or the respect of my friends.

Almost everybody's had a few homosexual experiences, I said to myself. Why should I apply such strict standards to myself when so few other people would admit to them? The government had no right to pry into my private business anyhow. I was justified in lying, if only to protect myself—maybe it was even true that I didn't have homosexual tendencies.

I left the box unmarked and remained officially heterosexual. Years later, when I first began to really accept myself as a homosexual, I wondered how different my life might have been had I had the courage to admit it to myself back then.

Of course homosexuals know they're homosexuals. One reason this assumption is so common is that straight people tend to think of gay people as enormously different from themselves, different in ways that are almost impossible to understand, sympathize with, or ignore. They believe that homosexuals have such different interests and needs that they must experience a whole gamut of emotions different from those familiar to heterosexuals.

There is no difference. When a gay person feels lonely or hurt, he is experiencing the same things a straight person does under similar circumstances. When a homosexual is happy, his feelings are no different from those of a happy heterosexual. When two men or two women love one another, it is as beautiful and important to them as when a man and woman fall in love. There are no special or different feelings which alert one to the fact of being homosexual. Rather, it is simply that one feels the basic human emotions of love and attraction more strongly for a member of one's own sex than for a member of the opposite sex.

One's first question about sexual orientation may be raised by as obvious a thing as a strong feeling of sexual attraction for a member of one's own sex. On the other hand, the ebb and flow of emotion may be subtle and confusing. At one point one may feel a stronger attraction toward women, at another, toward men, or the feelings may be blurred by ambivalence. Some people first begin to question their sexual identity when they become concerned because they are unaware of feeling any sexual attraction toward either sex.

What does it feel like to be sexually attracted to someone of the same sex? Precisely the same as it does to someone of the opposite sex. The same sexual stirrings are there, the same sense of excitement in the presence of the other person. Most of us feel a mild degree of attraction at times for members of both sexes, but even if we are able to acknowledge these feelings, we find it difficult to believe that they differ only in intensity—and not in quality—from those of individuals whose sexual orientation differs from our own.

Some homosexuals and many heterosexuals believe that homosexuality is a matter of choice, that homosexuals could function as happy heterosexuals if they only had the gumption to switch. While homosexuality may be a matter of choice for some individuals, it is a choice only in the sense that they may or may not be willing to accept themselves as homosexual.

Many people have both heterosexual and homosexual experiences, but most of them know that they find one or the other basically more exciting, more fulfilling. Some may not be able to accept it, some may manage to live counter to their preference, but for most people sexual orientation has very little to do with choice.

You can sometimes learn to enjoy things you did not expect to enjoy, but unless you fool yourself you cannot claim to prefer what you don't prefer. Many people of a homosexual orientation find that they can and do enjoy heterosexual relations. Some give up the gay life entirely. But that is not necessarily to say that they have come to prefer heterosexual relations. All too often what they really prefer is the relief of living a heterosexual life in a heterosexual society that shows little inclination to tolerate alternatives.

Often straight people think they do not understand what goes on in a homosexual's mind, what it feels like to be a homosexual. Barriers of mis-understanding lead us to believe that other human beings differ from us in essential ways, and these barriers can be removed only when people begin to talk to one another and know one another.

There has been little communication between the gay world and the straight world. Homosexuals have been studied like laboratory specimens. They have not been asked what they think about themselves, how they feel, what their hopes are. The gay world has been analyzed, criticized, and dis-sected from the *outside,* but few have thought to ask those who live within it what it is like.

This book is written from the *inside.* It is the view of a world straight society seldom sees or understands. It is an examination of the myths straight people have about gay people—and the myths gay people have about themselves.

I cannot claim to speak for all homosexuals, for we are a diverse group. I cannot attempt to speak for gay women, for male and female homosexuals also live in different worlds, face different social problems, and see themselves through different eyes. Lesbians are speaking for themselves today.

I speak for myself. I speak as a young man who once wondered who and what he was, found that he was a homosexual living in a society which did not like homosexuals, and learned that this was not enough to keep him from carving out a life of his own. Neither as a specimen in the laboratory, nor as a case history in a psychology text, but as someone who has been in love and been alone, laughed and cried, and known the feelings you have known—I speak to you as one human being to another.

## LABELS

We label things and we think we have understood them. Not infrequently the label takes on greater significance than the thing it was intended to describe.

The word "homosexual" is used in many different ways quite apart from its actual meaning: *of the same sex*. People commonly characterize some individuals as homosexuals, as though homosexuality were a quality which could define a human being. They will sometimes explain a person's actions by saying that he or she is a homosexual, as though this explained one whole realm of human behavior. Actually the word is not nearly this precise or informative.

Homosexual love implies love between two men or two women; if a man makes love to another man, we usually label him a homosexual. But some men make love only to other men, some make love to both men and women, and many men make love to women most of the time, having sexual relations with other men only rarely. The way we usually use the word "homosexual" does not make this clear.

Kinsey* found that approximately 4 percent of the American male population was exclusively homosexual. What does this mean? To qualify as an exclusive homosexual one must never have had even the slightest sexual experience with the opposite sex. Furthermore, the exclusive homosexual has never felt any urge to become involved with women, and he has had no fantasies concerning heterosexual relations.

For the majority of people whom society considers to be homosexual, the matter is not this clear-cut. More frequently, individuals who come to identify themselves as homosexual have had both homosexual and heterosexual experiences, as have a large percentage of those who come to identify themselves as heterosexuals. Kinsey found that 50 percent of the population had experienced conscious homosexual urges sometime during adulthood— 37 percent had engaged in homosexual relations to the point of climax. Certainly not all these people consider themselves to be homosexual, nor does society judge them to be.

Individuals who mature early sexually are more likely to have both homosexual and heterosexual experiences than those who mature late. Sexuality seems to play a more important part in their lives, and they are more likely to seek sexual satisfaction with a partner of either sex than to go unsatisfied. A young man may have equal amounts of heterosexual and homosexual experience during late adolescence before settling down into one or the other pattern of sexual orientation. Who is to say at the time whether he is heterosexual or homosexual?

Homosexuality is viewed so negatively in our society that people are seldom willing to wait and see what sexual orientation an individual eventually develops. If a seventeen-year-old boy gets caught engaging in a homosexual act, he may be given the benefit of the doubt: it's just part of growing

---

*A summary of Kinsey's data is found in the Appendix. The estimate of 8 percent of the adult U.S. population as actively homosexual used in this book is a conservative one. If this seems surprising, check the figures.

up, it doesn't mean anything. But if he gets caught a second or a third time, most people will assume that this is evidence of a permanent pattern. His parents may become sufficiently worried to send him to a psychiatrist.

Where homosexuality is concerned there is a tendency to assume a degree of permanence totally unjustified by the evidence. The man who qualifies as exclusively homosexual at one period in his life may completely abandon homosexual relations, marry, and raise a family later in life. Is he still a homosexual? Was he ever a homosexual? An exclusive heterosexual may develop a preference for homosexual relations late in life without any previous indications that such a development might occur. Was he really heterosexual for years, or did he have a hidden streak of homosexuality all along?

The situation is even more complex with regard to people who have both homosexual and heterosexual experiences. Intermittent homosexual episodes are by no means restricted to adolescence. Many men pass through periods in their lives when they prefer homosexual relations and later revert to a heterosexual orientation. Some homosexuals carry on heterosexual affairs and even marry, only to find that their homosexual interests become dominant again with the passage of time.

Society, whether in the form of the cop on the beat, the psychoanalyst, the prying employer, or the gossipy neighbor, tends to be arbitrary in deciding who is and who is not homosexual. Certainly many of the people who are judged to be homosexual do not actually consider themselves to be so.

Because the labels are arbitrarily applied, it is particularly difficult for an individual to decide for himself whether or not he is gay. Society may have labeled him a homosexual, but he may not feel like one. On the other hand, he may be accepted as the very model of heterosexuality, and yet still be personally perplexed about the homosexual urges and experiences which nobody else suspects. What justifies a person in identifying himself as a homosexual, regardless of what others think?

Many people will go to enormous lengths to avoid seeing themselves as homosexuals, no matter how extensive their homosexual activity may be. Others, honestly uncertain, will avoid coming to any decision on the matter, fearing that to do so will involve a commitment one way or the other. If there is any doubt, it often seems more prudent to consider oneself a heterosexual: to identify oneself as a homosexual is no easy thing. Many people straddle the fence for several years as I did, identifying themselves as homosexuals at one time, heterosexuals at another, never quite certain where they stand.

The first hints of my homosexual inclinations came shortly after puberty. I found that from time to time I would be aroused by another boy. The excitement was not distinctly sexual: I wasn't really certain what it was. But I would feel myself drawn to another boy, want to be around him, want him for a friend. There was a certain fascination with the male body, a particular masculine beauty that affected me more deeply than comparable feminine beauty. It never occurred to me to think of myself as a homosexual—I'm not sure I had any clear idea that there was such a thing.

Throughout adolescence I had both homosexual and heterosexual experiences. For several years mutual masturbation was quite common in my neighborhood, until it began to be viewed as kid stuff. I had both heterosexual and homosexual fantasies, but as time went on the latter began to predominate.

As I grew older I found that my strongest emotions centered on my male friends. I went through several intense crushes before I finally began to wonder whether I was homosexual, but I was not yet ready to accept the idea. Through the last years of high school and during college I lived a double sexual life, becoming more and more involved in the gay world, while continuing to date women. I enjoyed my heterosexual experiences somewhat, but never found them really thrilling or satisfying.

There was just no comparison between men and women for me: emotionally and sexually men were vastly more stimulating. Only once, during an intense heterosexual affair that lasted several months, did I ever again seriously doubt that I was homosexual, in spite of my continued ambivalence about the matter. When I finally did accept myself as a homosexual, an enormous burden of confusion and uncertainty was lifted from me. I knew who I was and I knew where I stood. Life might not be any simpler as a homosexual, but at least I was no longer at odds with myself.

During the years of uncertainty I read a great deal about homosexuality and acquired a wide variety of labels to apply to myself. There were many different ways to view myself and my sexual orientation depending on which label I could convince myself applied to me, which "kind" of homosexual I was.

I placed great faith in these labels at the time, for they seemed to make it possible to deal with homosexuality on an intellectual rather than an emotional level. Everything was laid out in neat categories. Some varieties of homosexuality were not considered as serious as others, and I sometimes found comfort in convincing myself that I was not a *real* homosexual at all.

I had had far more than my share of homosexual experiences—it was difficult to pass the whole thing off as adolescent experimentation. But did this mean that I had to be homosexual? How deep did the feelings lie, how far did they go? Perhaps I was basically a latent homosexual who had just happened to let his guard slip every once in a while: an overt latent homosexual, so to speak. On the other hand, I had not accepted my homosexuality by any means. Perhaps it would be better to think of myself as a latent overt homosexual.

I dated girls, more out of duty than desire, but perhaps I was bisexual. This would not be so bad. My sexual tastes and experiences did not seem to fit the classic symptoms of oral or anal fixation—if anything, I was manually fixated. I could be suffering from an extended adolescence, or maybe a regression to an immature level of functioning. Could it be that I feared women rather than desired men? Did I have an inverted Oedipal complex or some male version of an Electra complex? Perhaps, in truth, there was nothing the matter with me at all: I might be a latent overt heterosexual, or even an overt latent heterosexual. Certainly I did not *have* to be a plain and simple homosexual, did I?

Probably the two most familiar categories used to describe homosexuals are "latent" and "overt." Medically, psychiatrically, and legally, a person is an overt homosexual if he has been caught in a homosexual act or admits ever having engaged in one. Theoretically, one becomes an overt homosexual as soon as he engages in any form of homosexual relations to climax, whether or not the rest of the world knows about it. Under this category more than a third of the American male population can be classified as overtly homosexual.

The concept of latent homosexuality raises even greater problems, for it is usually interpreted to mean that one need not even be aware of homosexual urges or fantasies to be considered a latent homosexual.

"Latent" and "overt" have been with us for years; recently the term "obligatory homosexuality" has gained popularity. With the new emphasis, at least verbal, on sexual freedom and candor, it has become less fashionable to decry homosexuality per se. After all, many people have had a brush with homosexuality at some point in their lives. In swinging circles, for example, one is often encouraged to get more out of sex by experimenting, and some people are willing to admit confidentially that they swing both ways from time to time.

In order to distinguish all these "normal" experiences from *real* homosexuality, the concept of obligatory homosexuality arises. The obligatory homosexual is a *real* homosexual—a person who is not just experimenting or fooling around. He actually prefers men to women, so much so that he rarely or never pursues heterosexual relations.

Oddly enough, I've never heard anyone speak of obligatory heterosexuality. The heterosexual who has little interest in homosexual sex and therefore devotes his time to seeking heterosexual experiences is not considered bound within the confines of a particular sexual orientation. The homosexual, however, is viewed as operating under dire compulsion. It is never made clear why one should seek something one is not interested in merely to prove that one can do so. I should have sex with women because I prefer men?

A vast array of labels are used to distinguish between supposed varieties of homosexuality. New ones crop up all the time. They are almost invariably disguised value judgments rather than neutral scientific definitions.

"Obligatory homosexuality" is a loaded term, implying that no one would choose a homosexual life-style unless obligated to do so, while other patterns of sexual behavior are presumably free of any such compulsion. Furthermore, the labels often come in pairs: some forms of homosexual behavior mean you're a homosexual, while others do not. It all depends on the circumstances under which our society tolerates homosexual activity and those under which it is inexcusable.

Homosexual "experimentation," for example, is not considered important; "situational" homosexuality means a homosexual act took place under circumstances which justify our pretending it was not really homosexual. "Latent" homosexuality is acceptable; "overt" homosexuality is unacceptable.

Most of these labels are a product of social attitudes concerning homosexuality. They do not reflect the true diversity and complexity of heterosexual and homosexual behavior, and they do little to clarify the nature of homosexual experience.

The strict separation between heterosexuality and homosexuality, the seldom-questioned assumption that the two are mutually exclusive and contradictory, makes it difficult for many people to be certain whether they should consider themselves homosexuals or not.

The act of finally identifying oneself as a homosexual is ultimately a personal one. It does not really matter what labels society applies—it is the way you think about yourself that counts. A few people never have any doubts that they are anything other than homosexual, but most gay people and many straights spend a number of years trying to arrive at an understanding of themselves.

Usually it is a matter of experience. One person will find that most of his experiences are homosexual and these are the ones he prefers. He may see no point in not identifying himself as homosexual. Another man may conclude that he is heterosexual for much the same reasons, in spite of having had occasional homosexual experiences. The person who has the most difficulty in establishing his sexual identity is the one who is unable to view any of his sexual experiences in perspective, sometimes clinging to the hope that he might be heterosexual, sometimes dwelling on the possibility that he might be homosexual.

Is there any way to know for certain? How much homosexual experience qualifies one as a homosexual?

## EXPERIENCES

Labels aside, just what is a homosexual, anyway?

The criteria society applies to determine whether someone is to be considered a homosexual or not are seldom helpful in assisting us to reach a conclusion about ourselves. How much and what kind of homosexual experience reasonably leads a person to identify himself as a homosexual?

Adolescent homosexual activity is quite common. Whether it be a circle-jerk at Boy Scout camp, mutual masturbation over a *Playboy* centerfold, locker-room horseplay, a wrestling match that begins to stir sexual excitement, or an adolescent crush that develops strong sexual overtones, the average boy has at least one experience that would be clinically called homosexual.

Even when no open sexuality enters an adolescent friendship, it is often hard to deny that some sexual feelings are present. The excitement of finding a best friend, the intense loyalty such friendships can inspire, the resentment when too much attention is paid to others—these are things most of us can recall feeling for our closest friends. Although these feelings and experiences may often occur well beyond adolescence, we generally dismiss them as "part of growing up." But where does a friendship cross the line and constitute homosexual love, even when there is no sex involved?

Even in adult life, there are various circumstances under which homosexual behavior is tolerated because it doesn't seem to mean much. Homosexual experiences of this sort are usually considered instances of "situational homosexuality," which breaks down into two basic categories, one based upon a lack of desire or intent to become involved in a homosexual act, the other based on a lack of anybody besides members of the same sex to get involved with.

Most people are familiar with the "Christ, was I drunk last night" syndrome. Standard procedure here is to become so drunk that one could not possibly be held responsible for one's acts, or even be expected to remember them. This is not uncommon between friends who have never acknowledged any homosexual element in their relationship. College roommates, fraternity brothers, and old buddies on camping trips have been known to drink themselves into such a state that one thing leads to another and they find themselves in bed together.

The next morning is awful. Your head is splitting, you feel sick to your stomach, and then, as if that weren't enough, you begin to remember. Did it really happen, or was it a dream? Does the other person remember, and what does he think of you now? Usually the situation is handled by quickly establishing that nobody recalls anything out of the ordinary. If this works, face is saved all around, and many people soon do forget. Sometimes, however, the memory cannot be suppressed and is so disturbing that the friendship cannot be saved—which is sad, since sex when you're that drunk is not usually all that much fun anyhow.

Another common variation involves sex while sleeping. If for some reason two men or boys are sleeping in the same bed, quite a bit may go on between them under the cover of sleep. Sometimes they are just barely awake and are not really aware of what they are doing. Other times it seems to be part of a dream involving heterosexual activities. In any event it too is usually easily forgotten, unless one partner has seriously misjudged the availability of the other. You have to be a pretty sound sleeper not to notice somebody playing with you.

Situational homosexuality is also permissible under circumstances of deprivation of the opposite sex; isolated military or scientific outposts, long voyages at sea, incarceration in prison, or attendance at all-male military academies or private schools. Many men find combat buddies during their military service for whom they develop a lasting affection, even though the intensity of the relationship or the memory of it may fade. Something about being in danger makes it very reassuring to be held and cared for, whether by a man or by a woman.

Situational homosexuality is no different from any other sort, except that society is willing to look the other way. The fact that *all* homosexuality—and all heterosexuality, for that matter—is situational, being dependent upon the availability of a sexual partner, is usually overlooked.

Homosexual activities are sometimes justified as an expression of "bisexuality." This is taken to mean all sorts of things. Some people say Freud claimed that all human beings were bisexual and had both masculine and feminine components in their personalities. True, but what does this have to do with who you sleep with? Others carry the notion so far that they interpret "bisexuality" to mean that a person has some sort of hermaphroditic indeterminate gender.

More often, "bisexuality" is assumed to represent some sort of fifty-fifty balance between homosexuality and heterosexuality: I like them both just as well, it makes no difference to me. This is unlikely. Many people have both homosexual and heterosexual experiences, but it would seem more sensible to speak of *ambisexuality* than bisexuality, as though there were two distinct and easily separated types of sexual activity.

There could be some people who feel absolutely the same about heterosexual and homosexual relations, but I have never met one. Most people give evidence of a clear preference for one or the other, although they may not admit it. Usually they seek out one type of sex more often than the other, or their greatest emotional involvement and enjoyment seems to lie with one or the other. These days, bisexuality does not carry the stigma of homosexuality. If one appears to view it casually oneself, some people will even consider it rather glamorous and daring. Not a few basically homosexual individuals find it easier to think of themselves as bisexual.

The homosexual experiences discussed so far would usually be considered acceptable even though overt. Many less explicit experiences lead people to wonder whether or not they may be homosexual. Where one has had a few isolated homosexual experiences in the past but has settled firmly into a heterosexual way of life with no regrets, little reason remains to question one's sexual identity. But for many people the situation is not this simple.

One may successfully adopt a particular sexual life-style and yet continue to be aware of other sexual impulses. This is true of homosexuals as well as heterosexuals, but does not usually pose a threat to the former. Some heterosexuals accept occasional homosexual impulses as perfectly natural. Others are greatly disturbed by sexual impulses that do not coincide with their image of themselves.

How do these impulses manifest themselves? Some people may find an infrequent dream about engaging in homosexual relations upsetting. Others may be aware of more or less intense homosexual feelings for a close friend. Most of these would seem perfectly innocuous if homosexuality were not such an emotionally charged subject in our society.

Some individuals are so terrified by homosexuality that they become preoccupied over what are certainly minor instances of homosexual attraction, and begin to worry about their sexual identity. Far more explicit impulses, fantasies, and feelings are common. Some men have detailed fantasies about becoming involved in elaborate homosexual experiences, but would not dream of putting them into practice. Some individuals are unable to maintain an erection or have satisfactory heterosexual relations without concentrating on a homosexual fantasy which they find especially exciting.

A great deal of guilt and anxiety over homosexual fantasies arises because such a strict distinction is made between heterosexuality and homosexuality. Some people find it highly disturbing to see any signs of sexuality that run counter to the approved heterosexual orientation. They assume that the slightest trace of homosexuality means they are homosexuals.

Homosexuality is viewed in anything but a neutral light in American society, and very few people are able to accept homosexual experiences with complete equanimity. Attempts at denial or suppression are more common. The individual who has had a number of homosexual experiences may feel guilt, which only magnifies his fear of discovery, and may seek psychiatric treatment in the hope that it will purge him of the feelings he cannot accept in himself.

It is not easy to decide whether a particular person who has had a fair amount of homosexual experience should be called a homosexual or not. There are people who identify themselves as homosexuals who have had less homosexual experience than some of those who never doubt that they are heterosexuals. Some people obviously fool themselves about their sexual orientation because they find it impossible to accept themselves as homosexuals. Others with an equal amount of experience view homosexual relations quite casually and are probably completely honest with themselves and others when they say that they are basically heterosexual. Why make an issue out of it?

Because our society makes an issue of it.

All sorts of different systems for deciding whether or not an individual should be characterized as a homosexual have been devised. Some rely upon the ratio of homosexual to heterosexual experiences, others upon the comparative emotional reactions that these different experiences evoke. Under some systems, the main focus falls upon sexual fantasies, rather than actual sexual behavior.

None of these systems are much help in deciding for oneself whether or not one is a homosexual. It's something you *feel*. Most people who are uncertain or perplexed really know deep down whether or not they are gay. More often than not, their confusion is based on uncertainty as to whether they *have* to be gay. In any event, if one's homosexual activities are discovered or suspected, the question of whether or not one is a homosexual is no longer a private matter. Society will make the decision.

## COMING OUT

We know roughly where our society has drawn the line between heterosexual and homosexual. Where do we as private individuals draw the line with respect to ourselves?

If you have had a homosexual dream or fantasy, are you a homosexual?

If you had adolescent homosexual experiences, are you a homosexual?

If you have had a few homosexual experiences as an adult, are you a homosexual?

If you spent a period of your life as a homosexual, but now find heterosexual relations more rewarding, are you a homosexual?

If most of your sexual experiences have been homosexual, yet from time to time you have had relations with the opposite sex, which are you?

Granted that sexual behavior ranges across a broad continuum, does it really make sense to distinguish between homosexuals and heterosexuals at all?

The distinction between homosexuality and heterosexuality is arbitrarily defined; definitions are applied on the basis of public evidence. Most of us are aware of having preferences one way or the other and think of ourselves as either heterosexual or homosexual. At some point in our lives we reach a point at which our sexual orientation becomes a major part of our personal identity.

The person who thinks that he might be homosexual is not likely to embrace the idea with much joy at first. He knows that society strongly disapproves of homosexuals, he may have guilt feelings himself, and he can assume that life is likely to be more difficult as a homosexual than as a heterosexual. Even if he has an overwhelming preference for homosexual relations and has had extensive homosexual experience, he may hold back from the final admission to himself that he is homosexual. He may view his behavior as part of a phase that will someday come to an end, or he may feel that with a great deal of self-determination and control he can develop the heterosexual interests that he presently lacks. Many homosexuals go through an enormous inner struggle before finally accepting a homosexual identity and life-style.

In the gay world, this whole process is referred to as "coming out." There are various degrees of coming out. One has come out in a sense the first time one takes one's homosexual interests beyond the point of fantasy and actually becomes involved in a homosexual experience. In a more powerful sense, one has really come out when one accepts one's homosexuality.

In most cases, coming out is a long, slow process that begins with the first awareness of homosexual interests and feelings of attraction for members of the same sex, often during adolescence. The first indications of homosexuality need not appear this early, however, but can develop at any time during one's life. In either case, coming out is no easy thing.

Were ours a more tolerant society, individuals who felt homosexual inclinations would not have to be afraid to act on them. There would be no need to hide, no need to attempt to develop a heterosexual orientation if it did not come naturally.

Even after a person has come out in the sense of having had his first real homosexual experience, it may be years before he ever comes to actually identify himself as a homosexual. Some people find it unbearable to think of themselves as being gay; society has told them all their lives that homosexuality is wrong and they are unwilling to recognize or accept it in themselves.

At this point many homosexuals attempt to go straight, believing that in time they can develop an "acceptable," heterosexual preference. More often than not, they fail. The whole notion that if a homosexual forces himself to engage in heterosexual relations he will eventually come to prefer them through sheer force of habit is sadly erroneous. Habit may lead a homosexual to follow one particular type of homosexual life-style rather than another, but it cannot make him something he is not.

The same myth is responsible for a large part of the hostile treatment homosexuals receive in our society. When sexual orientation is believed to be a matter of choice, it becomes easy to see the homosexual as a criminal or sinner, deliberately refusing to conform to the standards of his society. Parents and friends find it hard to understand or accept homosexuality when they assume that it is deliberately chosen. They may wonder what motivated the "choice," interpret it as selfish or malicious, and believe that it can be revoked simply by making another decision.

The greatest cost is that paid by the homosexual himself. As long as he still believes that it is possible for him to choose not to be homosexual, and devotes himself to a desperate struggle for heterosexuality, he can never come to terms with himself. He is unable to establish his own identity because he is unable to accept himself. He has always been told that it would be better to be someone else, and that he could be if he tried.

This is why the act of identifying and accepting oneself as a homosexual marks a major turning point in so many lives. The inner conflict is over and one is suddenly free to be himself. There may be many difficulties in living life as a homosexual that would not have to be faced as a heterosexual, but the reverse is probably true as well. More important, one is no longer at war with himself. The energy which was devoted to denying one's self can now be re-directed toward building a happy life. For some people this is anything but easy, but at least they know who they are, and this is a start.

Does this mean that if one is once a homosexual he will always be a homosexual? No, it simply means that he has very little control over the matter one way or the other. The factors that influence sexual orientation are so numerous and complex that there is no way to accurately predict the future course of anyone's sexuality.

There are some people living their lives as homosexuals who would be happier if they realized that they are heterosexuals. There are some people living their lives as heterosexuals who would be happier if they realized and accepted the fact that they are homosexuals. But everyone will be happier accepting himself as he is in the present and letting the future take care of itself.

# How Do You Get to Be a Homosexual?

People who have come to identify themselves as homosexuals may nevertheless continue to disguise the fact from others. Unless one lives in one of the gay ghettos in a few of the larger cities in the nation, there are usually good reasons for hiding it. If one is obviously or openly gay in any but the most liberal of communities, he stands a good chance of verbal abuse at the least, physical attack or arrest at the worst. If one permits his employer to find out, he may quickly be out of a job. If he tells his friends, they may cease being friends.

Probably the most difficult part of coming out in public is facing one's parents. In a few families, the discovery of a son's or daughter's homosexuality presents no difficulties. Some parents feel that their children are entitled to their love no matter how drastically they fly in the face of social convention. But in most cases, the admission or discovery of homosexuality puts family relationships under a severe strain. Some parents withdraw their love and affection; a few even legally disown their children. Some Orthodox Jews even go through a ritual period of mourning, as if their child were dead. Most parents, however, simply have no idea how to handle the situation or the painful emotions it raises in all those involved.

Resentful of the issue their child has forced them to face, hurt, even repelled, many parents become angry at what they are unable to see as anything but willful perversity. Nevertheless, they are likely to blame themselves and wonder where they went wrong.

How did it happen?

## SEDUCTION

Like heterosexuality, homosexuality is something that one is usually aware of long before he ever has any overt sexual experience with it. It is just about as sensible to blame seduction for homosexuality as it is to blame seduc-

25

tion for heterosexuality, yet this is one of the more common theories about the origin of homosexuality. Who has not heard the familiar fairy tale of the ominous stranger, dressed in a trench coat, pockets filled with candy, lurking around the playground, luring small boys to moral disaster from which they never recover?

This myth persists, in spite of the fact that the vast majority of cases of child molestation involve heterosexuals and are often incestuous. And what do we mean by seduction, anyway? If we are talking about coercion, we are again talking about something statistics show to be extremely infrequent among homosexuals. Compare the incidence of female rape with the incidence of male rape; the latter is extremely rare.

If we are talking about mere suggestion, what makes one young person susceptible and another not? If a teen-age boy is seducible, it is usually a pretty clear indication that he has already discovered homosexual interests within himself and is pleased to finally find himself in a situation where he can do something about them. Considering all the sanctions against homosexuality in our culture, it should be rather obvious that homosexual inclinations generally precede acquiescence to homosexual seduction.

The seduction myth would have it that young boys are lured into homosexual experiences by an older homosexual who forces them to perform fellatio on him or compels them to let him perform the act on them. Having once had such an experience, the young boy develops an overwhelming liking for it, seeks it out, and eventually becomes actively homosexual in order to find partners—or victims—for himself. Those who believe this myth apparently think the seducer stupid enough to put his penis in the mouth of someone violently opposed to having it there. It seems unlikely that even the most talented homosexual could raise an erection in a terrified child. There seems to be an underlying notion that homosexual sex, rather than being repulsive and unnatural as is usually claimed, is so exotic that even an unwilling minor encounter with it will turn a child into a permanent "pervert."

The assumption that a few homosexual experiences can so strongly shape a young person's sexual tastes is highly questionable, unless those tastes are well developed to begin with. Were suggestion and seduction as powerful as all that, it seems unlikely that there would be any homosexuals at all, considering the great lengths to which our society goes in promoting women as the only acceptable sex partners.

In the vast majority of cases, there has to be a predisposition for homosexuality if seduction is to have any chance at all of leading to a homosexual life-style. Furthermore, considering the effects of heterosexual rape on young women, and the fears which such an experience can raise of any future heterosexual relations, it would seem that few things could be more effective in turning a young boy against homosexuality than an unwelcome homosexual seduction.

Seduction is hardly the word for what actually goes on in most cases. The teen-age boy who feels a strong attraction for other boys or men is likely to devote a good deal of thought and effort to finding some situation in which he can manage to be seduced. The urge to have a homosexual experience is just as strong in the homosexually oriented youth as the urge to have a hetero-sexual experience is in his straight counterpart. Heterosexual kids know enough about their sexual drives to actively seek satisfaction—is there any reason to believe that gay kids don't?

The myth of seduction fails both in logic and in fact. Some gay people say that they have been gay all their lives, and that they spent years wanting to have a real homosexual experience before they ever managed to arrange one. Others will speak of a period of ambivalence during which they were not sure whether they were gay or straight, but go on to tell how they sought out homosexual experiences and soon found that their ambivalence vanished and their gay preference became unquestionable.

The stories many gay people tell about how they had to plan and scheme simply to find a safe opportunity to have their first real sexual encounter seem humorous on one level, yet sad when one considers the unnecessary years of loneliness and frustration. Many individuals who have considered themselves homosexual since early adolescence find no way of expressing their sexual interests until well into adulthood. But some find ways of realizing their fantasies, and such first experiences can be memorable.

I had had a few experiences with mutual masturbation by the time I was fifteen, but I had never really had a romance. I found myself developing a strong crush on a close friend but didn't know whether my feelings were reciprocated. There was a charged feeling in the air when we were together; when we touched, it was electrical. But did he feel the same things? I didn't dare make a move.

One afternoon we were alone in my home after school and happened to end up upstairs in my bedroom. Oddly enough, we were both quite tired and made a point of mentioning how nice it would be to take a nap for a little while. I told him he could use my bed—I could sleep on the floor or sack out in my brother's room. He wouldn't have any of that: there was plenty of room for both of us on my bed, no reason for me to be uncomfortable. Well, all right.

Before long, we were under the covers together making love. He fell asleep afterward and I lay there for an hour or so watching the afternoon sunlight fall on his face, looking at the beautiful lines of his eyebrows, his mouth, his cheek, watching him breathe. It was a moment to hold and cherish, never to be forgotten.

Most first experiences take place among youngsters of approximately the same age, but high school is seldom a very encouraging environment for a young homosexual. It is a rare adolescent romance of any sort which survives into adulthood. Generally the young homosexual quickly realizes that he must move outside the circle of his peers and his high school friends if he is to find the sort of relationships he wants and needs. A homosexually oriented adolescent may seek out older boys or men he thinks are gay. He may also begin to frequent the nearest cruising areas, where homosexuals meet, if he has heard of them and is able to locate them.

The influx of young homosexuals into the gay world occurs not because older homosexuals strive to draw them in, but very simply because it is the only place they can be themselves. While the heterosexual youth can spend his high school and college years dating and having romance after romance with complete public approval, the young homosexual must leave his regular social circles to find any sort of emotional satisfaction and acceptance.

It is no easy thing to strike out on one's own like this. Often a great deal of anxiety and guilt is involved. Social and real or anticipated parental pressures on the young boy have often made him feel ashamed and ambivalent about his homosexuality. As a result, when he encourages an older homosexual to become involved with him, he may often protest—if he is discovered —that he has been seduced or molested.

It wasn't my fault, he made me do it, says the boy, often with the encouragement of his parents. What else can he say, when to admit that he *is* homosexual will lead to family agonies he shudders to imagine? It wasn't his fault, there's nothing queer about our boy, his parents sigh with evident relief. What else can they say when to acknowledge that their son might be homosexual will lead them to blame themselves?

Not all instances when an accusation of seduction or molestation is made are as easy to understand as this. Occasionally young sociopaths set out to destroy the reputation and career of someone they particularly dislike or who they feel looks like a homosexual. Against an accusation of homosexual advances or molestation, the *victim* has little possible defense. Who is more likely to be believed: the suspected criminal, who obviously has something to gain by lying, or his poor young victims, who are so repelled and upset by their experiences that they may even be unable to agree on the details? Lillian Hellman's play *The Children's Hour* poignantly illustrates the havoc such child's play can wreak in the lives of heterosexuals as well as homosexuals.

The adolescent who has accepted himself as homosexual and wishes to become involved in the gay world seldom finds it easy. It is not simply a matter of standing on the street corner for five or ten minutes waiting to be picked up by the local homosexual. Unless he lives near a large city, the average high school boy is seldom aware that the gay world exists. Many young men find few opportunities to practice their homosexuality until they finish school, go off to college, enter the service, or get a job.

By the end of my senior year in high school, I had heard that there were gay bars in Greenwich Village, so I decided to take a train into the city to see what I could find. At first I couldn't even find the Village—the subway system completely baffled me. When I did find the Village, I had no idea where to look for the bars, so I spent the evening wandering around aimlessly, hoping that something would turn up. Finally something did.

A young guy with a beard had been following me for about a quarter of an hour, but made no move to catch up and approach me. I walked as slowly as possible, stopping to tie my shoelaces, pausing at corners and peering in all directions as though lost, glancing back and trying to look available. Was he really following me or was it just my imagination? Finally he moved in while I waited at a corner for the light to change.

Quickly I pulled out a cigarette, nearly breaking it in the process, and began to fumble for matches as though I didn't have a pack in my hip pocket. (I had heard that this always worked.) Sure enough, the fellow offered me a light, struck up a conversation, and invited me up to his apartment to look at slides of his vacation.

I ended up in his flat, drinking warm wine out of a dirty coffee cup, and watching an endless series of painfully boring slides. I began to wonder whether he was gay after all—maybe he was just lonely.

Finally, showing uncharacteristic courage, I casually mentioned that I had heard there were a number of gay bars in the Village. This seemed to break the ice, and we soon ended up in bed, where I first learned that beards can be damned abrasive. I took the train home that night and had a difficult time the next morning explaining to my parents why my cheeks were so scratched and red: must be a heat rash of some sort.

Adolescence can be a lonely and painful period of life for the boy who has discovered that he is homosexual. If his parents suspect the truth, he may be under constant pressure to demonstrate an interest in heterosexual relations which he does not feel. Some boys leave home before they have finished school because they find their family situation unbearable or because they have heard of the gay life in the big city and can think of no other way to find the companionship and acceptance they need.

The underage boy who leaves home in search of the gay life is too young to get into the gay bars if he manages to locate them, and it is difficult for him to meet homosexuals anywhere else. Unless he looks a good deal older than he is, he will be recognized as jailbait and carefully avoided by most gay people. Parents often send the police to look for runaways, so few homosexuals will risk any involvement with them. Too often, the young homosexual who has fled to the city hoping to find companionship and affection ends up hustling simply in order to have food money, and a place to sleep.

Youth is at a premium in the gay world, but this does not mean that homosexuals are attracted to children. There is no question that a good-looking young man about twenty is usually considered most desirable—this is the age at which heterosexuals seem to consider young women most attractive. Most homosexuals, however, are drawn to those of roughly their own age, simply because they have more in common with them.

If a boy of sixteen or seventeen comes to the city and is forced to hustle for a living, his greatest hope will be to find an older homosexual who is willing to risk an involvement with him to get him off the streets. Occasionally this will happen. Some young men manage to find a healthier environment and finish their education when an older homosexual takes them under his wing. Frequently by the time the boy has grown a little older the difference in age between him and his benefactor makes the relationship unstable and he will seek a younger companion. There are some homosexuals who have helped several young men find their way in life, but who themselves end up alone.

A very fine surgeon I know has had an endless stream of young men wander in and out of his life, mostly boys who have joined the Navy at the earliest possible age and then found that it is not all that exciting a life. He has provided a few of them with cars and spending money that the average kid would hardly dream of enjoying, and yet he has gotten very little personal reward out of these relationships. Most of these young men consider themselves heterosexual and wouldn't consider having sex with him—they conveniently view the relationship as platonic. After a few months or years they vanish, seldom to be seen again. Who has taken advantage of whom?

Far fewer homosexuals risk involvement with adolescents than do heterosexuals, and not just because there are fewer homosexuals. The enormous social pressures on the homosexual make it necessary for him to exercise far more discretion in sexual matters than heterosexuals. The risks involved in approaching someone who is not homosexual are considerable, but those involved in approaching someone underage, even if he is homosexual, can be even higher. The law will come down with a far greater vengeance on the homosexual discovered in such a compromising situation than it is ever likely to on a heterosexual in similar circumstances. How many young men twenty-one years old, for example, have sexual relations with young women under eighteen? How many of them are prosecuted for statutory rape if the affair comes to public attention? The situation is rather different for homosexuals. Gay people tend to be well aware of their vulnerability to unequal application of the law.


## PSYCHIATRY

Popular notions concerning the "causes" of homosexuality have ranged from demonic possession to seduction. In recent years, the majority of the attempts to isolate causative or curative factors have originated in the psychiatric establishment.

It would be unfair to lay the blame for all or even most of modern psychiatry's excesses on Sigmund Freud. His tumultuous relationship with his longtime friend and collaborator Wilhelm Fleiss led him to no small amount of confusion and concern about his own sexual identity, and he carefully refrained from committing himself to any final judgment on homosexuality and its origin. Nor would it be fair to criticize the psychiatric and psychoanalytic profession as a whole.

Some psychiatrists and analysts in recent years have challenged the dogmatic appraisal of homosexuality as a form of mental illness. Some have been instrumental in helping their homosexual patients build constructive and rewarding lives *as homosexuals,* in spite of the many pressures to which our society subjects them.

But such practitioners are too few and far between, and the psychiatric establishment has done more than any other institution in our society to perpetuate the public's confusion, misinformation, fear, and hostility regarding homosexuals. None of the elaborate psychiatric theories proposed over the last several decades have contributed anything of real significance to our understanding of homosexuals.

The seduction theory, used to explain the development of homosexual tendencies in young boys, is rarely applied when a person's first homosexual experience occurs later in life, especially after a history of frequent heterosexual experience. But if seduction is not the cause of late-blooming homosexuality, what is?

One of the most popular psychiatric theories rests upon the idea of fixation at various levels of sexual development.

Although Freud conscientiously avoided the attempt to develop any master theory to explain homosexuality, his theory of stages in psychosexual development was rapidly adapted by his followers to explain homosexuality. The basic theory behind the argument was that in growing to adulthood, each child passed through several stages during which different parts of his body provided the prime focus for sexual feelings.

First the child passed through an oral stage, during which sexual excitement and gratification centered on the mouth. As he grew older and gained control over his bowel functions, the sexual importance of the mouth diminished and anal functions took on primary sexual importance. Next, the child entered the phallic stage, during which he took an intense interest in his genitals.

The phallic stage was characterized by a fascination with the organ itself, its appearance, its functions, and, in a vague, childlike way, its fantasied potential. More important, the male child was believed to take increasing interest in the mere fact of his possession of a penis, while female children lacked one. This was to lead to fears that the penis might vanish or be taken away.

It is here that the Oedipal phase was said to begin. Fear and anxiety about castration were believed to rise to such an unbearable intensity that the child suppressed, and finally repressed, his newly awakened sexual preoccupations and entered the phase of latency, during which his conscious interest in sexual matters was supposed to be minimal. When hormonal and physiological changes began to occur, the boy was said to be entering the final phase of genital sexuality, in which he had a fairly accurate idea of what his genitals could and couldn't—should and shouldn't—do, and sought to put them to use.

To enter the genital stage, however, was not to realize it. Only those who progressed to the point of engaging in heterosexual genital intercourse, and preferably to marriage and child rearing, could be said to have made an adequate genital development. The most preferred form of sexual behavior in our culture was defined as the only proper form of sexual adjustment, the goal of a confusing and arduous process of sexual maturation.

How does this psychoanalytic theory of sexual maturation apply to homosexuality?

Since by this theory the ultimate goal of human sexuality is heterosexual genital intercourse, preferably involving conception, any sexual behavior that deviates from this course represents a failure of development, a fixation at some earlier stage. Even heterosexual behavior that deviates from the standard of genital intercourse is considered a partial—but permissible—regression to earlier levels of development. So long as the behavior is heterosexual and genital intercourse takes place with some regularity, it is acceptable.

Where is the homosexual fixated? With homosexuality being as diverse as it is, the explanations are so diverse as to be meaningless.

The theory of psychosexual development is used to explain homosexual behavior of all varieties. The exclusive homosexual who started young and never had any interest in or experience with the opposite sex, according to this theory, never passed beyond some crucial stage, usually determined by his sexual tastes. The homosexual who comes out later in life, perhaps after a good deal of heterosexual experience, has regressed to an earlier stage of development.

Not all homosexuals do the same things in bed. They engage in a wide variety of sexual practices, including fellatio, anal intercourse, mutual masturbation, and various combinations of these, as do many heterosexuals. Nor does each homosexual restrict himself to only one of these sexual acts. Preferences vary, but most homosexuals engage in different sexual acts with different partners and experiment with different sexual acts and "roles" with the same person when they enter into a relationship.

What does this make of the theory of fixation? Are homosexuals fixated simultaneously at all different stages except the ultimate one, or are they fixated at one stage one night, another the next, depending on what kind of sexual act they perform? Why is the "active" role in anal intercourse an indication of "phallic fixation," while the "active" role in vaginal intercourse is a sign of "genital maturity"? Why is it "oral fixation" if a man blows a man, but a harmless regression if a woman does so? Just where is the homosexual who also enjoys heterosexual intercourse fixated?

It would seem to be rather apparent that the people who can most credibly be accused of fixation are those who have the narrowest sexual experience. At the top of the list would be the heterosexual who never strays beyond genital intercourse.

The real value of Freud's recognition of infant sexuality was severely undercut by the imposition of artificial, culturally determined pigeonholes in which to fit the different aspects of sexuality which were socially unacceptable in adults. Children do indeed have sexual feelings, but the impression that these appeared in discrete stages and passed in succession until finally repressed in latency reflects our cultural pattern of child rearing, rather than any rigid law of human sexual development. The theory was matched to the social requirements of one cultural tradition and stripped adult sexuality of all those dimensions which our Judeo-Christian tradition had defined as nasty and inappropriate.

The theory of psychosexual development is closely linked with another theory that is often presented as an explanation of homosexuality: the theory of sexual identification.

At a superficial level, there is little to quarrel with in the theory of sexual identification. Certainly children identify with their parents, adopt many of their characteristic mannerisms and some of their personality traits. Male children tend to adopt more of these aspects from their fathers, and female children from their mothers, but few children can be said to have identified solely with one parent.

The theory runs into trouble when it is applied to explain homosexuality. Homosexuals, it is argued, are the product of faulty identification. Perhaps it is a matter of cross-identification: the young child identifies with the parent of the opposite sex and adopts a sexual orientation "inappropriate" to his gender. There may be what is referred to as an inverted Oedipal complex: the child is overwhelmed by sexual feelings for the parent of the same sex. Or homosexuality may develop as a failure to resolve a standard Oedipal complex. The boy must be so terrified about possible retribution for his sexual attraction toward his mother that he will redirect it toward his father and other males.

The issue becomes still more confused when sexual roles are brought into the picture. It is assumed to be axiomatic that the male sexual role is "active" or "aggressive," while the female role is "passive." This leads to the most incredible casuistry. The person who inserts something—a penis, a finger, a tongue, or a dildo—is taking the masculine role, unless perhaps his or her partner suggested the idea, in which case the latter may well be considered the sexual "aggressor," playing out the masculine role. The person who allows something to be inserted into him or her is taking the feminine role, unless, of course, etc.

The sexual identification theory is even more inadequate when homosexuals are asked about their sexual identity. The vast majority of male homosexuals see themselves as men and have no desire to be otherwise. The vast majority of female homosexuals see themselves as women and have equally little desire to alter the situation. After all, to be homosexual implies that one is attracted to members of the same sex, and not, as some people continue to believe, that one wishes to be another sex.

But we have yet to exhaust the tortuous meanderings of the sexual identification theory. Family dynamics are immediately trotted out to bolster the argument.

Is mother too domineering, too strict? Then the baby will fear her and develop a lasting aversion to women. Or perhaps the child will decide that his mother has a good thing going and try as best he can to act like a dominating woman himself. Is father away at the office too much, is he too passive, too weak-willed? Then the child will have no real man to identify with and will come to see himself as a woman. Or, perhaps, repelled by his bossy mother, he will spend his life trying to seduce a substitute for the father he could never really depend upon.

The number of variations on this approach which have been put forth as major insights into the causes of homosexuality stagger the imagination. Probably the most widely known and popular version of this theory has been that of the "clinging mother." However you define a "clinging mother," it is undeniable that some homosexuals must have had one. So must some heterosexuals, unless a clinging mother is defined as one who has only homosexual children.

The sexual identification theory is deemed useful because it can provide an endless stream of alternative explanations for homosexual behavior, none of which can be proved or disproved by scientific evidence.

But the theories claiming to explain the origin of homosexuality have by no means been exhausted. Some speak of characteristic patterns of ego defenses and personality structure; others emphasize self-image, narcissism, or an ingrained neurotic need for failure and humiliation. Some analysts have pointed to paranoia as a psychological concomitant of homosexuality, as though homosexuals in our society had no real reason for feelings of paranoia and persecution.

Some researchers have claimed that homosexuality is hereditary. This notion first achieved scientific stature after it was discovered that in some insect species there was a sort of neuter gender, the worker which did not reproduce. It was not realized at the time that other factors than genetics alone were involved in this phenomenon, so it was simple to draw the conclusion that homosexuals could be equated with insects. After all, they didn't know what sex they were, they were neither men nor women, and they didn't reproduce. It must be heredity. Actually, studies of identical twins have failed to produce any evidence that there is a gene for homosexuality.

There seems to be no limit to the proliferation of theories regarding the causes of homosexuality, but this is more a sign of the enormous anxiety our society generates about homosexual behavior than an indication that any wealth of meaningful and relevant data exists. The research techniques upon which most of these theories are based are shockingly and inexcusably unprofessional.

These theories can be discredited on intellectual and scientific grounds alone, but they appear in an even worse light when their effects upon individual lives are considered. Few people enjoy being psychologically dissected like laboratory specimens. The homosexual must deal with this treatment constantly in situations ranging from esteemed and learned professional journals to vulgar everyday conversations.

Sadly, not a few homosexuals accept one or another of these theories and spend years in self-mutilating introspection and self-criticism, striving to suppress and erase major portions of their personality in order to conform to "expert" diagnoses.

These theories take a toll not only on homosexuals but also on many heterosexuals. Some individuals suspect themselves of latent homosexual tendencies because their childhood seems to have matched this or that classic syndrome presented in a textbook on abnormal psychology. The parents of homosexuals flagellate themselves over where they went wrong, how they failed as parents, and go through years of guilt and self-punishment for imaginary faults over which they could have had no control anyway.

If we must continue to seek some sort of causal explanation for homosexual behavior, there is no need to turn to the contradictory array of psychiatric theories. A far more adequate understanding of homosexuality and its general development can be acquired through the application of a little common sense.

## GROWING UP GAY

In a sense we already know what causes homosexuality, and that is the lack of specificity of our sexual instincts. Every human being is the product of a unique genetic heritage and set of experiences. There is no one way one gets to be a homosexual—there are as many ways as there are homosexuals. The same, of course, is true for heterosexuals.

A predisposition for homosexuality may well have its origin at the genetic level for some people. Physical appearance and constitution may be formative in a social context. People inside and outside of the family will react and respond to a child in different ways, depending upon his or her looks, temperament, talents, and intelligence. There may even be a genetic basis for individual differences in sensuality, preferences for particular types of sexual stimulation—who knows? But none of these possibilities alone is likely to account for the development of any particular child as a homosexual.

Similarly, factors of both a sexual and a nonsexual nature may influence the development of a child's sexual orientation, tastes, and activities, as well as his personality in a more general sense. Circumstances beyond anyone's control may make one year more influential than another in predisposing a child toward a particular sexual orientation. For each child, important periods of growth, the acquisition of new skills and learning, the development of new physical capabilities, and the elaboration of social interactions occur under different circumstances.

Relationships within the family may lay down general predispositions toward members of the two sexes, but it is highly unlikely that homosexuality or heterosexuality is predetermined. Parental attitudes toward sex and the manifestations of those attitudes in relation to the child may again lead to general predispositions, but the fact that siblings from the same family background often show an enormous diversity in their adult sexual behavior makes it unlikely that anything final is determined in this way.

The general outlines of a child's developing sexual orientation are probably laid down during his first five years of life and are less likely to undergo any basic modification the older he gets. This does not usually mean that his adult pattern of sexual behavior is determined, however. Only in the case where innate constitution, experiences, and interaction with the family have reinforced one another and produced an overwhelming predisposition for one orientation is the opposite orientation likely to be ruled out. Such a child may become an exclusive heterosexual or an exclusive homosexual, but social experiences in the coming years may make it impossible for him to adopt either a homosexual or a heterosexual pattern of adult behavior.

More commonly, both homosexual and heterosexual predispositions of different strength will take shape during these first years. Without any further influence, the child would be most likely to adopt a sexual pattern based on his dominant predisposition. Later experiences, however, may lead him to temporarily or permanently adopt a sexual pattern at odds with his dominant predisposition.

As the child begins to develop a social life outside the family, as he learns how to interact with his peers, the opportunity for new experiences may have some influence on his sexual development. If the experiences are sexual, their influence will be conditional on a number of factors, including whether they were enjoyable or threatening, whether they occurred during a period of tranquillity or anxiety, how the other child or children involved reacted to them, and how parents and other adults reacted if they were discovered. Again, nothing is preordained.

With the advent of puberty the possibility for sexually formative experiences is probably increased. Sex becomes a socially legitimate concern for the young person. He becomes increasingly aware of the sexual aspect of the adult world; he may get his first detailed information or misinformation about the mechanics of sex; and his parents are likely to become suddenly more aware of his sexuality, expressing greater interest, concern, and protectiveness than he has been accustomed to.

At the same time, his private sexual world becomes more elaborate. He may begin to masturbate and find that some fantasies are more pleasurable than others. His sexual ideas, fantasies, activities, and techniques may be influenced by the neighborhood lore passed around the circle of his peers. Yet there are unpredictable things he will discover for himself—parts of his body that are particularly erotic or sensitive, feelings for which he has no precedent, and ways of relating them to his personality and experience that are ultimately personal.

Part of his sexual development is out in the open, subject to direct attempts at influence by those around him, but another part of it is deeply personal and very unlikely to surface: it is in his own hands. His parents are seldom aware of the existence of this private sexual world, much less its details, and there is little they can do in any case to affect it deliberately.

If the young boy is going through adolescence in an environment where sexual activity is not restricted—an unlikely case for either heterosexual or homosexual relations in our society—he may be able to bring his inner sexual world into harmony with his external sexual behavior. Real sexual experiences will temper his fantasies, and a fair degree of congruence between them may result.

On the other hand, as is more often the case, if sexual activity is discouraged, his inner sexual makeup is likely to become the dominant focus during adolescence and have an important influence on his future sexuality. Fantasies which for lack of other varied experience become the center of the adolescent's sexual interest may shape the nature of later sexual behavior, whether it turns out to be heterosexual or homosexual. We can probably trace the development and consolidation of fetishes, sadomasochistic tendencies, and other so-called perversions to this sort of situation.

For some adolescents, a large number of earlier factors may already

have predisposed them toward a particular sexual orientation. Such a predisposition may lead to a lasting sexual preference depending on the adolescent's first real sexual experiences.

The heterosexually predisposed young person whose first heterosexual
experiences are disastrous, unsuccessful, or followed by consequences with
which he cannot cope may enter a homosexual phase or develop a lasting
homosexual orientation out of fear of heterosexual relations. If there is a high
premium on success in heterosexual performance, failure—or the fear of it—
may lead a heterosexually predisposed adolescent to turn to homosexuality
or to reject sexuality of any type. If, on the other hand, the first heterosexual
experiences are rewarding and fulfilling, he will have little reason to explore
the realm of homosexual experience.

Much the same is true for the adolescent who is largely predisposed
toward homosexuality. Social disapproval of homosexuality may be so
frightening that the young person will feel bound to attempt to choose a
heterosexual life-style. He may attempt to deny his homosexual feelings or
repress them. He may believe that an intellectual decision to opt for heterosexuality will eventually lead to the disappearance of homosexual impulses
as the "habit" of heterosexual sex becomes more and more firmly ingrained.
To combat his homosexual tendencies, he may demonstrate exaggerated
heterosexual behavior in the attempt to distract himself and others from any
sign of homosexual inclinations.

If the homosexually predisposed adolescent does have actual homosexual experiences, the quality of these and the repercussions that may follow
them are likely to affect the future course of his sexual behavior. If his first
homosexual experiences are pleasant and rewarding, the young person may
find the satisfaction of his homosexual desires far more important to him
than the social disapproval it is likely to entail. If, however, the first homosexual experiences are uncomfortable, or unpleasant, if they are frightening,
unenjoyable, or followed by discovery and public humiliation or punishment,
this too may lead to an attempt to reject homosexuality and adopt a heterosexual pattern, or perhaps celibacy.

When homosexuality is rejected out of fear, guilt, or a combination of
painful and disturbing early experiences, those who attempt to adopt a
heterosexual orientation are occasionally successful. After an early flirtation
with homosexuality, sexual interest in persons of the same gender may fade
and never reappear.

It is more likely, however, that the homosexual interests will be sub-
merged, perhaps for a long period, only to surface again in later life. The
early homosexual inclinations may have been so effectively suppressed or
forgotten that their reappearance will strike unexpectedly and seemingly
without explanation. Depending on the strength of the revived interest and

the personality of the individual involved, he may either deny them, engage in covert homosexual activities along with his heterosexual activities, or enter into a fully homosexual way of life.

But not all homosexuality which develops later in life can be traced to an earlier, conscious homosexual predisposition. If a person's heterosexual sex life becomes unsatisfactory, he may engage in homosexual relations to fulfill his sexual needs. Most people have both heterosexual and homosexual predispositions, and when their sexual preference is frustrated, secondary sexual interests may rise to temporary prominence, only to fade when the source of frustration is removed. In the case of a person who has been living according to his secondary predisposition because his primary predisposition was suppressed, a lasting change in sexual orientation may result. This applies to both heterosexuals and homosexuals.

Married men sometimes become involved in their first homosexual experiences in this way, when marital sex is curtailed or becomes unsatisfying or too much a matter of routine, lacking any special excitement or satisfaction. While an affair with another woman may be seen as clear-cut infidelity, an affair or quick sexual encounter with another man may seem perfectly legitimate.

Similarly, it is no more improbable for a male homosexual to have brief and occasional flings with women. Strict exclusivity in either type of sexual orientation is less common than a predominant interest, which in no way excludes a foray into new territory every once in a while.

A heterosexual's reaction to occasional instances of homosexual activity depends on his basic predisposition, personality, and values. The episode may be transitory, or it may lay the groundwork for an increasing preference for homosexual sex. The nature of the first homosexual experiences and their consequences is again of major importance.

If homosexuality is really a matter of the subtle interplay of numerous haphazard influences, the question may arise: Why does only about 4 percent of the population adopt an exclusively homosexual orientation? If so many factors seem to operate with random effects, should we not expect roughly half the population to be homosexual and half to be heterosexual?

In societies in which there are no taboos against homosexual relations, we do not find a fifty-fifty division between exclusive heterosexuals and exclusive homosexuals. Exclusivity of either type is comparatively infrequent. Rather, a far larger proportion of the population engages in both types of sexual activity, regardless of a preference for one or the other.

Were our social attitudes toward homosexuality to change, any significant increase in the number of exclusive homosexuals would be unlikely. Because the way we raise our children is designed to produce heterosexually oriented adults, there would probably still be many more individuals with dominant heterosexual predispositions than homosexual ones. In a society that was truly sexually neutral, we would expect about half the population to have predominant homosexual interests and half to have predominant heterosexual interests, while in only a small percentage of the population would either of these predispositions be exclusive.

One of the most prevalent myths about homosexuality is that it is somehow the parents' fault—that, had the child been brought up correctly, he would never have developed any interest in homosexuality. The absurdity of such a notion should be clear by now.

Parents have no control over the genetic makeup of their children and surprisingly little control over the range of social and sexual experiences they will encounter throughout their development. There is no way to know which specific things might predispose one's child toward homosexuality, and no way to perfectly control one's own actions, were such things known.

There would be no basis for these self-punitive and essentially inappropriate feelings if homosexuality were defined in our society as an alternative rather than a flaw. So often parents and their homosexual children become trapped in a vicious emotional double bind. The parents are unable to accept their children as they are—society has told them that to do so would be wrong. Because they feel guilt for not being able to accept the child as he is, as well as responsibility for his development, they are not fully able to accept or respect themselves. By the same token, the homosexual, denied acceptance by his parents, often finds it far more difficult to carve out a life of happiness.

But who would want his child to be homosexual? How many people could honestly see homosexuality as a viable sexual alternative and consequently not care one way or the other whether their child turned out to be gay or straight? Not very many today.

Even if one has no personal antipathy toward homosexuality, the treatment of homosexuals in our society is something few would wish to see their own child subjected to. The basic response is much like that which many people of a basically liberal stripe feel with regard to interracial marriages. They may have nothing against them in principle, but when it comes down to the hard fact of a son or daughter marrying someone of another race, they become deeply concerned about the treatment the young couple can expect from a society which preaches but seldom practices racial goodwill.

But regardless of whether parents wish their children to grow up to be homosexuals or not, the matter is out of their hands. The most any parent can hope for his child is that he will find happiness and love. To deny one's child the validity of his love, homosexual or heterosexual, is to strike most deeply and cruelly at the very center of his being.

If the ability to love and be loved and the ability to lead a full and rewarding sex life are major goals in emotional development and maturation, it should make no difference whether love and sex are found in a homosexual or heterosexual context.

Probably the most effective single way of assuring that one's child will be an unhappy homosexual or an unhappy heterosexual is to make sex an issue of overriding concern and importance. The child whose early sexual experience during the years leading up to puberty and throughout adolescence becomes a source of parental supervision, concern, and conflict, is unlikely to develop a happy and fulfilling sex life of any sort. The rule with regard to sexuality is a simple one: Hands off—let your child find himself.

# Where Do Gay People Meet?

Many straight people don't mind the fact that there *are* homosexuals so much as they mind having to see them. After all, everyone has the right to his own type of sex life—so long as he keeps it private. But homosexuals are always flaunting their sex lives, parading them before the public eye, forcing others to become aware of them. Society should not be expected to tolerate this. If homosexuals would keep to themselves and stop intruding on the lives of those who do not share their sexual interests, they would not have much more trouble getting along in our society than anyone else—or so it is said.

It is not surprising that the gay world often seems sordid and unappealing to straight people. They cannot understand why hundreds of homosexuals will crowd into a sleazy bar until all hours of the morning. They find it not only repulsive but incomprehensible that anyone would think to find romance in a public bathroom.

In order to understand why gay people meet where they do, it is necessary to pause and consider where gay people do *not* meet one another. Because homosexuality is not tolerated in our society, gay people are not free to gather and be themselves in many places. Most gay people still believe it is necessary to disguise their homosexuality, so it is often difficult for them to recognize one another in public. When a young man realizes he is gay and wants to meet other homosexuals it can be enormously difficult.

I was in high school when I first heard that there were gay bars, but I had no idea how to locate one. None of my classmates considered themselves homosexual as far as I knew, and I was not even sure how to go about meeting other gay people.

I could not go up to a male friend in the hall between classes or telephone after school for a date. I could not simply go up to someone and ask whether or not he was gay. I could go to the movies with a friend, but it would have been foolhardy to casually try to hold his hand, put my arm around him, or try to kiss him, no matter how much sexual activity was going on among the other couples in the balcony.

In high school, there was no homosexual prom, no gay dances: if you wanted to go to a dance, you went with a girl or you went alone. The gossip column in the school newspaper contained some pretty remarkable items, but never anything about two homosexual lovers. I couldn't stand on the corner watching all the guys go by, and I couldn't wander around town with a group of friends, making suggestive remarks to attractive young men.

The situation was much the same in college and later when I had a job, but by then I had found my way into the gay world and had less difficulty meeting other gay people. Through the years I had many romances, but very few dates. There was a limited number of places a homosexual couple could go, especially if they wanted to be openly affectionate. We could go to the theater and watch a movie or play about heterosexual romance, but it would be risky to make out. We could go to a nightclub if we were willing to play it cool, but we certainly couldn't dance together. It might have been nice to bring a date home to watch TV and meet my family, but I doubt they would have welcomed him.

Still, I had it easy.

I grew up in the suburbs of New York, and although it took a while, I finally found out where the gay bars were located. When I started classes at Columbia, I couldn't approach anyone in class or on campus, but I could always hop a subway down to the Village and meet gay people. By this time, my parents had also moved to the city, where many of their friends lived, but I didn't have to worry about covering my tracks: New York offered all the anonymity I could possibly want.

Young gays who do not grow up near large cities face many more problems than I did. They may never know that the gay world exists unless they happen to stumble on it, and even so their gay world is more likely to consist of a popular men's room than thirty or forty gay bars. They will find it infinitely more difficult to meet other homosexuals than anyone living in the city. Even when they do encounter other gay people, they cannot depend on any protective anonymity in a small town. Many conclude that the only solution is to leave home and move to the city.

I said I had it easy. I moved right into the circle of the bars and did not have to learn to make my way in some of the more difficult meeting places of the gay world. Because of this, my sensibilities were rather delicate and my skills rather limited: I never tried to meet someone in a tea room (a public rest room where homosexual contacts are made), and I never learned how to cruise the streets with any success. For a while, like many other "respectable" gays, I looked down on those whose haunts differed from mine. It never occurred to me that perhaps they were as pleased with their lives as I was with mine—with good reason.

It's difficult for everybody to fully sympathize with others whose lives, interests, and tastes differ radically from their own. As a gay person, I know this particularly well. But there is something self-serving about those straights who criticize gay people for meeting in unconventional places while making it impossible for them to meet anywhere else.

The straight world is not designed to meet the needs of gay people; in many ways it is designed to deny our existence. We are barred from the comfortable, genteel places where other people can meet one another, socialize, and relax: these are for heterosexuals only. We find one another when and where we can.

## WHO

Many straight people have no idea where homosexuals are likely to be found. Since most gay people have no trouble passing for straight, homosexuals are a largely invisible part of the population. It seldom occurs to straight people that there are gay people all around them—at work, at church, at the ball park, at the beach, even in their own families.

There are homosexuals everywhere, but their invisibility is so pervasive that people who first become aware of their own homosexual interests often have trouble seeing them, too. Most people's first homosexual experiences are with friends who know as little about the gay world as they do. Occasionally an older friend will know of a local gay bar or cruising area and pass the information along. Frequently a young homosexual first finds out where to meet other gay people by listening to straights—*Got to do something about these damn queers. Fairies all over the park last Sunday. The bus station's always filled with them.*

Finding the gay world is hard enough, but learning how to get into it can be even more difficult. Even if you're lucky enough to have a friend who can tell you where to go and what to expect, you never feel at ease the first few times. You don't know what standard procedure is, how you should act, or what will and will not be taken for granted. You find that half the things you were told were misleading and the other half were too vague to be useful.

If you've located a gay bar, you have to learn the art of indoor cruising. How obvious can you be in showing interest in somebody else? How do you start a conversation? What is expected when somebody buys you a drink? How do you tactfully discourage somebody uninteresting? How do you find out whether you and another person are sexually compatible before you go home together? There's a lot to learn in the bars, but at least you don't have to worry about whether anyone else is gay or not (unless there is some reason to suspect that a police decoy may be present).

Aside from the bars, most homosexual encounters hinge on initial identification: is the other person gay? Identification is not important only because police enticement and entrapment are common or because straights may become abusive or violent if they are mistaken for homosexuals. It is important because the vast majority of homosexuals haven't the slightest interest in approaching anybody who is not interested in homosexual relations.

The popular myth that homosexuals spend most of their time trying to seduce heterosexuals is one I could never quite understand. Homosexuals have no more interest in wasting their time seeking sexual relations with men who are not interested in them than heterosexual men have in seducing women who are revolted by sexual intercourse. There simply isn't any point to it. The reason for cruising is to find a sexual partner, not to cause a scene. Cruising is a process of identification, and the straight person who is approached by mistake has usually given one of the standard indications of interest and availability without realizing it or intending to do so.

There are a number of signals gay people use to identify one another in cruising, and they differ very little from those which heterosexuals employ. We all use our eyes in various ways to convey sexual messages: a frank once-over of another person's body can reveal sexual attraction, a sensuous, heavy-lidded glance can spell bed in no uncertain terms. A man may catch a woman's eye on the street and hold it a little longer than would be customary if he had no interest in her. If she returns his glance, slackens her pace, or drops a cliché, she is signaling him that it is all right to strike up a conversation. Homosexual cruising is not usually this straightforward and simple.

How do gay people cruise? The first step usually is a glance, catching another man's eye for a little longer than men are generally expected to look at one another. This conveys special interest or even intimacy, because there are many unconscious social rules about how men are supposed to behave toward one another, how long they may look at each other, how close they may stand to each other, when it is appropriate for them to touch, etc. Any violation of these rules signals a departure from standard procedure and may be used as a cruising technique.

The average straight may not even notice the special glance directed at him: he's not expecting it from another man and is simply not attuned. If he does notice it, he may ignore it or return it in surprise or hostility. Another homosexual interested in making a contact will usually give a clear response, looking back long enough to indicate that he was not simply startled. Either or both of the gays may now make the message more explicit by giving the other the once-over, or by glancing at his crotch. In a gay neighborhood or other well-known cruising spot, this may be all the identification necessary.

If the responses are ambiguous or the homosexual on the make is cruising a predominantly straight area, the process of identification will take longer. The cruiser may pass his man and glance back—if the other fellow is returning the glance it's a good sign. The two may look each other over for a while before deciding to start a conversation. They may amble along the sidewalk, pausing to look in a shop window while one of them passes the other, stopping to light a cigarette or buy a paper. If both decide that they want to pursue the matter, they will just happen to end up in a conversation. Unless there is some last-minute reason for uncertainty, they will quickly dispense with any verbal fencing and go somewhere where they will have some privacy.

Once in a while signals get crossed or something unexpected happens and a homosexual finds himself about to proposition someone he is no longer sure is gay. A casual and friendly conversation usually clarifies the situation. If the stranger mentions a wife or girl friend or says anything else to indicate that he is not likely to be interested in homosexual relations, the homosexual will take the hint and look elsewhere. If the homosexual has nothing else to go by, he may casually mention homosexuality in some abstract context to see how the other person reacts.

There are times when it seems impossible to determine whether another person is gay or not. A passing reference to homosexuality may elicit no response whatsoever or it may evoke a tolerant, friendly remark which in no way indicates whether or not the speaker himself is homosexual. A specific question about a bar can help. Often heterosexuals who enjoy occasional gay sex will know precisely what's going on but be too bashful or embarrassed to openly indicate their interest. A gay person may sense this but not be quite sure enough to risk a direct approach.

Under different circumstances, other signals and techniques are used. In tea rooms there is quite a ritual involved in signaling availability and interest in sexual relations. The average straight who does not normally exchange searching glances with other men, look at their genitals, play with his own, or loiter around the john when he's through will very likely not be approached or see any overt homosexual activity in a public bathroom. Devotees of the tea-room scene take every possible precaution to avoid attracting the attention of the unsympathetic and uninterested.

The elaborate procedures involved in identifying another homosexual may seem strange to some straight people who assume that homosexuals are easily spotted. Various things are supposed to be sure indications of homosexuality; this stems from the myth that all gay people are alike.

All male homosexuals, for example, are supposed to be effeminate. Some people even attribute homosexuality to glandular disorders in some men which result in the development of female secondary sex characteristics. By this theory homosexuals can be identified by their physical appearance: wide, rounded hips, flabby, breastlike pectorals, thin, fragile limbs, tiny penes, hairless chests, and high, piping voices. Not so.

Homosexuals as a group are indistinguishable from heterosexuals. There are gay people of all races, builds, colorations, temperaments, nationalities, religions, classes, and backgrounds. Considering that 8 percent of the American population is actively homosexual, it would be extraordinary if they all looked alike.

There are homosexuals who are effeminate and heterosexuals who are effeminate. What we refer to as effeminacy is quite distinct from femininity and is nothing more than a collection of traits which are often attributed to women. These are not innate; they are products of social learning, sometimes adopted unconsciously, sometimes affected. The lisp, often stereotypically attributed to homosexuals, was considered delightfully feminine and alluring in eighteenth-century England. Few women or homosexuals lisp today—it is no longer fashionable.

Heterosexuals with slim builds, high-pitched voices, or mannerisms considered effeminate are frequently tagged homosexual and must deal with some of the problems homosexuals face. Straights with a taste for flashy clothing are just as likely to raise a few eyebrows as any gay blade. Don Juan types are often mistaken for homosexuals because of their sometimes flamboyant dress and special intimacy with women. Most people are familiar with the stereotypes of the foppish dandy or ladies' man.

Gay people are often said to dress effeminately. It is true that many gay people will choose clothing that differs somewhat from prevailing heterosexual fashions, but whether or not their clothing is effeminate is a matter of opinion. Considering that such "effeminate" gay fashions as loafers, button-down collars, tapered slacks, and bell-bottoms were soon adopted by straight men, the matter is certainly open to question.

The belief that there is something peculiar about the way homosexuals dress rests on the assumption that they wish to create the same expectations in others as heterosexuals do. The homosexual who does not wish to call attention to himself will dress as a heterosexual of similar occupational and economic status would be expected to, but when he is out to meet other gay people, it would be self-defeating to look as though he were straight. For gay people, clothing is sometimes useful for identification, although not all gay people take advantage of this.

Fashions come and go in the gay world, just as they do in straight society. At any particular time there will be various criteria for deciding whether or not somebody "looks gay" and just how gay he looks. Gay styles tend to differ just enough from the current straight fashions so that gay people can provide a clue for other homosexuals without necessarily revealing themseves to the unhip. Those who want to broadcast the message in no uncertain terms, of course, may play the current style to the hilt. Under most circumstances, however, few gays dress any differently than straights.

With all the techniques involved in identification, it might seem that each homosexual must be very aware of all the other homosexuals with whom he comes in contact, but this is not generally the case. Gay people themselves often accept the myth that they all look alike and that if somebody doesn't look gay, he's straight. Some gay people are not very successful at cruising simply because they do affect a very straight image and other gays never give them a second look.

Many gay people fail to recognize one another because of their earliest experiences as homosexuals. Never having heard about homosexuality, they assume that they are unique in their feelings. When they do hear of homosexuals for the first time, they are usually portrayed as uncommon and easily recognized—there is no hint of the diversity or size of the gay population. Even when a homosexual enters the gay world, the atmosphere of secrecy and the need to dissemble that often prevail result in a sort of closet mentality. Too many gay people are left feeling unnecessarily isolated and alone.

## WHERE

Although an openly gay subculture is found only in larger cities, there is virtually no place in America where there isn't something gay going on. From covert meeting places in rural areas to gay ghettos in urban areas, the network of communication provides the person who identifies himself as a homosexual with the opportunity to learn from other homosexuals the nature and extent of the gay world.

Contact with the gay world is by no means limited to those who consider themselves gay. Acknowledged homosexuals constitute a minority of those who engage in homosexual activities. The man who considers himself straight, but occasionally seeks out a homosexual as a sex partner, may realize how extensive the gay world is without wanting to become more deeply involved in it.

Similarly, not all homosexuals gravitate toward the center of gay activities in the major cities of the nation. Some are content to stay where they are, develop preferences for the part of the gay world that they first encounter, or deliberately avoid further involvement due to fear of discovery or personal inhibitions.

The peripheral parts of the gay world, far from the active and open life of the major gay ghettos, provide the setting for most of the sexual contacts between homosexuals and "heterosexuals." Here the gay identity is weakest. Some people consider themselves heterosexuals, some bisexuals, and some recognize their homosexual preferences without accepting themselves as homosexuals. The more strongly a person identifies himself as a homosexual, the more deeply he is likely to become involved in the gay world.

The young homosexual living in the country or a small town is unlikely to be aware that the gay world even exists until he has made contact with it at the periphery. His first contact usually takes the form of the discovery that there is a place reasonably near home where homosexuals meet furtively.

There may be a park, a bus station in a nearby town, or a highway rest stop which is notorious as a homosexual meeting place and well known to local heterosexuals, from whom the young homosexual may first hear of it. In some towns the knowledge is not so widespread. There may be a place where a few of the older high school boys go to get picked up or hustle for spending money, and a young gay may hear about it from a friend. Occasionally a young man will be picked up by a homosexual while hitchhiking and learn of local activities by pumping him for information. Once in a while, a young homosexual stumbles on a popular cruising area by chance.

What sort of cruising spots are likely to be found outside of the city? Where a town is too small to provide cover for homosexual activities, a car is usually a necessity for those who want to make homosexual contacts. There may be a state park nearby where homosexuals from neighboring towns can meet. There may be a tea room located in a rest stop at the intersection of two major highways. A great deal of homosexual activity often goes on at truck stops. There may be a dirt pulloff along the highway where contacts can be made and consummated on the spot or in a nearby secluded area, perhaps on a back road. Diners and restaurants at truck stops sometimes have a mixed clientele and serve as meeting places, along with bars, motels, or sleazy resort areas between moderate-sized towns.

The main criterion for these meeting places is that they be far enough away from the center of things to be out of the public eye and relatively free from the attentions of the police, yet close enough to populated areas so that a reasonable number of homosexuals can gather there. For this reason, they are generally located among several neighboring towns or at the junctions of heavily traveled thoroughfares. They come and go quite quickly—for a summer one spot will be heavily visited, while the following year it will be dead. When the local or state police begin to take interest in a particular meeting place, activity there will quickly fall off.

These out-of-the-way places exist only for the purpose of making contacts. There is rarely a sense of any gay subculture: people do not gather to mingle or converse. The pretense is maintained that everyone is straight and is there for "legitimate" reasons. The atmosphere is usually impersonal, and even most of the regular visitors will pretend not to notice or recognize one another. Part of the reason for this is that much of what goes on involves heterosexuals who know they can find homosexuals there who will be willing to provide them with a quick sexual release with a minimum of reciprocation.

The young homosexual who comes upon this sort of scene has certainly not found an attractive entrance to the gay world. Most who remain regulars at these meeting places have either come to prefer impersonal sex or have remained on the fringe of the gay world because they are unable to accept their homosexuality. The small-town gay who enters this scene may think it characteristic of the gay life everywhere. If he feels guilt about his homosexuality, it may seem that this is the most he can expect from life.

Not all young homosexuals whose first contact with the gay world is furtive and impersonal are willing to accept this as permanent. From some of the homosexuals they meet, they will hear of the larger gay world, and many decide to seek it out.

Medium-sized cities sometimes have a private club, a gay bar, or a mixed bar where homosexuals meet regularly, though discreetly. Young men from rural areas may settle here rather than head for the gay ghettos of the larger cities, but in the long run the ghettos have the greatest attraction for homosexuals from all over the country.

The gay life in a medium-sized city is not nearly as open or diverse as that in the major ghettos. In a mixed bar there is seldom any open evidence of homosexuality: the gays pass for straight and dare not rock the boat. There may be a regular group of local homosexuals who spend most of their evenings there, talking to one another, hoping for the appearance of a new face, or a homosexually inclined visitor from out of town, perhaps a salesman passing through. There are usually a few regular straight patrons of the bar who indulge in occasional gay sex, usually after drinking heavily, but all the homosexual activity is disguised.

If there is a gay bar, it will often cater to both male and female homosexuals, something that is much less common where there is a large gay population. This is one of the few situations in which the paths of gay men and women are likely to cross outside the gay movement, and it is here that they are most likely to understand and sympathize with one another.

These bars are often run-down places in the poorer sections of town, occasionally serving as truck-stop restaurants during the day and gay bars at night. They are anything but liberated in most cases. There is rarely any dancing or the open display of affection that can be found in the bars of larger cities. Everybody may be gay, but nobody is supposed to act gay. These bars are just barely tolerated by the police, and viewed as a necessary evil to keep the local gay people out of the public eye. The bar is permitted to remain open only so long as its clientele do not become "objectionably" open about their homosexuality.

In addition to a mixed or gay bar, a medium-sized city usually has several established cruising areas, perhaps a public park or a few blocks of a main city street. There are likely to be a number of tea rooms in town, usually including the bus and train stations. A magazine stand, a diner, or the balcony of a theater may be known as a good place to make a pickup. Naturally there is a great deal more information about the rest of the gay world, and some will decide to move on to the gay ghettos where a more open gay life can be enjoyed.

Closer to the heart of the gay world, an increasing number of alternatives are available to gay people and the gay community becomes more visible. The big cities have a complete cross section of the gay world. There are tea rooms and other meeting places for impersonal sex both inside the city and in the area surrounding it, as well as mixed bars, gay bars, gay baths, private clubs, gay restaurants, and bars which cater to special elements within the gay community. There are gay cruising areas and places where homosexual prostitutes can be found. There are heterosexuals who engage in gay sex, people who consider themselves bisexual, homosexuals who are unhappy with their homosexuality, gay people who remain in the closet and pass for straight, as well as gay people who lead an openly gay life.

The gay ghetto differs in some ways from other minority ghettos. Because homosexuals can usually pass for straight if they wish to do so, gay people are not forced to live in the ghetto. Although many landlords will not rent an apartment to anyone they suspect of being homosexual, most homosexuals can avoid suspicion if they are willing to lead a secretive life. Furthermore, there are some neighborhoods outside of the ghettos where a homosexual can get an apartment without taking any great pains to hide his homosexuality. He is only expected to be reasonably discreet.

It is difficult to say precisely how a gay ghetto forms, for there seems to be a circular process involved. A particular section of the city may happen to have a larger than average homosexual population, possibly because anti-homosexual sentiment in the neighborhood was less than elsewhere, or because the area included a gay bar or popular cruising area. As the gay population increases, gays from other parts of the city are drawn to the area to meet other homosexuals. New cruising areas may develop or the existing ones may become more heavily visited. Because of the increased potential clientele, new gay bars may open and become popular.

The nascent ghetto becomes increasingly attractive for gays from other parts of the city: there are more people to meet, there is more going on, the gay life is more open because there is generally less hostility from the straights living in the area. Straights come into contact with gays more often, get to know some of them personally, and depend on them as customers for local business. As space becomes available, more gays will move to the neighborhood. The gay population may rise to as high as 30 or 40 percent of the total in some areas, and the number of homosexuals is further increased by nonresident gays who spend a great deal of time in the area.

Although the gay life in the ghetto is more open, there are also a number of drawbacks. Police harassment is generally much higher than elsewhere

—there are supposedly no homosexuals on the police force and few policemen choose to live in the ghetto itself. The police do not know the homosexuals who live in their precincts as neighbors but as criminals. Because there are more gay bars and cruising areas, the police feel required to pay more attention to homosexuals than is typical in other parts of the city, and the homosexual residents resent the police-state atmosphere that sometimes develops. The police seem more like invaders than protectors of the gay community.

Because of its large homosexual population, the ghetto becomes a target for those who dislike homosexuals. Straight gangs sometimes harass, beat, rob—and occasionally murder—homosexuals. It is not uncommon for a carload of young men to drive around the streets of the ghetto until they spot a solitary homosexual, stop the car, jump out and beat him up, and then vanish. Muggers are attracted to the well-known cruising areas at night, and the crime rate is usually higher than elsewhere. Because of the dubious legal status of homosexuals themselves, they receive little protection from such attacks.

The gay ghetto is a mixed blessing. Some people question whether it should even be called a ghetto at all. Homosexuals move there voluntarily, the living conditions are not usually inadequate, and the homosexual residents can always leave it if they choose. While it is true that gay people move to the ghetto voluntarily, they usually do so as much because they are not really welcome elsewhere as because there is more going on in the ghetto. It is far more difficult to meet other homosexuals outside of the ghetto, and unless one is wealthy it is expensive to live outside and commute to it regularly. In the last analysis, the community spirit, the feeling of living among one's own kind in the midst of a hostile society, is probably what best qualifies these heavily gay areas as ghettos.

New York's Greenwich Village is probably the archetypal gay ghetto, but most of the nation's large cities have at least one, and often several. In New York, large concentrations of gay people are found outside of the Village as well: the Upper East Side, the West Side in the seventies and eighties, Brooklyn Heights, etc.

The gay world is not rigidly bound within the city limits in major gay population centers. There are often gay beaches, parks, and resorts within commuting distance of the larger cities, and some of these have acquired a national reputation. Griffith Park near Los Angeles is probably the most famous cruising area in the country, and Fire Island's Cherry Grove and the Pines are probably the plushest gay ghettos in the world, though, surprisingly, not the most liberated.

An enormous number of options are open to the young homosexual who grows up in the big city or who comes to it in search of the gay world. At the heart of the gay world, gay people are more diverse than anywhere else and a wide variety of life-styles is available. No two gay people, of course, live identical lives, but a number of different common patterns are discernible with regard to the places where gay people seek out sexual partners and who those partners are likely to be.

## HOW

How does the average homosexual live in one of the larger cities of the nation with a high gay population? There are so many distinct life-styles available in the city and they differ so greatly from one another that there is little value in speaking of the *average* homosexual in this context. Although the gay world is more open and extensive in the cities than elsewhere, by no means all gay people are deeply involved in it. Differences in background, personality, and sexual tastes mean that the gay world breaks down into many discrete segments among which communication is often minimal.

Involvement in the gay world does not necessarily mean that a person is living an openly homosexual life. The vast majority of those involved attempt to disguise their homosexual activities from everyone who is not gay, and are said to be "in the closet." They may maintain an elaborate façade to avoid discovery. Some enter "marriages of convenience" with women who understand that they are primarily homosexual, but who still wish to marry them for companionship and whatever sort of sexual relations they are able to work out together. Others may date women in order to maintain a straight image, even if they have no interest in them sexually.

Most gays who are in the closet, however, do not go to these lengths in order to disguise their homosexuality. Many simply pass themselves off as bachelors who have little interest in marriage but who are essentially heterosexual. This may mean telling an occasional tale about an affair that never took place, expressing an artificial but casual interest in women, or devising some other excuse. If asked whether they are gay, most who are in the closet will deny it; some will even disparage homosexuals.and use antihomosexual humor as a screen for their real feelings.

The average closeted gay who is not disturbed by his sexual orientation simply sees no reason to call attention to it, since he knows that life will be easier if it remains undetected. He makes little effort to maintain a façade, but avoids speaking about the homosexual side of his life. He adopts a straight image and never mentions the bars he visits or the affairs he has to anyone but other homosexuals. He may even live with a lover without the fact ever coming to light.

Many different types of gay people consider themselves out of the closet. Some have never made any pretense of being straight and may have entered an occupation in which homosexuality is tolerated—the theater, for example. Others are self-employed and have no need to worry about discovery.

More people who are open about their homosexuality, however, have had to come out of the closet, often after a great deal of soul searching. There are various degrees of being out of the closet. For some gays, it simply means that they have decided that they will take no special pains to hide their homosexuality and will admit it if questioned. For others, it means telling their close friends and family that they are gay, while leaving those about whom they care less in ignorance.

In recent years, "coming out" has taken on the additional connotation, in light of the gay liberation movement, of a political act, an insistence on the right to an open and public life free from discrimination and harassment.

Being in or out of the closet does not necessarily indicate whether or not a person has accepted his homosexuality and views it as a valid sexual preference and life-style. A few individuals who are quite open about their homosexuality still consider it a curse. The majority of gays who remain in the closet, however, do so simply because they see little reason to risk good jobs, respectability, and a comfortable life, no matter how much better they might feel about themselves if they had no need to lead two lives, one public, one secret.

The degree of involvement a person is likely to seek in the gay world depends primarily on the way he views himself. Those who do not consider themselves homosexual, but who enjoy homosexual sex, are the least involved. In homosexual slang, these people are referred to as "trade," and they are most likely to be involved in the segment of the gay world related to impersonal sex, often in public places.

Impersonal sex is frowned upon in our society. Most people feel that sex should involve at least some affection, if not love. But many people prefer to have sex with a minimum of personal involvement and communication, often finding that they are less inhibited under such circumstances. Some fulfill their emotional needs elsewhere and simply require a convenient sexual outlet with no strings attached. Some find impersonal sex exciting in itself, because of either an inability to handle emotional involvement with others, or a taste for the risk that usually characterizes sexual encounters in public places. Finally, some people limit themselves to impersonal encounters because they do not want to be more deeply involved in the gay world, either because they have not accepted their homosexuality or because a deeper involvement may increase the risk of discovery.

In every large city, impersonal sex can be found in many places. Not all public rest rooms, of course, serve as tea rooms where homosexual contacts are made. But because of their accessibility, bus and train station rest rooms attract a fairly sizable group of regular visitors, many of them commuters. These places are among the most well-known tea rooms in many cities, as are men's rooms in subway stations, popular hotels and department stores, and cheap theaters.

Tea rooms are not the only place where impersonal sex takes place. Theater balconies and parks where a great deal of shrubbery offers some privacy are often popular spots for cruising and quick sex. Each city has its own specialties: in New York, for example, "the trucks" down by the water-front provide places where dozens of people crowd into the back of parked vans and have sex in the dark with people they may never see or speak to.

Gay baths and health clubs in large cities are less public or semipublic and a good deal more comfortable. In New York, after-hours bars provide unlit back rooms where an enormous amount of impersonal sex goes on.

Although there are a few individuals who really enjoy impersonal sex in public places because of the risk of discovery, most of the people who pursue this scene do so because of its convenience and the anonymity in-volved; they have no wish to be caught in the act and arrested. Some homo-sexuals frequent tea rooms because they believe that to go to the bars will increase chances of their being discovered. Others first came out in the tea rooms, are familiar with the cruising procedures there, and prefer them out of habit.

The tea-room scene involves only a small part of the gay population. It is the most common type of involvement sought by men who consider themselves primarily heterosexual.

Most of the apparently heterosexual individuals who frequent the tea rooms are perfectly ordinary individuals, more often than not married with families. Many men from all walks of life, from the blue-collar worker to the highly paid executive, make a quick stop at a nearby tea room a regular part of their daily routine. Most of these men do not consider themselves homo-sexual—they are merely taking advantage of the opportunity for free, uncom-plicated, readily available sexual release.

Some of these people cannot be said to have any significant homosexual inclinations. If heterosexual sex were as easily and cheaply available, they would much prefer to find their sexual outlet with women. Some men become involved in the tea-room scene for short periods when heterosexual relations are particularly hard to come by, or when their financial position makes it impossible for them to employ the services of female prostitutes.

Others are less than honest about their degree of involvement. Imper-sonal homosexual encounters become the main focus of their sex lives for some men, with the result that they lose interest in sexual relations with their wives or other women. Some continue their involvement in tea-room sex for years, eventually providing unreciprocated sexual services for others, regard-less of whether or not they finally come to identify themselves as homosexuals. Others become more deeply involved in the gay world and begin to frequent the baths or bars.

Just what goes on in these impersonal sexual encounters? In the tea rooms, fellatio is by far the most common act. Usually the heterosexual who gets a blow job will not reciprocate in any way, for to do so would place him in a homosexual role. Straight men who go to the baths or seek impersonal sex in other places where more privacy is to be had often prefer to be fucked, even though they enjoy taking the "active" role with women.

Those who consider themselves heterosexual do not necessarily restrict themselves to impersonal sexual encounters. Out of town on business, some men make a pickup at a gay bar rather than hire a prostitute. Others who view themselves as bisexual may carry on one or more homosexual affairs for several years while remaining happily married.

Homosexual experiences need not pose any threat to a marriage. For some men, a homosexual experience is nothing more than a casual diversion which has nothing to do with infidelity. Not a few wives are unbothered by their husbands' homosexual activities, while another woman would be another story.

Sex of an essentially impersonal nature is also found in the gay world where prostitution is involved, although not all sex which is paid for need be like this. In every major city there are areas where "hustlers"—male prostitutes—can be picked up. Usually several blocks on a number of major streets are more or less well known as places where young men will loiter or wander back and forth waiting to be picked up. They may also be found near transportation facilities, in a hustlers' bar or a few cheap restaurants.

Who becomes a hustler? Although young gays who have left home for the city sometimes end up hustling, most hustlers do not consider themselves homosexual. The typical hustler thinks of himself as straight and justifies his activities on financial grounds: it's a good way to make money without being tied down to a regular job. Hustlers will often maintain a relationship with a woman, as though to establish their heterosexuality beyond any doubt. Many refuse to reciprocate in any way when they have sex with homosexuals and others insist upon taking an "active" sexual role.

The average hustler maintains a tough, masculine image. Sometimes he will beat up and rob a customer if he thinks he can get away with it. As these Midnight Cowboys grow older, lose their looks and their appeal in the sexual marketplace, many come to consider themselves homosexual, or at least bisexual. Some hustle because they feel threatened by close relationships with other gays, which may make it difficult for them to continue considering themselves nonhomosexual. In other cases, the payment of money for homosexual activities makes them seem less homosexual, more acceptable.

The use of money to legitimate homosexual activities is also common among many supposedly straight individuals who are considered "trade." The runaways who often get picked up in bus or train stations frequently look for a small "loan" or the purchase of a meal or a ticket to another city before they feel comfortable having sex. Soldiers and sailors on leave will often pick up extra spending money this way.

In some cities, cruising is done by car and many predominantly straight individuals are involved. Most of them expect some token payment in order to justify their homosexual acts: gas money, toll money, a couple of bucks for extra cash.

Not all who hustle for a living consider themselves straight or affect a "butch" image. Some young homosexual transvestites who hustle on the streets or in bars often succeed in passing for women. Often they will maintain the illusion by engaging only in fellatio, rather than other sexual relations which would reveal their real gender.

Homosexual prostitution is not limited to the streets. In large cities, call boys are usually available. Often billed as male modeling studios or massage parlors, some houses of male prostitution even offer picture catalogues from which customers may select a sex partner. The whole operation is extremely discreet and usually quite expensive. Wealthy homosexuals or "heterosexuals" who are extremely worried about discovery are the most frequent patrons. Sex with these professional call boys is usually a good deal less impersonal than that which can be had on the streets.

One additional area of largely impersonal sex is usually referred to as "rough trade." A few homosexuals are particularly drawn to men who are predominantly straight and appear to be dangerous: aggressively masculine individuals in especially "masculine" professions — construction workers, policemen, petty criminals, ex-convicts. Again, this is usually a case of heterosexuals who enjoy homosexual sex but are unwilling to reciprocate. Occasionally, a homosexual will misjudge a partner of this type and end up being beaten, robbed, or murdered. When this happens, torture or mutilation of the victim is not uncommon.

The vast majority of homosexuals have little interest in prostitutes or predominantly heterosexual individuals. Most prefer others who consider themselves to be homosexual for sex partners, and sexual relations tend to be casual rather than impersonal. Contacts made in gay bars or popular cruising areas are usually reciprocal and much friendlier. Sex is casual in the sense that two individuals will not expect a relationship to develop between them or even to see one another again, but the partners take some interest in one another, usually chatting for a while and getting to know one another before and usually after having sex.

Cruising can take place anywhere, but certain areas in most cities come to be known as established homosexual cruising areas. Gay sections of public

parks or streets near them are often heavily cruised, as are the streets of the
gay ghettos.

A whole life-style can be built around cruising. Many gays take apartments near popular cruising areas and find all their sexual partners there.
Some gays will cruise a few times a week, while others feel a need to have sex
every night, sometimes more than once. This is usually a matter of personal
taste and differences in sexual drives, but there are some homosexuals who
cruise compulsively, driven by loneliness and anxiety to seek comfort and
company in sex, yet rarely satisfied or emotionally fulfilled by their sexual
encounters. Many of those whose main sexual outlet is cruising fulfill their
emotional needs elsewhere and see cruising as an expression of sexual
freedom.

The gay bars also center primarily on casual sex, although it is here
that most gays feel they can find a lasting relationship if they want one. The
bars also serve as the main social institution of the gay world. Friends will
often go out to a bar together or run into one another there.

Prior to the rise of the gay liberation movement and the appearance of a
more active gay press, the bars were the only link between homosexuals in
different cities and different parts of the country. Using a guidebook listing
gay bars in other cities, a homosexual who was traveling could easily locate
the gay bars on his route.

In the largest cities there is a wide variety of bars to choose from. New
York has well over a hundred gay and mixed bars as well as many after-hours
clubs which cater primarily to homosexuals. Some bars serve distinct segments of the gay community: hustlers, transvestites, leather fetishists, and
sadomasochists. Most bars, however, have a generalized gay clientele. Although a few bars cater only to whites, blacks, or Puerto Ricans, most are
racially and ethnically integrated. Some of the bars are plush and elegant,
some feature dancing, entertainment, or food, but most are dingy dives
where drinks are overpriced and the floors unswept.

Each bar has an atmosphere all its own which depends on its physical
layout and decor as well as its location and its regular clientele. In the gay
ghettos, the bars tend to be free, more openly gay. In other parts of town,
the bars are often more restrained, less visibly gay. The bars which cater to
wealthier gays are often more formal and more expensive. Some bars welcome only those in suits and ties. Elsewhere, there is a broader variety in
dress, although each bar tends to draw people with similar tastes. In one bar,
the look will be very collegiate, in another, more flamboyant.

Some bars appeal mostly to older gays, while others—especially the
dance bars—attract a young crowd. Those frequented by older gays usually
have a less liberated atmosphere. There is less open display of affection, less
open cruising. The generation gap is reflected in the gay world, for younger

gays have experienced a great deal more freedom from the start than those who came out ten or twenty years ago.

Regular bar clientele ranges from the closeted individual who visits bars only rarely for fear of discovery to others who may make the rounds of several bars every night. Some go for relaxation; others go to the bars primarily for sex and stay until closing time in the hope of meeting someone.

When the bars close, many of those who are still there go elsewhere in search of sex. In cities where bars close comparatively early, impromptu parties may be arranged. In larger cities it is more common for people to head for a nearby cruising area where they can hope to meet other gays who have just left the bars. For many, a long evening has left them a little less choosy, a little more available. And many others continue the search elsewhere.

The baths range from elegant to tacky, but all of them are geared primarily to impersonal sex. Some people do take time to get to know one another, and most baths have lounges or refreshment areas especially for this purpose, but the bulk of activity goes on in the steamrooms or private cubicles which can be rented for various periods of time. There are unlit orgy rooms, usually called "dormitories," which contain a number of beds for group sex. People are crowded in together in the dark and may go from one person to another or become involved with several at one time. In the private rooms the standard procedure is to lie on the bed with the door left partially open as an invitation to someone passing in the corridor.

Sex is easily available in the gay world, but the environment sometimes leaves much to be desired. In most cities the gay bars are located in the poorer sections of town or in industrial districts where they will not be directly in the public eye. Consequently, they are sometimes dangerous to get to and are often in older buildings which are neither safe nor sanitary. In a number of larger cities, such as New York, the bars are controlled by organized crime and have an underworld atmosphere. In many cities they are regularly visited by police decoys or subject to police raids.

Some gay people frequent the bars only until they have developed a circle of friends and then meet most of their sex partners at private parties. Depending on the people involved, these parties range from sedate gatherings for cocktails and dinner to well-organized orgies. Entrance to the party circuit is often hard to gain, especially among the gay jet set. The wealthiest and most prominent homosexuals tend to look down their noses at the average gay as unsophisticated and uninteresting, and may find a hustler more entertaining to invite as a surprise guest.

In the last two years the enormous growth of the gay liberation movement has made a new life-style available to homosexuals in many parts of the country. Being a political homosexual can be a full-time occupation, regardless of the type of gay organization one joins. Most organizations offer social events, dances, discussion forums, and consciousness-raising groups, in addition to meetings and organized political activities and demonstrations.

Gay communes have been established in various parts of the country, and there have been several attempts to found exclusively gay communities outside of the city. In a few cases this has been tried by encouraging large numbers of homosexuals to move to underpopulated areas where they can hope to exert a major influence in local politics—Alpine County, California, for example. Wealthier gays have attempted to pool their resources in a few instances and finance gay housing developments. Neither of these approaches has met with much success to date.

The generation gap and a great difference in values has been evident between homosexuals in the movement and the majority of the gay population, which has so far remained uninvolved. Some movement gays are critical of those who remain in the closet, although most see them as trapped by circumstances and regard them sympathetically. Some of the more radical gays in the movement consider the bars oppressive and the more established sexual life-styles unliberated.

The militantly visible gay movement is so new that it is difficult to assess the reaction of the larger gay population to it. An increasingly large segment of the gay population responds favorably, supporting the overall goal of equality for homosexuals, but reluctant to risk exposure or make a major commitment of time and money. Other gays feel that the movement is doomed to failure in our antihomosexual society. Some think it irrelevant: movement types are too serious, even puritanical, and would do better to take advantage of the gay world as it is, ignoring society at large. Finally, there are some gays who are entirely opposed to the movement, either because they have not accepted themselves as homosexuals, are afraid of rocking the boat, or they oppose change and reform on political grounds.

The role of the movement in creating new life-styles within the gay world has undoubtedly just begun. While the more established life-styles are unlikely to vanish quickly, the greatest change in the way homosexuals live, love, and see themselves is likely to appear in the movement. There is no way of predicting now how great an influence the gay movement will have on the gay world as a whole.

Many homosexuals find a place for themselves within the gay world that meets their needs and provides the framework for a happy life. Many find lovers and drop out of the mainstream of gay life with no regrets. It is impossible to say that any one life-style is typical of homosexuals or is preferred by the "average" gay person. Straight society's stereotypes have little to do with real gay people.

# How Do Homosexuals Really Feel About Women?

There are probably more myths concerning male homosexuals' feelings about women than any other kind. Homosexuals are described as hating women, fearing women, understanding women, and wishing to be women.

People often say homosexuals don't know what sex they are, but what they usually mean is that male homosexuals are not really men. Homosexuals are often viewed as imitation women, expected to behave like women, share interests and emotions with them, and respond to men much the way they do.

Most of the myths about homosexuals' feelings toward women can be traced to this inaccurate notion. Some feelings are attributed to homosexuals because they are feelings that women are expected to have for one another. Others are attributed to homosexuals because it is assumed that they will feel just the reverse of what "normal" men are expected to feel. Actually, the stereotypical emotions attributed to homosexuals reveal many of the stereotypical notions held about heterosexual men and women in our society.

## HOMOSEXUALS AND WOMEN

Little boys don't like little girls. One of the first indicators of homosexuality is believed to be an "abnormal" interest in girls at an age when "well-adjusted" boys can't stomach them. Grown men like individual grown women, but do not generally enjoy spending much time in groups composed only of women. Adult homosexuals are expected to enjoy being "one of the girls," to be perfectly comfortable mingling primarily with women, chatting, gossiping, trading tips on matters of feminine interest. In any service occupation which involves dealing with women on a regular basis, those who choose it are likely to be taken for homosexuals: who else could stand it? Hairdressers, fashion designers, interior decorators, salesmen in women's-clothing stores, are quite often assumed to be primarily homosexual.

Such societal expectations lead many homosexuals to enter these fields,

63

where they can expect a greater degree of tolerance, even acceptance. But while homosexuals may be disproportionately represented in these professions, certainly not all who enter them are gay.

The average man does not enjoy working with women on a regular basis. He is expected to find women difficult to understand, their motivations obscure, their moods and emotions complex, sometimes incomprehensible. Homosexuals, on the other hand, are often believed to have a special understanding of women, a special sympathy for their feelings and needs. A woman may be able to confide things to her hairdresser that she would never mention to her husband.

There is some truth in this. While the majority of gay men have no more desire than heterosexual males to spend most of their time with women, some gay people do find women easier to get along with than men.

There are reasons for a special rapport between homosexuals and women on both sides. The homosexual does not see women as prospective sexual partners. Although he may feel a mild attraction toward some women or simply note that they are particularly attractive, his major interests lie elsewhere. Since no real sexual interests are involved, he need not be alert for a chance to become involved in some sort of sexual liaison.

If he is in an occupation which is popularly considered to be "homosexual," his female patrons will be less inclined to make overtures toward him. There is little pressure on the homosexual; he need not feign interest where it is not felt, as a heterosexual male might be expected to do to protect his masculine image. The homosexual may find himself under greater pressure with other men, as he attempts to hide his feelings of attraction.

Part of the reason our society prefers to think of service professions which cater primarily to women as "homosexual" is that women are thought to be safe with homosexuals. A man may dislike homosexuals intensely, but he need not feel that it is a threat to his masculinity or his sexual prerogatives if his wife spends an afternoon at the beauty parlor or has an interior decorator at the house for the day. Homosexuals are a threat to men, not to women.

Because women do not constitute their main sexual interest, homosexuals in our society probably do have a greater potential for understanding and sympathizing with them. Fewer pretenses and deceptions are required on both parts, and homosexuals frequently find more areas of basic human communication with the opposite sex than the typical heterosexual male is likely to find. Many gay men develop close and lasting friendships with women.

Women often respond more favorably to homosexuals than straight men do. While a few women feel threatened when a man fails to be aroused by them or relate to them in a basically sexual context, the average woman is likely to feel quite at ease with a homosexual—unless his homosexuality is made explicit and she feels called upon to react to it with a moral judgment.

While some people believe that homosexuals have a special affinity for women, others assume that since men like individual women, homosexuals must dislike them. Some people even find a way to merge the two expectations, explaining that homosexuals only appear to get on better with women because they are more adept at manipulating and duping them, secretly holding them in contempt all the while.

Just as there are heterosexual misogynists there are homosexual misogynists. But homosexuals who dislike or even hate women are a small minority within the gay population, and this is one of the least credible generalizations applied to homosexuals as a group. Male homosexuality is an attraction to men, not an aversion to women.

Aside from those who work closely with women, the most characteristic attitude of male homosexuals toward women is probably one of indifference. The average homosexual is not likely to seek out female companions; he prefers to spend his free time with gay friends or in search of sex partners. If his social life does bring him into contact with women from time to time, he will treat them much as he would treat any straight person. He will be unlikely to open up very much unless he has some reason to believe that they will not be put off by his homosexuality or become hostile toward him.

While some women feel threatened by the homosexual's lack of interest in them and become quite hostile at the first suspicion of homosexuality, there are others who lavish a particularly great amount of attention on men they suspect of being homosexual. Even if these women have perfectly adequate sex lives, they see homosexuals as a challenge. They may feel a need to demonstrate power over men by arousing them sexually, whether or not they have any real desire to sleep with them. When the homosexual man fails to respond as expected, he becomes a particularly vexing challenge.

Even more common than this phenomenon, though, is the woman whose sex life is neither adequate nor satisfying. In the simplest case, a lonely single or married woman may find herself drawn to an attractive unmarried man who she is unaware is homosexual. Since it is usually taken for granted that an unmarried man is heterosexual and interested in meeting women, the homosexual often has few defenses against this sort of approach unless he is willing to disclose his homosexuality.

If a heterosexual man is approached by a homosexual there is nothing to stop him from delivering a curt and public refusal at the very least. But there are many situations in which it is awkward for a homosexual to discourage the advances of a woman who has become interested in him. At an office party, for example, the homosexual who has not made himself known to his employer and fellow workers may feel called upon to play along with an attempted seduction to avoid drawing attention or suspicion to himself, regardless of how uninteresting or unpleasant he finds such a heterosexual involvement. Occasionally such attempts will be pursued well beyond the limits of ordinary courtesy and discretion. The homosexual who does not wish to reveal himself can do little under the circumstances. For gay women, as might be expected, the situation is even worse.

Similarly, some women—frequently they are lonely women whose fear or bad experiences with men lead them to unconsciously search for a "safe" relationship with a man—are especially drawn to homosexuals. Some gay men enjoy these relationships, but most find them a real nuisance. Again, there may be major difficulties in discouraging such women from pursuing a romance where none is possible. Some women fall in love with homosexual after homosexual, never consciously aware that they have sought them out because they find them less threatening.

Others will become involved with men whom they know to be homosexual and persist in attempts at seduction regardless of how explicit the homosexual makes his lack of interest. Known in gay slang as a "fag hag," such a woman often operates under the assumption that the homosexual is gay only because he has not yet found the *right* woman. She is convinced that his homosexual interests will vanish once she has successfully initiated him into the glories of heterosexual sex. The missionary zeal which some of these women will devote to this sort of unwelcome "cure" can be highly offensive to the homosexual man. (Gay women face a similar problem with men who believe that all a lesbian really needs—and secretly wants—is a good lay to straighten her out.)

Not a few of the misconceptions about homosexuals' attitudes toward women stem from the common belief that homosexuality precludes any sexual interest in women at all. Just as many primarily heterosexual men enjoy occasional homosexual sex, many homosexuals enjoy occasional sexual relations with women. Most homosexuals experience at least a mild attraction toward women from time to time, although they may have no intention at all of ever acting upon it; other interests and attractions are far too important for it to be worthwhile.

Some homosexuals who wish to hide their sexual orientation date and have sexual relations with women on a regular basis and not without a good deal of enjoyment. During lonely periods in their lives, some gay men will involve themselves in a heterosexual affair or share an apartment with a woman who also finds herself at loose ends. A number of homosexuals marry women later in life, more for love and companionship than for sexual relations, simply because they have given up hope of finding a male lover or because they have found that their increasing age has made it difficult for them to find sexual partners.

Male and female homosexuals usually move in different circles and have little contact with one another. Except in small cities, there are usually separate bars for gay men and women, and the life-styles of the two groups differ greatly. Gay men usually know little about the problems faced by gay women, for lesbians are even more invisible than male homosexuals in our society.

Just as the social distance between the straight and gay worlds breeds stereotypes and misconceptions about homosexuals, the separation between gay men and women sometimes leads each group to adopt stereotypes about the other. A few male homosexuals have a strong dislike of gay women, and a few lesbians have an equally strong dislike of gay men. Most homosexuals, however, have few feelings one way or the other about homosexuals of the opposite sex, and when they do happen to become acquainted, their common experience as homosexuals in a straight society draws them more closely together. As the gay movement has grown and women have taken on an increasingly independent role within it, an encouraging tendency toward solidarity between gay men and gay women has become evident.

While many male homosexuals do have friendly relations with straight and gay women, homosexuality is no guarantee of a special understanding of women. Some of the worst "male chauvinists" are gay and consider themselves experts on women while they labor under the most stereotypical delusions about them. Much of the tension in the past between gay men and gay women stemmed from the fact that gay men treated gay women as though they were just another type of male homosexual, rather than individuals whose lives, interests, needs, and values were quite different.

The relationship between heterosexual and homosexual males is in some ways more interesting than that between homosexual males and women, for feelings run stronger on both sides. Homosexuals—by definition—are far more interested in men than in women, and straight men tend to be quite a bit more hostile toward homosexuality and homosexuals than are straight women. Even women who do not approve of homosexuality are likely to see it as a minor evil, a peculiarity that causes more difficulty for those "afflicted" with it than for society at large. Straight men, on the other hand, are far more prone to see homosexuality as a direct affront to themselves and their masculinity. The very existence of homosexuality suggests that men as well as women can be sexual objects, and most men are uncomfortable with this possibility.

It disturbs most straight men to think that other men may find them sexually attractive, so it is often easier to view homosexuals as people who don't know what sex they are or as imitation women. Straight society's blindness to the existence of "masculine" homosexuals and the many myths about homosexual "effeminacy" can be traced in large part to this feeling.

## EFFEMINACY

A surprising number of straight people believe that they know a good deal about homosexuals without ever having met even one personally.

Long before either they or I had any idea that I myself might be homosexual, for example, my parents believed they knew enough about homosexuals to be able to identify them and point them out to me. They certainly didn't make a practice of this, for they had no special reason to take much interest in homosexuality at the time.

One summer my family was on vacation at Atlantic City. As we walked along the boardwalk, my father called our attention to two individuals, walking in our direction, hand in hand.

Both had platinum-blond hair just a shade beyond belief. They wore slacks that looked sprayed on, shirts or blouses—it was difficult to say which —of some silvery silky material, and as they drew closer, we noticed that they had on bracelets and little golden earrings. As they passed us, rolling their hips and giggling, I was astonished to see that their eyes were heavily made up —to the point of caricature—and that their faces seemed to be covered with a heavy layer of pancake makeup.

"Those are homosexuals," my father said, quietly enough so that they would not hear.

Years later, when I first began to ask myself whether I might be homosexual, I was unable to put these two strangers out of my mind. I had become perfectly aware that I was far more interested in boys than in girls, yet I did not feel like a girl myself. I wasn't sure whether I was fooling myself or not. Did other people see all sorts of feminine traits in me that I hid from myself?

I wondered whether my behavior, my taste in clothes, the way I carried myself, would change over the years if I accepted myself as a homosexual. Would I follow some inescapable pattern of development that would eventually transform me into a barely recognizable feminine version of myself? A few years later, after I had come out into the gay world and begun frequenting the bars, I was constantly on the alert for signs of such a development in myself.

Partly, I did not want to look like the two homosexuals who had been pointed out to me—because this did not fit my image of myself. Partly, I was afraid that becoming so visibly "homosexual" would ensure that everyone I met would immediately identify me as gay—and that was something I myself had not yet come to accept with much grace. When I walked around town, I would be uncomfortably aware of my gait: was there a little too much hip in my walk, was I swishing a little bit? I used to walk around trying to move my hips as little as possible, trying to keep them in a rigid imaginary line absolutely parallel to the ground. The resulting unnatural gait probably led many people to believe that I suffered from the effects of some devastating childhood paralysis, but at least they would not take me for a homosexual.

I had met a few other homosexuals who had much in common with those my father had pointed out, but most of the gay people I met in the bars looked no different from the men I met anywhere else. Some of them—the ones I found myself most attracted to—looked a good deal more virile than the average man on the street. In time, I came to realize that there were homosexuals of all sorts and that being gay did not mean that I had to dress or act in any particular manner other than that which came most naturally to me. From then on, I walked a little easier.

Straight people who have not had much contact with the gay world often believe, as I did, that all homosexuals are effeminate. Most jokes about homosexuals derive at least part of their humor from representing homosexuals as some odd variety of artificial woman.

In some cases the myth of homosexual effeminacy takes on the most exaggerated and ridiculous proportions: all homosexuals wear blond wigs and makeup, many wear women's undergarments under their everyday straight attire, most wish only to be women and even buy artificial plastic vaginas to maintain the illusion.

Numerous effeminate traits are attributed to homosexuals. They walk with a swishy gait, rolling their hips and behinds like grotesque parodies of voluptuous pinup girls. Their wrists are limp, their hands nervous and fluttery, and when they sit, they cross their legs delicately at the ankles. They are coy: they bat their eyelashes, titter and giggle, and when affronted put on grand airs. They are emotional creatures, given to temper tantrums and sudden bursts of pitiful weeping.

Homosexuals are said to be effeminate, not merely in their behavior, but in their interests and psychological makeup as well. They are flighty, silly, irresponsible, and all too often bitchy, ready to gossip about others behind their backs at the first opportunity. They fancy frills and decorations. Their apartments are grotesqueries of froufrou bric-a-brac and au courant kitsch. They have more cosmetics in their medicine cabinets than can be found in the average beauty salon, and they use them to embarrassing excess with minimal success. They know nothing of serious matters, politics, finance—the real world—but are in a constant tizzy over the latest fashions, the newest screen idol, the up-and-coming smash musical comedy.

All these traits and many others are presented as examples of homosexual effeminacy, and few people question them. Considering that effeminacy is defined as having or showing qualities generally attributed to women, the unquestioning acceptance of all these traits as effeminate, whether actually displayed by homosexuals or not, seems somewhat shocking today. Are these really the ways in which America expects women to behave? Does this strange combination of affectation and vacuity really characterize either femininity or homosexuality? Until quite recently, few people seemed inclined to doubt it.

One of the most embarrassing things about popular notions regarding homosexuals is that they so often reveal popular notions regarding women.

In our society there is probably no more widespread and unquestioned myth about homosexuals than that of their supposed effeminacy. Until quite recently, many young homosexuals entering the gay life labored under the same delusion. They tried to match themselves to the myth, affecting characteristics they supposed to be typical of homosexuals. Trying to live up to the expectations of the role provided for them, they became much as society expected them to be.

If it is true that a greater percentage of homosexuals than heterosexuals are effeminate, it is because the prevailing social expectation demanded it. But "effeminacy" is a catch-all term reserved for almost all behavior that falls outside our conception of the masculine role. Even a man who expresses his gentler emotions readily may be judged unmanly or effeminate by some.

Effeminacy is socially defined. It has little to do with the difference between masculinity and femininity. Elements of both are to be found in everyone, once we go beyond the narrowly defined limits of sexual roles. Nor is femininity, whether in homosexuals or heterosexuals, a negative characteristic; it may well be the most natural expression of an individual's feelings and identity. One person may be more expressive and demonstrative, voluble and excitable, warm and emotional than another. Only when these and other traits are linked together and defined as undesirable do they acquire any value outside of themselves. It may well be that because of our society's negative attitudes toward women and the feminine role, the accusation of effeminacy is used as a criticism directed at some individuals, homosexual and heterosexual alike.

Not surprisingly, social expectations often have an effect on homosexuals.

Unlike other minority groups, racial, ethnic, religious, or economic, the homosexual is not brought up within a tradition. He has not been raised to be a homosexual, he has been given no basic grounding in a subculture he can call his own.

In the case of a Jew or a black or a member of any other minority group, the child grows up in a family and is usually in a community that shares his minority status. From his earliest years, he is immersed in a subculture in which his identity develops, a minority tradition which shapes his values, goals, style of behavior, ways of relating to other members of the minority and to the world at large. There are models in the community—siblings, peers, and older persons—with whom he can identify.

The homosexual, in contrast, was not born into a homosexual subculture and is unlikely to know that one exists. He is usually aware of his own homosexual interests long before he has any idea that other homosexuals exist, and rarely has an opportunity to meet other homosexuals and pattern himself on them. He becomes aware of sexual feelings which nobody else seems to share, and he quickly learns that it is dangerous to let it be known that he has them.

The young homosexual sees himself as different, but he does not know precisely how or why. Having become aware of his homosexuality, he has no idea where to go from there. Society has provided none of the guidelines, activities, or support which are available to the young person who becomes aware of heterosexual interests.

The heterosexual adolescent knows a great deal about heterosexuality and the existence of other heterosexuals. The message is promoted almost overpoweringly through advertising, television, films, books, and humor, as well as through the overt behavior of the adults in his world. The homosexual has no such guidance in building an identity.

The story of the young homosexual who wonders what he is and whether there are others like him is so familiar in the gay world as to be trite. One friend told me that as a young teen-ager he developed an intense crush on one of the actors in a television soap opera. He couldn't miss the show for a day. Watching the actor embrace and kiss the women on the program, he would imagine what it would be like to be held by him himself, but he had no idea what to make of these fantasies and feelings.

There was no likelihood that my friend could ever have seen a man being held and kissed by another man on television or anywhere else. There was no way to conceive of a homosexual role that was essentially masculine—only women were attracted to men and received their attentions in return.

He did not even learn that there were such things as homosexuality and homosexuals until years later. When he finally came out into the gay world after college, he learned that the actor he had worshiped was notoriously gay. "If only I could have known back then," he said, "it sure would have made things a lot easier."

The first information about homosexuality that the young homosexual is likely to get reaches him in the form of the dirty jokes and put-down remarks circulated among his peers or overheard from adults. When homosexuals are portrayed as grotesquely effeminate and repulsive, objects of derision and snide humor, he begins to wonder, Is *that* what I am?

Rather than speak to anybody about his inner feelings, he is likely to try to find out more about himself by reading books that deal with homosexuality. He may thumb through the text of a book on abnormal psychology, carefully looking up each reference to homosexuality as a sickness or perversion, or he may be lucky or unlucky enough to locate an entire book on the subject expounding one or another unflattering "explanation" of homosexuality. In any case, he encounters nothing positive with which to identify and may indeed acquire enough biased misinformation to cause him severe and lasting emotional problems.

When he first comes out into the gay world, the young homosexual is likely to be easily molded by his first experiences with it. In the first excitement of finally finding other people like himself, he may do everything possible to make himself one of the crowd.

Anxious to fit in and find acceptance, the young homosexual may be rapidly socialized into the gay subculture. For the first time, he is likely to find a way of life with which he can identify and other homosexuals after whom he can style his dress, behavior, and attitudes. He encounters the basic elements out of which he can create his own gay identity.

The gay subculture is enormously diverse; gay bars differ from one part of town to another, from one city to another. Nevertheless, gay people themselves have stereotypes about what most homosexuals are like and what one can expect in adopting a gay life-style. Until recently, gay people questioned these myths about themselves as seldom as straight society questioned *its* beliefs about homosexuals, so when the young homosexual asked those he met after first coming out what he could expect in the gay world, the answers he got were not necessarily very accurate.

I remember my own early experiences after I first came out into the bars. Often the older homosexuals, who had more time on their hands, were most willing to impart a little inside information to the newcomer, and perhaps buy him a drink while chatting.

When I tried to get a clearer picture of what gay people were like in general, I was told that even the most masculine-looking individuals were regular queens at heart. Trying to look butch was just a façade, and the more a guy tried to disguise his effeminacy, the more effeminate he was likely to be. This wisdom was often reinforced by my mentors' behavior. If a particularly butch-looking stud happened to turn up in the bar, they would try to find some opportunity to put him in his place: *Oh really, Mary, who do you think you're fooling.*

I was also given to believe that homosexuals were among the most devious, two-faced people on earth. Everyone had at least one plot in the works, one vendetta to pursue, one pricelessly vicious remark to make to a cherished enemy or rival. Nor was the gay world they represented to me a particularly attractive place to spend one's life. There was no more hideous fate than to be homosexual, old, and poor. Looks were all that mattered, and once they were gone you paid for any love you got. There was no such thing as a lasting or happy gay relationship; infidelity and dishonesty were so commonplace that one was a fool not to play the game oneself.

These kind insights had no small influence in shaping my first few years in the gay world. Other young homosexuals might have gotten a totally different picture, but the one I got was anything but sunny. I despaired of ever meeting anyone with whom to build a life, and I worried about how *I* would face the loneliness of old age. I began to dress more along the lines of what I thought was expected of me, and I behaved, I'm afraid, just about as shallowly as I expected others to behave.

Like everybody else, gay people can often be the victims of their own myths. It took me several years of meeting a broader cross section of gay people, fine individuals whom I respected, admired, and sometimes loved, to realize I had been sold a bill of goods no better than that offered me by straight society.

In searching for an identity upon which to base a happy life, the young homosexual often has to travel a tortuous path. That so many make it and find themselves, and that the gay world is as diverse as it is, is a tribute to the resiliency and positive potential—and occasionally to the obstinacy—of the human spirit. The stereotypical thinking of both the straight and gay worlds persists, but surprisingly few gay people are willing to be turned into stereotypes themselves.

## THE FEMININE ROLE

The myth has it that male homosexuals are all effeminate. Some people even believe that all homosexuals secretly wish to be women. Neither, of course, is true.

Stereotypical thinking is difficult to avoid. As soon as one makes a generalization, he risks losing sight of diversity. No generalizations can validly be made about homosexuals as a group, except that they prefer members of their own sex as sexual partners. At the same time, various distinct types of gay people can be found in the gay world. The discussion of different types of people need not, however, imply stereotypes, if we keep in mind that the search for similarities often produces an artificial blindness to differences.

The fact that some gay people more or less fit our definition of effeminacy implies neither that all gay people are effeminate nor that those who are, are effeminate to the same degree and the same manner. A few homosexuals live up to society's least flattering expectations concerning effeminacy; others are among the most beautiful, warm, gentle, and gracefully feminine human beings one could have the good fortune to know.

On a number of occasions of acute organizational tensions in the movement, one young man did more than anyone else to soothe feelings and draw people back together. Ron is a beautiful, warm, loving person who has a special ability to reach out to other gays of all types and help them understand one another. It is a gift, I think, that comes from not being bound within the confines of any one sexual role: he is simply a very sincere, lovely human being. No matter how high feelings of division and anger are running, nobody can help but trust him and respond to his attempts to restore communication.

Ron is good in a crisis, but he really comes into his own when there is cause for exuberance and joy. At some of the first gay dances in New York in the summer of 1970, nonmovement gays, accustomed to nothing but the bars, felt somewhat ill at ease coming to an all-gay affair held in a public place, often a church. Ron had a particular knack for making them feel at home. At one dance he showed up in hot pants, a tie-dyed T-shirt with little silver wings affixed to the back, a gay-power balloon tied to his wrist, and flowers in his hair. Making his way through the crowd, he passed out little gifts: plastic wedding rings and other favors. At the march on the State Capitol early in 1971, he helped to raise spirits and quell anxiety about a confrontation with the police. Wearing an outrageously large 1950's garden hat, a wig, and a sort of silken boa, he passed through the crowd, stopping to hug a person here, camping with another there. This is not "effeminacy," it's freedom. We'd be lucky if there were more of it around today.

Most of the time, people appear at their best when they express their inner selves with integrity, seeking to realize their potential as individuals. Many men, both homosexual and heterosexual, find within themselves feelings, ways of relating to others, ways of expressing their emotions, that we tend to consider feminine, just as many women find elements within their personalities that are likely to be considered masculine.

Psychological differences based on gender are in fact not nearly so great as they are expected to be in our society. Many people deny themselves a richness and breadth of experience simply because they have been taught that one must adhere strictly to either a man's or a woman's role, and nothing in between. We are all a blend of masculine and feminine and are more likely to be at home with ourselves and the world if we acknowledge and explore that fact.

The uninformed say that homosexuals don't know which sex they are. Quite the contrary is true. If we are talking only about biological gender, only the most seriously disturbed individuals would be likely to confuse the physical fact of being male or female. If we are talking about sexual identity, it is still true that few homosexuals have any doubts about the matter. The vast majority of male homosexuals see themselves as men and the vast majority of female homosexuals see themselves as women. Few would have things any other way, and most are quite satisfied with the congruence between their gender and their sexual identity.

Male homosexuals are attracted to other men, not because they see themselves as or wish to be women, but simply bcause they find other men sexually exciting. The feeling of sexual attraction is the same, whether one is heterosexual or homosexual.

Many societies other than our own do not discourage homosexuality, but some of these provide a special feminine role for the homosexual. In these societies, homosexuality is acceptable in conjunction with transvestism: homosexuals are expected to dress as women and pattern their behavior on that of women. Sometimes special status or supernatural powers are attributed to homosexual transvestites and they are powerful figures within the community. In other cases no distinction is made between them and actual women —a man may take a transvestite as a wife without any social stigma.

Part of the myth of homosexual effeminacy can probably be attributed to a similar pattern in our own society, although there is nowhere near the same degree of social approval. While American society as a whole does not tolerate homosexual behavior, some ethnic groups within the larger population are more tolerant than others. Blacks and Latins have tended to be a good deal more accepting of homosexuals if they adopt an openly feminine role. It is the homosexual who does not visibly differ from other men who runs the greater risk of encountering hostility.

In our society, it is considered more "natural" for a homosexual to adopt feminine characterisitics than it is for him to maintain a masculine role. Transvestites, who may be either heterosexual or homosexual, are also more easily accepted if they are homosexual. A certain amount of transvestism is tolerated in our society: female impersonation, for example, is considered a legitimate part of the theater, although it is uncommon.

Sexual identity is not necessarily the same as sexual role. A man may consider himself male and still enjoy dressing as a woman from time to time. We tend to think of sexual roles as being almost instinctive, but they are actually quite fluid and can be consciously assumed. Most people occasionally mimic somebody of the opposite sex, adopt the appropriate mannerisms and tone of voice, without thinking anything of it. What they are actually doing is assuming another sexual role for a moment, and it certainly does not require a major effort.

For some people, experimentation with the opposite sexual role is pleasurable in a social context—a fun thing to do. For others, it has additional enjoyment in a sexual context and can provide a sexual thrill in and of itself. Transvestites are people of any sexual orientation who enjoy dressing as members of the opposite sex and adopting the mannerisms and behavior commonly associated with that sexual role.

The general ignorance about transvestites is just about equal to that about homosexuals. Many straight people assume that all homosexuals are transvestites, that all transvestites are homosexuals, and further confuse the issue by believing that both homosexuals and transvestites wish to be women. The real situation is quite different.

There are both homosexual and heterosexual transvestites, but those in the gay world have found an open acceptance that is denied their straight counterparts. The nonhomosexual transvestite is generally very much in the closet; there are very few circumstances under which it is considered acceptable for him to cross-dress openly.

Many straight transvestites are married, some try to hide their interest in cross-dressing from their wives, while others incorporate it into their marital sex lives. A heterosexual transvestite and his mate will occasionally live together as two women. Some straight transvestites will dress in women's clothing before having sexual intercourse. In such cases, the transvestism is likely to be a shared secret, a source of mutual embarrassment and guilt.

Unmarried transvestites may cross-dress in the privacy of their own homes. Sometimes they derive sexual pleasure from looking at themselves in the mirror, but they rarely appear in public. A few nonhomosexual transvestites become professional female impersonators or become involved in the social circle and activities of gay transvestites. Since they do not feel a basic attraction for members of their own sex, though, their involvement is likely to be superficial. Because the straight world does not tolerate transvestism, straight transvestites find it difficult to meet others who share their interests, and the straight drag scene tends to be a private one, quite different from the gay drag scene.

An interest in cross-dressing is not all that uncommon. Many young boys try on their mother's or sister's clothing at some time, yet develop no lasting interest in the practice. Similarly—especially in all-male institutions such as prep schools and military establishments—some individuals welcome the opportunity to dress and act as women in plays and other dramatic presentations. While some may consider themselves transvestites, most simply find it a fun thing to do once in a while, or consider it a lark. In the same vein, one or two men in every social circle may get a kick out of dressing as women at masquerade parties. This need not mean that they are secret transvestites; it may just indicate enjoyment in cross-dressing.

Sometimes it is difficult to make a distinction between transvestism and fetishism. Many men find the feel of women's underclothes highly stimulating; silk can be pretty sexy. Some men, heterosexual or homosexual, enjoy wearing women's underwear beneath their regular clothing. Others find it exciting to wear silk panties or other women's garments during sex.

Transvestism is certainly not limited to men. There are also female transvestites, but as in the case with female homosexuality, less attention is usually paid to the matter. Under many circumstances, it is not considered shocking for a woman to wear male styles; some men find a tomboy look particularly appealing. Recent fashions for women have appropriated many articles of men's clothing into the feminine wardrobe, and several times in history there have been exchanges—and sometimes reversals—in the style of clothing considered appropriate for men and women. Remember the wigs and ruffled sleeves of the founding fathers.

Male homosexual transvestites have a well-established place within the gay subculture. Elegant drag shows, beauty contests, and drag balls are regularly scheduled events in some large cities, and cross-dressing is a feature of some private gay parties. Some female impersonators become popular entertainment figures and culture heroines in the gay community, although not all female impersonators are gay. I was interested to discover what great appeal female impersonation seems to have for some straight people. Various drag reviews travel around the country and the audiences are seldom exclusively gay. The country-club set seems to have a fondness for these shows as a risqué form of entertainment. Even television today tries to milk a lot of humor out of situations in which comedians dress as women.

The gay transvestite encounters mixed responses in the gay world. In some circles the transvestite is admired for her outrageous courage in daring to flout society's sexual taboos so flagrantly while the majority of homosexuals are doing their best to keep out of the public eye. There is not as much irony as it might seem in the widely held feeling that it "takes balls" to be a transvestite. Many gay people believe the transvestite has contributed most toward creating a distinct gay subculture and developing the fine art of camp.

Nevertheless, the gay transvestite encounters occasional hostility from other homosexuals. The reasons for these attitudes are complex. Homosexuals in some social circles never come in contact with transvestites and know nothing about them other than the stereotypes they may have acquired. Others adopt the prevailing straight attitude that transvestism is "sick," while vehemently denying that straight society is right in viewing all homosexuals that way. For a few homosexuals, self-esteem seems to depend on being able to feel superior to somebody else. They view themselves as respectable and the transvestite as disreputable.

The transvestite, the "respectable" homosexual argues, gives all homosexuals a bad name: *they* are the queer ones, not us. What these people are really saying is that straight society's insistence on role playing and sexual conformity is justified everywhere but in the bedroom. Denied the right to be different themselves, they take comfort in scorning others for *their* differences.

Some homosexuals are uncomfortable in the presence of transvestites for other reasons. For one thing, most homosexuals are interested in sex partners who look like men and are thrown off balance by men who look like women. On a deeper level, many homosexuals have gone through major identity problems because of straight society's definition of homosexuals as pseudo-women. To be confronted with a homosexual who does look and behave like a woman can resurrect these earlier conflicts and threatening questions about one's own sexual status.

While many transvestites never appear in drag outside of gay circles, some enjoy being seen in public. For them, a major part of the pleasure in cross-dressing is to be seen and mistaken for a woman. It takes courage to cross-dress in public, and many street transvestites, in spite of their feminine appearance, are very well able to defend themselves if it comes to that.

The gay transvestite is more likely to be victimized by hostile straights or the police than by the average gay. Often more easily identified than other homosexuals, transvestites are frequently attacked in public. In many states, laws prohibiting "impersonation" or "masquerading" are used solely as an excuse for harassing or arresting transvestites, and the police will often interpret laws prohibiting "lewd and indecent" behavior to cover transvestism. For some, cross-dressing in public is an act of social protest and anger. Told that they are the lowest of the low—the "queer queers"—some transvestites throw it back in society's face as a challenge. Gay people who pride themselves on coming out openly in public now that the liberation movement has taken hold should remember that many transvestites have been putting themselves on the line for years.

It is often more difficult to come out and accept oneself as a transvestite than as a homosexual. Just as it takes some straight people a while to feel comfortable with gay friends, some gay people have difficulty making friends with transvestites until they overcome their own problems about sexual roles.

The summer I first came out in Albany, the Jewel Box Revue, a well-known female-impersonation show, had a long engagement at a well-to-do resort in the suburbs. I saw the remarkable performance several times—you simply could not tell that the performers were not women, and very beautiful ones at that. There were many apparently straight men in the audience, mostly with wives or dates, and they seemed to get as much out of the striptease as the men I saw in later years at heterosexual burlesque shows. There seemed to be an added thrill in the fact that when the last pieces of clothing were removed, a man stood before them.

I brought home a program for the review, filled with photographs of the performers in drag with their real names listed below, and took care to hide it where my parents would not discover it. I must not have taken sufficient care, for they did discover it and confronted me with it one night: why do all these women have men's names? The resulting scene—mostly a guilty overreaction on my part—was one that haunted me for years, making me uncomfortable about my own sexual identity and enormously uptight about the transvestites I met from time to time. I never really thought of transvestites as people after that until I met several in the movement and learned what beautiful and courageous human beings they could be.

In spite of the fact that many transvestites like to think of themselves as women and prefer to be addressed as women, not all want any physical alteration of their gender through sex-change operations. Some transvestites much prefer what we think of as the masculine role in bed and have no desire for a different set of genitals.

There are some transvestites and homosexuals who do wish they were women, or who feel that they are actually "women in men's bodies." In some cases this seems to derive from a confusion over sexual identity stemming from straight society's hostility toward those who deviate from the sexual "norm." *If I were really a woman, then it would be all right to sleep with men or wear women's clothing.* These cases should not be confused with those involving actual transsexuals, who have developed sexual identities at odds with their physical gender, and who are encouraged today to undergo operations for sex modification or alteration.

The public tends to assume that transsexuals are homosexuals looking for an easy way to find acceptance. Transsexuals themselves consistently deny this and have been supported by what little research has been done on the phenomenon. Public attitudes being what they are, to undergo an alteration of gender requires no small amount of determination and courage. It is anything but an easy out.

The sensitivity about sexual roles typical in society at large is reflected in the gay world in many ways. In earlier years, many gay people played "butch" or "femme" roles in imitation of those which straight society insisted upon. Although this practice has become uncommon today, it still persists in some social circles.

Many gays—myself included—have reacted to the stereotype of homosexual "effeminacy" by consciously and sometimes rather defensively seeking to create a "masculine" image. In most gay bars today you seldom encounter many people dressed in what would be considered an effeminate style.

Although most straight people think of homosexuals only in terms of effeminacy, some will speak about "butch" and "femme" stereotypes as though all homosexuals could be fit into one or the other category. According to them, the "butch" homosexual looks no more like a "real" man than the "femme" homosexual looks like a woman. Both are viewed as travesties of the standard heterosexual roles.

"Butch" homosexuals are said to be easily spotted by their exaggeratedly masculine attire. They look a little too rugged, a little too *macho* to be convincing. Somehow they always manage to overdo it, and their inevitable homosexual effeminacy shows through.

This stereotype is no more representative of the average homosexual than any other, and probably derives from a superficial acquaintance with one segment of the gay world—the leather and Western set. Just as transvestites often seek to personify the feminine role, there are some homosexuals who will deliberately exaggerate the masculine role. This is not typical of the average gay, but represents a particular scene within the gay world with which few straight people are familiar. Those who dress in Western style or wear a great deal of leather are not trying to blend into the crowd any more than a transvestite is: they are deliberately creating an image.

This form of self-conscious and overdrawn "masculinity" is a complex subject in its own right, and sheds light on the aggressive character of the masculine role in our society.

# How Dangerous Is the Gay World?

Many people say the gay world is a dangerous place to live. Although homosexuals sometimes run the risk of being beaten up or attacked by hostile straights, the greater danger is said to lie within the gay world itself.

"Butch" homosexuals, according to some straight people, are a particularly dangerous lot. They go to embarrassing extremes in the attempt to look masculine, and some of them act tough and aggressive in an attempt to hide their homosexuality. A few of them go further, and enjoy brutalizing their sex partners. They pick up an unsuspecting homosexual, take him home, and torture him. There is no way to recognize these sadists in advance, so homosexuals take their lives in their hands when they become involved with "butch" types.

Belief in this myth is not restricted to the straight world.

When I was still relatively new to gay life, I got occasional warnings about homosexual sadists, individuals who would pretend to be interested in conventional homosexual relations and then beat or torture their victims when they got them home.

I knew there were leather bars in New York, but I had been warned to stay away from them: just about everyone in the leather crowd was supposed to be involved in some form of sadomasochism—S&M sex. From time to time, a rough-looking number wearing a leather jacket and boots would saunter into one of the bars where I hung out, loiter sullenly for a while, looking too fierce to approach, play a game of pool, and finally stalk out, the very image of a rebellious, angry 1950's hood.

I was attracted to the look. In high school, I had secretly wished that I could run with a pack of toughs from the North End of town, instead of being the rather quiet and intellectual type I'd been. I used to wish that I could get away with wearing a leather jacket, be a Walter Mitty on a motorcycle. The guys in the gang didn't have to worry about being called queer, even though they spent most of their time together.

When I finally summoned up the nerve for my first trip to a leather bar, I wasn't certain what to expect. The motorcycles parked in front made me think I'd quickly be recognized as an interloper and bounced out on my ear.

It was still early and the bar was not yet crowded. A few guys were playing pool, others leaned against the bar, the wall, or the jukebox, as if to suggest that no real man would be caught sitting down when some action might break out at any moment. Almost everyone was wearing a leather jacket. Some wore leather pants and shirts, chains, heavy belts, motorcycle caps, and bike club insignia. A few wore jeans and boots, and I spotted an occasional cowboy hat. Nothing about the atmosphere suggested that this was a gay bar.

I tried to blend into the background, not wanting to be taken for the sightseer I was. By eleven o'clock, the place was packed. The atmosphere became heavy, hot, and sweaty—sensual and ominous. I had never seen such a collection of tough-looking people. I found a number of them very attractive, but the last thing I wanted was to call attention to myself. As far as I knew, I was in a den of sadists.

Having broken the ice, I began to go to the leather bars every once in a while. I enjoyed the milieu, but was still too nervous to become involved with anyone. Wild stories circulated in the gay world about the leather crowd, and I had no idea how much truth there was in them. I knew that some better-known straight "experts" on homosexuality had claimed the homosexual sadist was one of the most vicious, cruel creatures walking the earth, and I wasn't about to take any chances.

It was quite a while before I began to realize how distorted these outside appraisals of the leather crowd were. If I was in any danger in the leather bars, it was only because of the fairly remote possibility of a police raid and being roughed up by an overzealous cop whose sadism was sanctioned by law.

## LEATHER

There is no simple way of coming to terms with the leather scene. In some ways it appears to be a reverse form of transvestism; in others it appears to be essentially fetishistic. Although it is not directly linked to sadomasochism, more than half of the gay people who are into leather are into S&M sex as well.

The gay leather scene has its counterpart in the straight world, ranging from publicly visible straight motorcycle clubs to secret heterosexual clubs that offer their members an opportunity to engage discreetly in fetishistic and sadomasochistic sex. There are many other types of fetishes, but where leather is concerned, it is often difficult to tell where a fetish leaves off and a life-style begins.

If the leather scene and S&M sex are difficult to come to terms with, why bother? Straight people already have enough difficulty understanding and accepting even the most conventional homosexuals. If these things are kept well hidden when they occur in a heterosexual context, why should any homosexual admit that they constitute one important segment of the gay world?

Until recently, society did not care to know about homosexuals and most homosexuals were afraid to speak up for themselves. Now gay liberation has arrived, and increasing numbers of gay people are coming out of the closet, demanding an end to discriminatory treatment. As we leave the closet, straight people find that we are not as different and strange as they had been led to believe: we are human after all. Suddenly, it seems, we have an image to maintain—homosexuals are becoming respectable.

When the closet door swings open, it opens for everyone. Liberation is not just for the gay people whom society finds it easiest to accept, it is for all of us. There can be no such thing as a second-class homosexual, somebody who is expected to remain in the closet while more acceptable homosexuals take their place in society.

Gay transvestites have often been asked to accept the status of second-class homosexuals. Some gay people view them as an embarrassment and would prefer that they not come to the public's attention. Homosexuals involved in the leather and S&M scenes are an even greater embarrassment. They are never mentioned in movement rhetoric—straight society would never understand.

If I thought it necessary to present an artificially flattering image of gay people there are many things I would conveniently fail to mention in this book, but I do not. Either the time has come when we can speak honestly and openly about sexuality, or there is little purpose in writing or reading this book. If I had more personal experience with transvestism I would cover it at greater length than I have. Since I have had more experience with the leather and S&M scenes, I have no intention of ignoring them for cosmetic purposes. Few parts of the gay world are still so deeply hidden in the obscurity of the closet.

In cities where there is a large gay community, there is usually at least one leather bar, and often several. People come in wearing a great deal of leather or other rugged, butch-looking clothing. The atmosphere is tough, somewhat self-consciously masculine. A stranger entering unaware might think—except for the suspicious absence of women—that he had stumbled into the favorite watering hole for a number of local motorcycle gangs.

The leather bars have an etiquette which is nearly as demanding as that of straight society. No camping or blatantly effeminate behavior is tolerated. Dancing is unthinkable and any overt signs of affection are strongly discouraged. The colorful and flamboyant clothing which is typical of many other gay bars is unwelcome here; anyone who comes into the bar dressed in a less than aggressively masculine fashion is likely to be met with hostility. Women are usually barred, although a few bars will admit women who are into the scene themselves The whole milieu is one of *nobody here but us men.*

These bars cater to the leather, Western, and S&M elements in the gay community. The dividing line between these groups is very vague. Depending on the part of the country and the time of year, a leather or Western look usually predominates: In New York, for example, some individuals dress in denim, boots, and Western hats all year round, and there are always a few dedicated souls who will turn up in full leather, head to toe, at the height of the summer's heat. But generally the crowd wears leather during the winter and denim during the summer.

Not everyone who wears leather or Western dress is also involved in the S&M scene, but most people who hang out in the leather bars have had at least some experience with sadomasochistic sex. Because the bars have a reputation for catering primarily to the S&M set, people whose interests are primarily sadomasochistic rather than fetishistic are drawn to them and tend to adopt the prevailing mode of dress. By the same token, those whose interest is basically fetishistic have frequent exposure to the S&M scene and may decide to experiment with it.

The leather crowd is quite sensitive about its image. Considering the average gay too effeminate, people in the leather scene are generally intolerant of transvestites. Any suggestion that they are involved in a dressing-up scene themselves, that they are wearing leather and Western *drag,* had better not be made by an outsider. In private they do not take themselves so seriously, but one of the most important parts of the scene is coming on as though one always dressed that way. Certainly some of the leather people do dress this way all the time, but that is hardly true of the bankers, dentists, and business executives who lead quite a different life by day than they do by night.

If transvestites sometimes exaggerate society's feminine role, the leather and Western crowd carries the masculine role to an equal extreme. They are cowboys and motorcycle hoods, two groups considered to be particularly virile in our society, yet at the same time notorious for their homosexual inclinations. The television version of the winning of the West has been carefully mythologized, and the homosexual side of life on the range minimized. The more the cowboy was viewed as the archetypal American hero, the more conventional the portrayal of his sex life became. The motorcycle tough, however, still fulfills the role of antihero, and it is still quite common to hear "latent" homosexuality cited as the major force which binds the members of a gang together.

The exaggeration of masculine and feminine roles is not characteristic of most gay people, but this role playing takes place much more openly in the gay world than it does in society at large, and gay people tend to be more frank about it.

There are various reasons why a person might enjoy dressing up to play a role that has little to do with his everyday life. If he is attracted to others who favor the leather and Western bars, he will have to adopt the image himself if he is to have much success in meeting others there. He must visually define himself as part of the crowd, part of the scene.

It usually goes further than this. For many people, dressing in leather or in Western style is sexually exciting, both in terms of how one feels about the image one has created for oneself and how others react to that image. Most people have had this experience: if you have an outfit that you feel makes you look particularly sexy—a bathing suit you only dare to wear once in a while, a shirt which makes you look particularly virile—there's a certain thrill in wearing it that derives from the reaction you produce, or expect to produce, in others.

In the leather bars the game is far more direct. People often react more to appearance than to personality. You come into the bar dressed like a rough stud charged with animal passion: the response can be electric. People's eyes explore you. The atmosphere becomes sensual and erotic. It is as though you had stepped into a movie and were suddenly larger than life, half yourself, half the character you have created.

The element of fetishism increases the sexual tension. Some people become sexually aroused just by looking at your leather clothing, smelling its musky animal scent, brushing past you. There may be an exciting feeling of power and control, you have become a visual aphrodisiac.

If you yourself are turned on by leather, the sexuality of the situation increases. You feel the leather clinging to your flesh, a warm, erotic friction, a second skin that embraces your every motion. Its animal smell is intoxicating: you feel like a beast on the prowl, a new creature to whom your everyday standards simply don't apply.

Where does this taste for leather come from? As usual, the standard psychoanalytic explanation that fetishes result from traumatic experiences does little to explain the phenomenon. Few people who are into the scene have had any traumatic experiences with leather in their youth. Most frequently, a taste for leather starts at the level of fantasy and develops further once one has begun to wear it. In a sense, it is another form of coming out. A fascination for leather is not limited to the gay world, nor even to men. The people who specialize in leather clothing and goods insist that the heterosexual leather and S&M scene makes the gay leather scene look insignificant by comparison, although the former is kept much more under cover, indulged in private clubs. Some women are as aroused by dressing in full leather as men are. Women dressed in leather often play a stereotypical role in heterosexual sadomasochistic pornography.

What is there about leather that makes it so exciting for some people?

Beyond its appearance, texture, and smell, leather also has various psychological associations in our culture which may add to sexual appeal. It is often associated with sadomasochistic sex, brutality, and sexual abandon. Some people who are not actually involved in the S&M scene find a thrill in looking as though they were. Their appearance creates a whole different set of expectations and reactions in others which they may find more stimulating than those they encounter when dressed more conventionally.

Not everyone involved in the leather scene leads a double life of conformity by day and nonconformity by night. Some people build an entire lifestyle around their taste for leather and the motorcycle milieu associated with it.

Bike clubs are an important part of the leather bar scene. A string of motorcycles is always lined up in front of any bar that is a going concern. Inside there are likely to be banners with the insignia of the different clubs that patronize the bar, hooks for hanging helmets, and sometimes even a particularly tough bike on display. Some of the bike clubs are exclusively gay, some are exclusively S&M, while others are mixed or exclusively heterosexual. Not all motorcycle clubs have a sexual component—there are people who are interested in bikes alone. Even some exclusively gay clubs, many of whose members do not own motorcycles, will insist that there is no sex involved and sometimes deny their homosexual orientation. Again, it is often a matter of maintaining an image.

The bike clubs serve as well-established social organizations, planning excursions to other cities and abroad, conferences, cycle competitions, and social events. They are the backbone of the leather scene and can make or break any particular leather bar.

The leather crowd is notoriously fickle about its watering places. If too many sightseers show up, or if the bar catches on with the nonleather crowd, its future is limited. There is a fascination for the leather scene in the gay community at large, and when a bar acquires a reputation as *the* place for the leather set, many gays who are not into the scene will begin to frequent it out of simple curiosity or an attraction to the regular clientele. When this happens the bike clubs will move on to another bar. The leather crowd as a whole soon follows.

While outsiders and sightseers may find the atmosphere in leather bars clannish and hostile, those who have been around for some time enjoy a far friendlier atmosphere than prevails in most nonleather gay bars. Much more than the average gay bar, the leather bar serves as a focus for the interests and the needs of the segment of the gay community which frequents it.

In New York, the leather bars are the closest thing to community bars that can be found in the gay subculture. Prices remain low in comparison to other bars. Free brunches and bike washings are sometimes offered during the day, and raffles, films, and reduced prices on drinks are generally available various nights of the week. The cycle clubs post their schedules of events, and print club newspapers. Often a leather bar has connections with local businesses which cater to the clothing tastes of the leather set and the interests of the S&M crowd.

These bars have both their good and their bad features. While they demand a high degree of conformity in dress—some bars even refuse to serve those who are not "in uniform"— there is a greater acceptance of diversity in sexual interests and preferences. The atmosphere is comparatively nonjudgmental, and people are more frank about personal sexual tastes that would be viewed as shocking in other bars. Age is a good deal less important in the leather bars than elsewhere.

The leather scene blends into the S&M scene. At a typical leather bar, some of those dressed in leather have no interest in sadomasochistic sex, while more are interested in nothing else.

Like homosexuality and some of the other variations of sexual behavior discussed so far, sadomasochism is taboo in our culture, although it is far from uncommon among both homosexuals and heterosexuals. Gay people, having crossed one taboo sexual frontier, are often more liberated about their other sexual tastes, but many gays balk at leather and S&M. There is just as much confusion and misinformation about fetishism and sadomasochism in straight society as there is about homosexuality, and much of it spills over into the gay world.

You may have accepted yourself as gay, but to come out into leather is another major step. You've been led to believe that people with fetishes are bizarre, and to go beyond the realm of fantasy is no easy thing. If it seems peculiar to you that you should find it sexually exciting to dress up a certain way, you're sure that it will strike others who don't understand the feelings involved as even more peculiar.

But finally you take the big step, you get some leather and try wearing it. You find that it's just as much fun as you'd imagined it would be, but—more important—you find you're the same person you were before. You have not been suddenly transformed into some bizarre and warped creature with the most depraved of sexual tastes. Your tastes may be somewhat out of the ordinary, they may run counter to what society accepts, but they do not make you any worse a person or less deserving of respect for having expressed them. On the contrary, you may feel that you have been more honest with yourself than those who do not dare explore the entirety of their sexual makeup.

As you begin to view yourself in this light, your appraisal of others may change as well. Others may have sexual tastes that strike you as peculiar, but after all, they're as entitled to them as you are to yours. Furthermore, having come to see sexuality as a mode of self-expression, rather than self-definition, you may feel freer to explore other forms of sexuality yourself.

## S&M

Many people have misconceptions about the S&M scene. They assume that all sadomasochism involves pain and torture. How can pain be pleasurable, they ask, and how can anyone take pleasure in inflicting pain on someone else?

Although most people have heard of the Marquis de Sade and are aware that sadists and masochists exist, they seldom recognize the various forms of sadomasochism which are quite commonplace in our society.

Heterosexual pornography is replete with examples of sadistic and brutal treatment of women, but one need not turn to under-the-counter material for examples of sadomasochistic fantasy. The whole adventure genre of literature, especially detective and crime novels, plays on the sadomasochistic fantasies of the reader. Women are generally cast in a masochistic role, subject to beating, rape, and various forms of bondage. While the hero of such works usually plays the sadist in relation to women, he may well undergo excruciating torture at the hands of his enemies. The popularity of James Bond indicates the extent of public fascination with sadomasochism. The fantasies developed in this type of literature and films are essentially the same as those in many S&M relationships.

Other concrete manifestations of sadomasochism are quite evident in our society. Rape, basically sadistic in itself, is often accompanied by torture and disfiguration of the victim. Wife beating is often thinly disguised sadism, and child abuse continues to be a serious national problem. Sadistic treatment of newcomers to groups, whether neighborhoods, social circles, athletic teams, fraternities, or sororities, is an expected part of initiation. Sadism is even unofficially legitimate in some professions: police interrogation and the treatment of inmates in prisons and mental hospitals.

These manifestations of sadomasochism are predominantly involuntary. There is no choice or mutual agreement involved, and the masochist is viewed as a victim.

Many people assume that the S&M scene follows this pattern. They believe that most masochism is involuntary, and that sadists take particular pleasure in seeking out and preying upon unwilling victims.

It just doesn't work that way.

Those involved in the S&M scene play by certain rules. S&M sex should be voluntary—no one should be forced into a situation which he does not freely choose. A sadomasochistic sexual experience is expected to be satisfying for everyone involved, masochist and sadist alike. Though someone may play the role of a victim in acting out a fantasy, no one is to be victimized. People who will not play by these rules are not welcome in the game and are shunned by the regulars in the S&M crowd.

No two people are exactly alike: this applies to sexual tastes as well. In S&M sex, where sexual tastes are often more specific than elsewhere in the gay world, it is more important to establish in advance what each person's interests are if the experience is to be mutually enjoyable. As a result, quite a bit more preliminary communication is involved in S&M cruising.

This is accomplished in a number of ways. In the leather bars, it is impossible to be certain that someone is interested in S&M sex merely by checking out his basic mode of dress, since virtually everyone is wearing leather or denim. There are, however, more specific cues for the cognoscenti.

Those who are into S&M frequently wear keys hanging from their belts. On the East Coast, keys worn on the left indicate a preference for sadism, while those worn on the right indicate a preference for masochism. On the West Coast, the reverse is true. Similarly, gloves tucked into a pocket or fastened with a flap to the shoulder of a leather jacket, chains on either boots or jacket shoulders, are indicators of sexual preferences. A variety of lesser-known signs and symbols are also used, but most people in the scene don't hesitate to ask a potential partner about his interests if they are in doubt.

An individual's sexual tastes are rarely so rigid that he must search for the one person in a million who might share them. While there may be a particular S&M scene a person prefers, he is likely to find many others enjoyable. Some of the people in the S&M scene are perfectly willing to become involved in nonsadomasochistic sex if their partner isn't interested in it. Furthermore, although some individuals adhere to either a sadistic or a masochistic role, it is more common to experiment with both.

Just what is involved in S&M sex?

There is an enormous variety of sadomasochistic sexual practices. S&M sex may simply be "rough sex," an especially active tumble in bed, some wrestling around, and the hitting and biting, the fierce embraces, that most people reserve for the moment of climax.

Some S&M sex involves the deliberate intensification of bodily sensations associated with more conventional sex acts. Probably the most common form of sensual intensification practiced by the S&M crowd has to do with bondage or constriction. In essence, bondage boils down to a variety of means for applying pressure to the body and restricting its movement, ranging from wearing tight clothing during sex to being tied up or chained in a sexually stimulating manner. Sexual arousal is often intensified by sensations of pressure, constriction, or stretching; muscles tighten, limbs are extended, and the body is arched. Bondage heightens these sensations.

Psychologically, bondage may be sexually exciting because it has become associated with these pleasurable sensations, or because the implements used have a fetishistic appeal. The symbolic meanings attached to ropes, chains, handcuffs, and shackles probably cause some people to prefer one to another. Themes of bondage and restraint are not uncommon in the average person's dreams and fantasies, and these implements often have unconscious associations.

For some, the role of captive, prisoner, or slave is the source of sexual excitement. The feeling of helplessness and dependence, the need to trust the sexual partner, and the sensation of anxiety tinged with fear are stimulating to some people. Many people become sexually aroused when frightened or endangered, and brief sexual liaisons often form when strangers are thrown together during a natural disaster or other crisis. Some forms of S&M sex seem to play upon these basic feelings.

Enjoyment of bondage and constriction is also linked for some to pleasure in releasing sexual inhibitions. For most of us, these inhibitions are apparent not only in public, but are also carried over into the bedroom. Restraint is expected in sexual behavior; sexual abandon is frowned upon.

Sex may be enjoyed, but only in moderation. Many people are only comfortable making love in the dark where they cannot see one another's bodies. Many people try to make as little noise as possible during sex. To get really wild in bed, to thrash around and cry out in passion, is considered immodest and indiscreet. What if the children or the neighbors should hear?

Yet sexual exuberance is a basic part of human sexuality. In many societies sex is expected to be on the wild side. Biting, slapping, and scratching are common, and moaning or crying out in passion are signs of normal sexual satisfaction, not bizarre thrills. We have been conditioned to limit the expressiveness of our sexuality, and the inhibitions are enormously strong.

Some people find that bondage frees them of these inhibitions. When one is chained or bound, inhibition is externalized and the individual is freed to let his body do whatever it will within these artificial limits. One can writhe and strain in sexual ecstasy, feeling that his behavior is under control. We are all restrained in various ways, but some people experience greater freedom of expression by externalizing those restraints symbolically.

Beating, slapping, and mild forms of whipping are also used for sensual intensification. People unfamiliar with the S&M scene usually assume that these acts are always intended to be painful, but this is not the case. Generally they are intended to produce more excitement than real pain. Repeated blow which fall below the threshold of actual pain, but which produce a sharp, stinging sensation, can be sexually stimulating. The overall sensitivity of the body may increase noticeably, adrenalin may start to flow and increase sexual arousal, and some people even find that the deceptively loud sound of moderate blows may serve as a sexual stimulant.

Although S&M sex is more commonly a matter of intensifying sexual pleasure, some people do find pain sexually exciting, while others derive sexual pleasure from inflicting it. Those who enjoy pain in conjunction with sex do not experience it as unpleasant, although they may dislike pain under other circumstances. Those who enjoy inflicting pain derive part of their enjoyment from the awareness that they are inflicting pleasure as well. The sexual thrill associated with sadism is derived not only from acting out sadistic fantasies, but also from an appreciation of the pleasure and excitement aroused in the masochistic partner.

Sadomasochistic sex involving serious pain or injury is relatively uncommon and rarely the result of a casual encounter. Before people become involved in such a scene, tastes and limits need to be well defined, and a basic level of trust must be established. Usually this stage is reached only after a good deal of mutual exploration of milder forms of S&M sex.

The myth that homosexual sadists prey on other homosexuals has little basis in fact—gays are far more likely to encounter violence at the hands of straight hoodlums. Most gay people in the S&M scene are alert for signs of abnormality in those with whom they consider becoming involved. Heavy drinking, for example, doesn't mix well with S&M sex. You talk to someone for a while, observe his emotional responses. You make your sexual interests clear and try to get a general picture of his. If there's anything about him you don't trust, you drop the whole thing right there.

Equally unfounded is the myth that the homosexual sadist—or any sadist, for that matter—is necessarily vicious, cruel, and unfeeling, while the masochist is weak-willed and self-hating. A certain amount of role playing does take place in the bars to facilitate preliminary communication and arouse sexual interest, but there is no way to spot the typical sadist or masochist in everyday situations. Often the tough-looking character most people would assume is a sadist actually prefers a masochistic role. The sadist may in fact be a more than usually tender, affectionate, and warm human being, just as the masochist may be aggressive, decisive, and self-confident.

Generally the masochist sets the limits of an S&M scene and guides its progress from start to finish. Most sadists find pleasure in re-creating as nearly as possible the particular fantasy the masochist prefers.

A great deal of S&M sex involves a controlled acting out of sexual fantasies. People tend to think of sadomasochism as anything but controlled, conjuring up visions of screaming victims desperately anxious to escape the clutches of tormentors whose passions drive them on to more and more dangerous abuses. If this were true, few people would acquire a taste for S&M sex and those who did would not survive long. Common sense would suggest that people do what they do sexually, not out of perversity, but because they actually find pleasure in it.

## FANTASY

For all people sex is mixed with fantasy. From the earliest sexual experiences with masturbation through the broad range of adult sexual behavior, fantasy generally accompanies and often heightens sexual pleasure.

Although some people are ashamed of or disturbed by the fantasies which come to them during sex, very few can deny or repress their imagination completely.

Fantasy is of varying importance to different people. For some it hovers at the brink of consciousness, vague, never explicit. For others it is sharp and clear, only a shade less tangible than reality. It plays a minor role in the sex lives of some individuals; others are unable to have satisfactory sexual relations without concentrating on a particular well-developed fantasy that helps increase and maintain sexual arousal.

Fantasies arise out of personal experiences, individual emotional needs, and each person's reactions to the social environment in which he finds himself. Many of the most common S&M fantasies are inexplicable without reference to our society. Often they suggest things we would prefer to ignore.

S&M fantasies are frequently built around roles of domination and submission. "S&M," usually taken as an abbreviation for sadomasochism, is also frequently interpreted in the context of the slave and master relationship through which many fantasies are expressed.

The roles of slave and master correspond to those of masochist and sadist respectively. The requirements of the roles determine the set of rules by which the partners will play out their particular fantasies. The slave plays a role of obedience and submission. The master has the right to order him to do whatever he pleases and to discipline him if he fails to obey.

To an outsider observing such a sex scene, the slave might appear to be at the mercy of the master's every whim. The fact that the slave is not only expected to obey, but to do so with the utmost courtesy and servility, subject to punishment should he decline, might lead some people to forget that the roles are voluntarily chosen and maintained.

The slave and master fulfill each other's expectations and needs. The master, for example, has a clear idea what situations the slave enjoys, what things he likes to be ordered to do, when he can be expected to deliberately balk, risking punishment, and what kind of punishment best matches the requirements of his fantasy.

Both partners are likely to get more out of their sex scene if it is play-acted as though compulsion were involved, for the fantasy must be made to seem real if it is to have its maximum impact and pleasure. Actually, the slave-master relationship could hardly be other than voluntary. No one is likely to be chained or beaten unless he allows it.

Some sadomasochistic fantasies involve a good deal of violence and pain, but even these are far more controlled than they appear to be. A masochist may like to imagine that he is being beaten or whipped as punishment for some deed or character flaw. He may like to pretend that he is at the sadist's mercy, that he is being raped or forced to engage in sexual acts which he actually enjoys, or that his life is in real danger. He may scream in apparent agony, plead with the sadist to stop, beg for mercy, cry that he can't stand the pain, and make every apparent effort to struggle to break free—while actually enjoying the scene enormously. There is little point in being tortured if you can't act as if you're being tortured.

The sadist and the masochist must develop a high level of communication. By his choice of words, tone of voice, and behavior, the masochist must be able to make it clear whether his protests and expressions of pain are in earnest or only part of the fantasy. The sadist must remain alert to the nuances of his partner's behavior.

Punishment or discipline is as likely to be symbolic as physical in many forms of S&M sex. Fantasies of degradation and humiliation are not uncommon, and various forms of symbolic appeasement, such as bootlicking and exaggerated self-criticism, may become an integral part of the game. Name-calling and vilification play a role in some S&M scenes.

Many sadists and masochists have isolated and controlled parts of their personalities to their advantage. By acting out their sadomasochistic impulses sexually, some people are able to reduce the influence of these impulses on other areas of behavior.

A person with strong masochistic tendencies may act them out in real life, losing one job after another, living from calamity to calamity. Another person may confine his masochism to sexual relationships, where they produce pleasure rather than misery, and lead a successful and unremarkable life. One person may find himself in trouble with the law when his sadism runs away with him, while another, who is more conscious of his sadistic tendencies and provides for them in his sexual relations, will have no difficulty controlling them.

Sadomasochistic sex can serve as a means of acting out inner conflicts and anxieties that would otherwise make it difficult to lead a stable life. It is some-times easier to handle a situation one fears when it is acted out under con-trolled circumstances. A masochist may be able to demonstrate through fan-tasy that he can cope with the hostility and aggression of others, and even exert control over it. A sadist may be reassured to find that he can act out his anger and aggression without losing control, destroying others, or isolating himself. Both may discover that situations which provoke the greatest anxiety when imagined are actually quite easy to deal with when acted out. For some people, S&M sex seems to serve as a pleasurable form of sexual psychodrama.

The S&M scene has other seldom recognized positive features. Gener-ally viewed as cruel and brutal, S&M sex is often based on a greater degree of trust and tenderness than more conventional sex. An S&M relationship usually requires a great deal of mutual trust and responsibility. You do not open your inner world of sexual fantasy to just anyone, you do not trust just anyone not to abuse your vulnerability once you have set your defenses aside.

A sadist and a masochist who have worked out a relationship fulfilling to both have developed one of the most far-reaching sexual relationships pos-sible. Linked together not merely by their external actions, they also share one another's most intimate and personal fantasies. For the masochist, a great love may come from the fact that he knows how completely and implicitly his partner can be trusted. For the sadist, an equally strong love may derive from the fact that another human being can trust him so deeply.

The S&M scene is not the frightening jungle that so many people imagine it to be. The people you meet there are ordinary, pleasant people with little but their sexual tastes to distinguish them from others. In spite of the fact that they comprise a sizable minority within the gay world, homosexuals who are into leather and S&M encounter hostility from many other gays.

Whether we are talking about transvestites, fetishists, sadomasochists, or homosexuals, it seems that wherever it is possible to distinguish a pattern of sexual behavior that differs from the average, people will say that it is unnatural, perverse, and should not be tolerated. People who engage in these different sexual practices are labeled sick, even by others who deviate from the expected norm. But when you meet gay people, transvestites, or leather and S&M people, you find out that they're not really all that strange. Aside from their sexual tastes, they're average people, leading average lives when society will permit them to.

Is being different the same as being sick?

# Who's Sick and
# Who Isn't?

I knew I was gay for many years before I finally accepted myself as a homosexual. I struggled with my homosexuality, sometimes hoping that I could suppress it entirely and lead a life as a heterosexual, other times merely hoping to gain enough control over it so that I could refuse to give in to my homosexual impulses and lead a nonsexual life.

It was not that my homosexual experiences had been unpleasant. If they had been, I would probably not have had much desire to repeat them. The "problem" was that they were all too pleasant: my earliest homosexual experiences brought me more happiness than I would ever find in heterosexual experiences.

My difficulty in accepting myself derived not from the quality of my homosexual experiences but from the fact that they were different from what was expected of me. They were disturbing because I knew they were defined as wrong, not because they felt wrong.

When my parents began to suspect that I was homosexual they were quite distressed. We had a long talk about the matter, and they explained that homosexuality was a type of sickness rather than a natural part of my life. There was no need for me to remain homosexual, and I would be much happier in the long run if I managed to overcome my homosexuality and lead a normal life. With the best intentions and at considerable expense, they arranged for me to enter psychoanalysis.

The first thing my analyst did was tell me not to worry: fortunately, I was not really a homosexual, he said. It would require some perseverance in order to develop my heterosexuality, but there were no major obstacles. I was to avoid any further homosexual experiences at all cost—they would only bring me unhappiness. I was not to masturbate, for this would weaken the strength of my "heterosexual drive." I was to remain alert for any signs of homosexuality in my behavior, my thoughts, and my dreams, and report them to him at once.

I really tried for quite a while. I stopped seeing the friends with whom

I had been having occasional sex. I had dated girls before, but now I did so as though my life depended on it. Each new heterosexual accomplishment—"How far did you go with her?"—was dutifully reported and analyzed in detail. When I failed to progress as far as heterosexual intercourse, my analyst suggested that I was unconsciously dating only those girls in my class who were not willing to go all the way. I was in tenth grade at the time.

I became increasingly introspective and found indications of homosexuality in almost everything I did. I avoided making friendships because affection seemed to be evidence of homosexual tendencies. I criticized myself for my dependence on the few friends I had. I found it impossible to be spontaneous: I had to be so careful not to allow any homosexual elements to creep into my behavior unnoticed that I was afraid to move or speak.

After a year and a half, I left therapy thinking I had been cured. I still had homosexual impulses, but I was able to prevent myself from acting on them. I dated young women for the last years of high school and the first years of college, but I got no particular happiness or satisfaction out of these relationships or the sex they involved.

During my first year of college I again began to act on my homosexual impulses, although I fought them as best I could and managed to limit myself to just a few isolated experiences. All the things I had learned about myself in analysis again came to dominate my thoughts. I realized that I was allowing my heterosexual drive to grow weak, that I was masochistically seeking out sexual experiences that would only make me unhappy, and that it was only my sadistic wish to punish my parents by shaming them that led me to find pleasure in homosexual relations.

There was no doubt in my mind that I was a very sick young man. I was right—it took me years to get over my psychoanalysis.

## NORMAL SEX

Explanations of homosexual behavior are frequently justified by reference to this or that "expert's" clinical experience in treating homosexuals. Few people ever stop to ask whether homosexuals who seek psychiatric treatment are representative of homosexuals in general.

Because homosexuals are sick by definition, the assumption is made that homosexuals who do not seek psychiatric treatment must be just as disturbed as those who do, perhaps more so, since they have not recognized their obvious need for help.

The willingness to accept "sick" homosexuals as representative of all homosexuals is not so surprising when we remember that most theories about heterosexual development are based on clinical experience with "sick" heterosexuals. People who are leading satisfactory and rewarding lives—as heterosexuals or homosexuals—are usually not represented in the statistical charts of psychiatric researchers.

We are inclined to accept theories about sexuality based on the experiences of people who are having emotional problems, because sexuality is viewed as the most common source of emotional difficulty in our society. We are encouraged to believe that all our problems can be traced to the sexual vicissitudes of infancy and early childhood. Sex has become the major focus of attention, the one factor that explains all the confusing details of human behavior.

Not surprisingly, heterosexuals who are finding life unsatisfactory often assume that they have deep-seated sexual problems and seek psychiatric help in dealing with them. Nor is it surprising that many homosexuals who find it hard to lead a happy life assume that their homosexuality is at the root of their problems. In a society as confused as ours is about sexuality, very few of us can avoid being caught in the crunch. Unfortunately, however, society has a special bone to pick with homosexuals.

Gay people—more than others—are encouraged to see their sexuality as an albatross around their necks. It is easy to make a good case for the idea that life would be easier as a heterosexual. The discrimination and hostility to which the homosexual is subjected often force him to lead a double life, and maintain a façade that makes it impossible for him to express himself or enter into honest and rewarding relationships with others. Worse than this, some homosexuals are never able to accept themselves, and bear a load of guilt and shame which comes to dominate their entire emotional life.

But there is no reason to think that the average heterosexual has it much easier in a society that is highly ambivalent about all sexuality.

Everyone in our society is forced to suppress or disguise many of his sexual feelings. A certain amount of conformity is demanded of us all. We are expected to express some opinions which we do not hold privately, and we often find it necessary to hide or misrepresent our real feelings about other people.

Guilt and shame about sexuality are not restricted to homosexuals. Our society approves only certain types of heterosexual acts and relationships, and most people find that a large part of their sex life is better kept private.

A strict and sexually puritanical upbringing is not something that only homosexuals have experienced. As infants, we all begin life with a broad range of erotic potentials. Many parts of our bodies are subject to erotic sensations and we are generally considered to be pansexual—Freud called us "polymorphous perverse."

But in our culture, restrictions are quickly imposed on this pansexuality. Our sexual development is defined in terms of which parts of our bodies we are no longer permitted to retain as a source of sensual enjoyment.

Beyond a certain age, we are discouraged from thumb-sucking and putting other objects in our mouths. Mouths are for food, not pleasure. A little later in our development we are usually discouraged from touching our behinds or our genitals. These areas are unpleasant and unclean.

The scope of our childhood sexuality is severely curtailed. As we grow older, our curiosity about sex is stifled: we are too young to know about such things. Sex is something that must be kept hidden and secret. Certainly we do not see our parents making love. In most homes some care is taken that we not even see them naked.

A mystery is created, and with it, the attraction/repulsion of what is forbidden. Small wonder that in our culture—though not in all—children enter a period of "latency" in which their sexual interests and activities are apparently suppressed.

But is latency really the innocuous period it is believed to be? True, the child's sexuality may cease to manifest itself within the family, but it is during these years that the child first begins to have social contacts with other children outside of the family. Would it surprise anybody if these social contacts sometimes involved sexual contacts as well? How many people can remember playing doctor and nurse and keeping it a big secret from their parents? A child need not even leave the house in order to have sexual experiences of which his parents remain comfortably unaware. Sex play between siblings is anything but uncommon. Most people with a brother or sister can recall at least one innocuous incident.

Sex is officially allowed to come out into the open again when puberty arrives, but only in culturally acceptable forms. During puberty the child must try to make sense not only of his increased interest in sex and the changes taking place in his body, but also of the private collection of diverse sexual experiences and confusing fantasies which he may have acquired during a not so latent latency.

In adolescence, pressure is brought to bear on the young boy or girl to conform to the sexual roles expected of them. Past sexual experiences which do not fit must be denied or repressed.

The young adolescent is expected to take a sexual interest in the opposite sex, but is not supposed to do anything about it until he is a good deal older. Masturbation is discouraged in most families, and even when it is considered acceptable it is something best kept secret. In spite of pressures to the contrary, adolescence is the period in which many people have their first homosexual experience if they are ever to have one. It is typically during adolescence that homosexual crushes appear and mutual masturbation becomes common.

The adolescent must shape his behavior to match society's demands; whole areas of experience must be closed off, rejected, and forgotten if possible. Guilt because of homosexual urges and experiences must be dealt with, usually at major cost to the adolescent's peace of mind. Guilt about hetero- sexuality even becomes a major problem for many. Told that he must adopt a heterosexual pattern, the adolescent boy is nevertheless blocked from doing so. Although our sexual mores regarding the young are relaxing, parents still discourage premarital relations at an early age: Whatever you do, don't get a girl into trouble.

Adolescent girls are in a similar bind. They are frightened with stories about the fate awaiting the mother of an "illegitimate" child. They are told that if they make themselves available sexually, no one will want to marry them later. On the other hand, if they walk the straight and narrow, their peers may warn them that they will be unpopular and never keep a boyfriend or land a husband. All talk of the sexual revolution aside, the average adoles- cent does not have it much easier today than young people did twenty years ago.

The agonies of adolescence do much to explain why so many adults in our society lead a limited and often unsatisfactory sex life. Sexuality has been charged with so much emotion, so many contradictory demands, that it is to be expected that frigidity and impotence are common problems. Hetero- sexuals and homosexuals are put through the mill together, but at least the heterosexual has the final comfort of social acceptance.

But even that social acceptance turns out to be rather narrow. Restric- tions are placed on whom it is all right to have sex with, where, what kind, and under what circumstances. Our double standard even parcels out sexual pleasure, determining when and for whom enjoyment of various sexual acts is appropriate.

The double standard also shapes our judgment of heterosexuality and homosexuality. It specifies that sexual acts which are legitimate in a hetero- sexual context are illegitimate in a homosexual context. It determines when a homosexual act will be labeled homosexual, and when some way will be found to classify it in other terms or ignore it. It provides a separate system of evaluation for the behavior of heterosexuals and homosexuals.

One of the most ticklish aspects of the double standard determines which sexual acts are to be considered normal and acceptable and which are not. In spite of changing attitudes, many people still feel that there is some- thing shameful about oral-genital sex. It is all right to enjoy getting blown, but it is not supposed to be particularly pleasant to give someone a blow job.

A similar situation prevails with regard to anal sex. From early child- hood on, neither men nor women are supposed to have any sort of real sexual sensitivity on their backsides. Nevertheless, people do, and heterosexual anal sex play and intercourse is far from uncommon. Again, it is not considered surprising that screwing someone up the ass might be enjoyable, but nobody is supposed to really enjoy getting screwed in this manner. A woman might let a man do it as an experiment or as a favor, but she would not be expected to like it.

Regardless of what is taboo and what is not, many people do pretty well what they please in private. But even those who have the courage to explore the extent of their sexuality in private may feel guilty or ashamed for breaking taboos which have been ingrained in them since their earliest years.

On the surface, it appears that very little besides frontal, supine, genital, heterosexual intercourse—missionary sex—ever goes on. Oral-genital sex, anal sex, sadomasochistic sex, fetishistic sex, and other more esoteric varieties are rarely admitted, even between close friends, no matter how widely they are practiced and enjoyed.

The unnecessary burden of guilt that our narrow sexual mores have imposed on so many of us, heterosexual and homosexual alike, is staggering. Poorly informed about sexual matters, brought up under the guidance of rigid principles of sexual decency, many people go through no small amount of personal agony simply to raise the courage to express their natural sexual inclinations in the privacy of their bedrooms. As if this were not enough, they must then face the anxiety of believing that they are among the few "deviates" who engage in such "unnatural" practices.

Sexual surveys make it clear that many heterosexuals enjoy oral-genital sex, anal sex, mutual masturbation, and the like. Yet to suggest that these can be enjoyed by two members of the same sex is, by our double standard, to speak of "perversion."

What homosexuals do in bed is precisely what heterosexuals do in bed; it is simply done with a partner of the same sex. It is sometimes argued that since homosexuals have only two of the same sexual organs to work with, their sexual activities cannot possibly be fulfilling. This argument is usually based on the assumption that the human genitals can and should be employed only in missionary sex. Unfortunately, this argument strikes deeply at those heterosexuals who see no point in restricting themselves to such an extent.

It is our cultural taboo on everything but the most straitlaced sexuality that makes homosexual relations seem so different from heterosexual ones. In terms of sexual enjoyment, it is generally the quality of the orgasms for the individuals involved rather than the manner in which they are achieved that is most important.

The popular attitudes that continue to treat homosexuality as a peculiar form of mental illness are so illogical that there is reason to wonder whether they serve an important function in our society that has not yet been recognized.

# THE MASCULINE ROLE

Why is homosexuality such a sensitive issue? Part of the answer can be found in the roles men are expected to play in our society.

Much has been written recently about *machismo* and the masculine role. It has been pointed out that the bulk of social, economic, and political power is concentrated in male hands, as if in accordance with some natural law. God is male—mankind is male. Although it is voiced less often now that attention has been drawn to it, an underlying assumption of male superiority is built into the fabric of our society.

The increasing attention focused on the masculine role has been one product of the feminist movement. Many women have concluded that the masculine role and the male prerogatives associated with it are responsible for the unequal treatment of women. Women have rightly complained that they are often treated as sexual objects. Some feel that they are forced into the role of domestic servants.

For more radical feminists, "the Man" has become a symbol of the drive for power and domination, the source of destructive aggression in our society and throughout the world. To some, he is the principal enemy in the final struggle for sexual freedom and equality.

Many men dismiss the critique of the masculine role as so much non-sense—feminists, they say, need nothing more than a good lay to set them straight. Others, however, find that many of the women's arguments strike home. They see that many of their expectations regarding women have been based on assumptions of male superiority. They will admit that in many ways they have treated women in a demeaning, sometimes dehumanizing manner, yet they are disturbed by accusations that they have done so deliberately.

The angry rhetoric has reached such a high pitch in some cases that even sympathetic men are no longer certain just what the feminists want from them. Are they to flagellate themselves for attitudes which have been inculcated in them since early childhood and which they never before suspected were anything but natural? Are they to assume the burden of guilt for a social system which has molded both men and women with neither the active consent nor the conscious complicity of either sex? If they are to change their ways, how are they to do so and where are they to begin?

It is difficult to deny that there are many ways in which women have been and continue to be victimized by a society geared to male needs and privileges. But the question must be raised whether our society really does serve men's needs and whether all the privileges reserved for men are in fact privileges.

There is no guarantee that the masculine role demanded by our society assures men maximum happiness and self-realization any more than the feminine role assures women fulfillment. Possibly, men are just as much victims of the masculine role expected of them as women are of the feminine role.

So much of our daily life is divided along gender lines that it seldom occurs to us that society could function any other way. In one sense, we live in a homosexually structured milieu. Both labor and leisure are divided into activities which are considered appropriate for men and others which are considered appropriate for women. The double standard which determines what sorts of sexual behavior are permissible to men and to women, and how they shall be judged, merely reflects and reinforces the more far-reaching segregation of the sexes.

Training for masculine and feminine roles begins early in life. In order to achieve the desired male or female product, some aspects of each child's basic makeup are suppressed—whole areas of potential behavior, emotion, and thought are closed off—while others are encouraged to expand and fill the resulting void.

Children are groomed for their adult sexual roles from earliest infancy in subtle and unconscious ways. When parents stop thinking of their children as toddlers and begin to view them as little boys and little girls, training becomes a good deal more conscious. It becomes important to separate the sexes, for example, and children are encouraged to find playmates of their own sex. Boys and girls will be taught very different sorts of things and encounter very different expectations. If a family is without a father, it seems particularly important to find another strong male figure with which the young boy may identify.

In our society, homosexuality is enormously important in defining—at least implicitly—the limits of the masculine role. At every stage of development, a homosexual role is counterposed to the desired masculine role, although this is not usually done consciously until a boy has reached adolescence. The homosexual role embraces all those forms of behavior which are not considered appropriate to the masculine role at any given age and consequently, it usually appears as a travesty of the feminine role.

How does the homosexual role bolster the masculine role? Because homosexuality is a clear deviation from the desired masculine role, any boy who is old enough to be aware of this will make every effort to avoid being defined as a homosexual. Chances are that his parents will rush to take corrective measures at the first hint of homosexuality or the effeminacy associated with it.

This does not mean that parents will suspect a seven-year-old boy of being homosexual because he likes to play with girls at an age when young boys are expected to dislike girls. It need never be this conscious. They will feel, however, that something is wrong and that steps must be taken to correct it. Social pressures encourage them to do so. The boy may turn out to be wishy-washy, and the neighbors may comment upon it. If the boss comes home for dinner and finds the boy playing with dolls, what will he think of the father?

The homosexual role as the incarnation of peculiarity and aberration packs an enormous emotional punch. Any deviation from the expected masculine role invites family, peers, and other significant individuals in the child's environment to try to pressure him back into a more acceptable pattern of behavior.

That which is expected of a boy who is fulfilling the requirements of the masculine role is defined for any given age. All other attributes and patterns of behavior will be seen as abnormal, and in retrospect are likely to be pointed out as early signs of developing homosexual tendencies.

When he ceases to be a toddler, the male child is expected to behave like a little man. It is no longer all right for him to cry—men don't cry. In many families, open affection is withdrawn from male children, while tangible expressions of love may be continued for female children through adulthood.

Mothers often become noticeably less intimate with their sons. In many families, fathers stop kissing their sons. Such intimate affection becomes uncomfortable and embarrassing—unmanly. A handshake seems more appropriate than a hug. Emotionality, warmth, and responsiveness are curtailed and blocked. Men are not expected to have the "softer" emotions, much less express them openly.

Most fathers begin early to lay the foundation for the aggressive and competitive drives that will be expected of their sons in later life. Wrestling and rough-and-tumble play replace more direct expressions of affection. Some fathers even try to teach their sons the rudiments of real fighting at this early age, encouraging them to play with toy weapons. Many men will feel guilty if they don't take the time to teach their boys how to play ball, worrying that a weak athletic background will leave them at a disadvantage in the competitive play of the neighborhood.

Other fathers are apparently concerned about the same thing, for competitive sports are adopted in the neighborhood, and a boy's status depends on the skills he is able to develop. The struggle for leadership is more common than teamwork and cooperation. Who is best? Who gets to lead the others?

Parents often worry about how well their boys make out in neighborhood play, for they sense that the status a youngster achieves in his neighborhood may influence the way he will see himself in years to come. Fathers may coach their sons and practice sports with them to improve their skills. A boy who is artistic, creative, or imaginative may have to neglect these areas of his personality in order to develop his athletic abilities. If he does not do so and is poor at sports, he may become an easy mark for neighborhood bullies and withdraw from the circle of his peers to become a solitary child or one who prefers to play with girls.

In childhood, little deviance from the boy's expected role is permitted. Girls have a good deal more leeway, probably because the feminine role has already been defined as less important. Parents may be mildly concerned if their daughter is a tomboy, but not nearly so much as if their son prefers the company of girls to boys. The role of tomboy is acceptable for girls in our society, but no analogous role is offered to boys.

So many demands are made on young boys that the years before puberty may be one of the most difficult periods of their lives, no matter how carefree we believe them to be. In some families the boy is expected to play the role of little man to such perfection that the pressures become too great for him. One common result of this may be stuttering, which appears in boys about five times as often as in girls.

Before they reach adolescence, boys are expected to dislike girls, to view them as frivolous and inconsequential creatures unworthy of consideration or respect. Probably the two worst insults that can be hurled at a young boy are either that he is a girl or that he has one for a friend. But when adolescence arrives, the expectations are suddenly reversed. Now the boy who is *not* interested in girls is a source of concern to his parents, who may worry about his deviation from the expected masculine role.

Our society acknowledges the possibility of latent homosexuality, but not of latent heterosexuality. The adolescent boy who is a "late bloomer," who feels no interest in girls while his peers are already dating, is placed under enormous pressures. He may immerse himself in study or sports, but after a while even these diversions will not justify his lack of involvement with the opposite sex. Remarks may be made about him. His parents may try to arrange dates for him, suggesting this or that daughter of family friends. He may find it necessary to pretend an interest in girls he does not yet feel, or to go on dates simply to prove that there is nothing strange about him.

Men are expected to prove their masculinity over and over again in order to retain their status. You cannot prove your manhood once and for all—it is always open to doubt. Young boys feel called upon to boast and brag, take dares, and pretend to be more courageous than they really feel. From an early age, men are taught that in order not to be vulnerable to attack or loss of status, they must maintain an aggressive image. Muscle-flexing and saber-rattling tend to be male habits. Automobiles become an important status symbol and means of demonstrating masculinity. Watch young men peel out of the high school parking lot.

Virility is equated with a strong sex drive. Once adolescence has been reached, a man should demonstrate a powerful interest in women for most of the rest of his life, regardless of what his real feelings are. In high school, dating helps to establish one's manhood, and it is important at least to give the impression that one has sexual relations on a regular basis. This is the source of many apocryphal stories about visits to prostitutes.

But maturity and marriage confer no proof of masculinity. Happily married men who have no desire whatsoever for extramarital affairs are expected to show an interest—if only as connoisseurs—in women other than their wives, whether they feel it or not. In some business circles one is at a distinct disadvantage if one hasn't got a few lurid tales to tell, man to man, about this or that broad. Some men allow an impression to form that they get around quite a bit, even though their lives are really quite sedate.

To a greater extent than is usually realized, women structure relations between men. The more attractive one's date or one's wife happens to be, the more highly one will be respected by other men. The status which inheres in the "conquest" of an especially attractive woman is one reason women in our society are often treated as sexual objects. Some men have little interest in women as anything other than pleasure-giving status symbols—their lives are structured by the relationships with other men to which these status symbols entitle them.

As they prepare to enter adult life, men are taught to perceive the world as a highly competitive jungle in which it is seldom safe to let down their guard. It's a dog-eat-dog world, and you're crazy not to look out for your own interests. Cooperation is nice in theory, but a lot of people will stab you in the back if they get half a chance. You've got to maintain an image. You've got to look too tough to tangle with.

I was cop-watching at a gay demonstration a few months ago when an attractive young patrolman happened to stroll into the area. It was a nice day, and he was obviously in good spirits, smiling and bopping along the sidewalk. Suddenly he spotted our posters, did a double take, realized there were homosexuals around who might be observing him. The smile was quickly replaced by an aggressively outthrust jaw. Chest expanded, shoulders back, he swaggered past the crowd looking just a little too inflated to seem genuine. It was all necessary—somebody might have gotten the wrong idea about him.

Men are taught to hide their tenderer emotions, which may be interpreted by other men as signs of weakness. They are not supposed to talk to one another about themselves, their personal feelings and doubts, for they dare not become too close. Touching is taboo, and the inhibitions against any open expression of affection between men are very seldom relaxed. Most expressions of affection between men take an aggressive form: the punch in the ribs, the slap on the back.

The masculine role is defensive. Men are to be hollow fortresses, safe from attack or loss of status from without, safe from inappropriate emotions and uncertainty from within. American men are not encouraged to know themselves any more than they are encouraged to know other men. We think of women as intuitive, possibly because they are permitted to stay in touch with their deeper feelings to a much greater extent than men.

It is seldom remembered that many of the privileges and advantages men enjoy are of dubious value and are acquired at a heavy cost. Does "the Man" really have it made in our society?

Men are cast in the role of breadwinner as much as women are cast in that of housekeeper. While raising children and doing housework may be tedious, intellectually stifling, and poorly rewarded, holding down a nine-to-five job is seldom as enjoyable or fulfilling as it might be.

Competition in many occupations is murderous. On the average, women live seven or eight years longer than men, who are subject to heart disease, ulcers, chronic backache, high blood pressure, and chronic nervous tension at a far higher rate than women. The male suicide rate is approximately two and a half times that for women, many more men than women become chronic alcoholics, and men are far more prone to disabling mental illnesses than women. In addition, men have the dubious honor of providing the cannon fodder for all the wars that some feminists attribute to willful masculine aggression.

In short, the average man is just as much a victim of the masculine role as the average woman is of the feminine role.

Both masculine and feminine roles are maintained by the dread of homosexuality—the role to which all behavior inappropriate to each role is ascribed—but a larger issue is made over the matter with regard to men, for the masculine role determines the social structure more directly and must be more closely guarded. This is why antihomosexuality is institutionalized in our society.

One of the most astonishing myths concerning homosexuals seems inexplicable unless interpreted in this light. As homosexuality has become an increasingly popular subject for controversial magazine articles, I have several times encountered one criticism directed at homosexuals which struck me as absurd: homosexuals inspire resentment because they have things so easy. They are irresponsible in shirking the duties of marriage and fatherhood, and this makes it less necessary for them to hold down high-paying jobs in order to support a family, while leaving them plenty of free time to lead a wildly promiscuous life.

My initial response was anger. It was bad enough for gay people to be treated as undesirable, second-class citizens and criminals in our society, but to then accuse them of having it soft seemed like the worst sort of doublethink. Nobody forced heterosexual men to marry and raise families. Nobody said that they had to tie themselves down to one woman and give up the promiscuous life they might have preferred.

In retrospect, I realized that while no person forced the average American male to do these things, the masculine role did in fact do so. The complaint represented less a resentful infatuation with the joys of the gay life than a dissatisfaction with the requirements of the masculine role and its supposed privileges.

But no matter how dissatisfied the straight man may be with some aspects of the role expected of him, he dare not stray, for he may be labeled a homosexual. Women have a slightly greater degree of latitude, but accusations of female homosexuality are almost as effective in keeping them in line. Some feminists will burst into tears when called lesbians. All behavior that deviates from the requirements of each sexual role is lumped together and called peculiar, deviant—and, ultimately, homosexual.

It may just be that it makes as little sense to define homosexuals as sick as it does to claim that there is no such thing as an unhealthy heterosexual.

## CURES

In the Middle Ages homosexuals were condemned as heretics, devil-worshipers who mocked God's natural order. As with witchcraft, there was only one cure for homosexuality, and many homosexuals were burned at the stake. The "faggots" of today fed the fires of ignorance in an earlier era.

We seldom speak of sin today—it has become *passé*. Those who fail to conform, those who deviate from the norm, are "socially maladjusted" or mentally ill, and we often set out to cure them with the same sort of missionary zeal that characterized medieval religious intolerance.

Our standards of mental health are more often based on the demand for conformity than on a realistic appraisal of what is required to lead a happy and productive life. There is little room for diversity. People are encouraged to eliminate their differences, rather than learn to live with them. Behavior which does not fit the common mold is labeled "neurotic," and neuroses are defined in advance as undesirable.

Sexual orientation for both heterosexuals and homosexuals is a very basic thing, a broadly based predisposition formed during childhood. It is not subject to simple manipulation. It goes to the root of the personality, and drastic measures are generally required to modify or alter it.

Many forms of psychoanalysis easily qualify as drastic measures, but their success in "curing" homosexuality has still been very limited. Many of those "cures" which do occur can be explained by an examination of the way in which an unfortunately large number of analysts practice their profession.

During the first months of therapy, the analyst provides the patient with a special language, a jargon through which he is expected to express himself.

The use of a new language is vitally important in order to avoid the verbal rationalizations which the patient has devised and come to accept in his natural language. The analyst suggests new interpretations or possible origins of the "problem" being treated. If the patient rejects these, he is blocking, repressing the truth, refusing to face reality. But finally he comes around if he is to be "cured." He realizes that the analyst was right all along. Brainwashing worked in Korea too.

Freud himself encountered this problem and had the integrity to grapple with it at least. When he realized that many of the unconscious, presumably repressed sexual fantasies which his patients managed to dredge up at his urgings were imagined rather than real, he laid down the law by fiat: imaginary material was as valid as true recollection; subjective reality could be used as the basis for treatment.

Unfortunately, many of his less conscientious followers neglected to ascertain just whose subjective reality was involved in treatment, their own or that of their patients. With dozens, frequently hundreds, of hours of therapy at stiff fees, this is perhaps understandable. If nothing else, it has provided us with interesting data on the types of fantasies which psychoanalysts often have about homosexual behavior.

If one closely examines the supporting data offered by analysts who claim to have developed techniques for "curing" homosexuals, one finds that the claims are enormously inflated. The following sort of picture usually emerges.

After screening several hundred homosexuals seeking psychiatric treatment, Dr. X selects fifty who seem "highly motivated" to change and whose homosexuality is not too "severe." After years of treatment, during which thirty may drop out uncured, he selects his final sample of twenty or so. More treatment, and eventually thirteen or fourteen of his patients decide that they have been "cured." We then find such glowing testimonials to psychoanalytic success as "Patient Q has already had three dates with women and has had fantasies about petting while masturbating; Patient Z is engaged to be married; Patient Y has not yet had any heterosexual experiences, but has refrained from homosexual experiences for two months."

These are our "cured" homosexuals. No follow-up is made to see whether the "cure" sticks or whether they're happier for having had it. Instead we find an article in one of the prestigious psychiatric journals announcing that a new method of treatment can guarantee a 67 percent cure for homosexuals, when the actual rate of what is called a cure is closer to 6 or 7 percent. Nevertheless, on the basis of his findings, Doctor X may write a book and be interviewed by the mass media for an "expert" opinion on homosexuals and the gay liberation movement.

What is manifestly clear in spite of all the claims is that homosexuality is very seldom "cured," even when drastic measures are employed. But if drastic measures are required, there will always be those who will offer them. In Europe, for example, lobotomies and other operations involving the removal of brain tissue suspected of controlling sexual behavior have been used to alter sexual orientation—in one direction only: from homosexual to something else. What else is altered, what happens to the patient's personality in the process, is left to the imagination.

Castration has also been found effective in reducing the strength of the drive for homosexual sex. The strength of the drive is reduced, but its object is seldom altered. Who knows what else is affected by such tampering? Attempts to "cure" homosexuals by injecting additional male hormones have only succeeded in strengthening sexual urges, resulting in a number of hyperhorny homosexuals. ESB—electric stimulation of the brain—is now being investigated as an important new way of altering the behavior of homosexuals and other mammals.

The most popular new "cure" in the United States at present is "aversion therapy," based on a conditioning process which Pavlov used on dogs. The homosexual patient is wired to electrodes and an attractive nude male is projected on a screen before his eyes. At this point, a jolting electric shock is delivered and is terminated only when the nude male has been replaced by a picture of a nude female. Other forms of aversion therapy are rapidly being developed, including the injection of chemicals which induce violent nausea and vomiting while a picture of a naked man is displayed before the homosexual.

The problem with this form of therapy is that it does not deal with the patient as a human being, but rather as an object which can be hammered into the desired shape. The conscious intellect is bypassed, and new instructions for behavior are burnt into the nervous system as though it were a tablet of wax, or a computer to be programed.

The results of such "therapy" are far from clear. While a number of "cures" appear to have been effected, there is again a lack of follow-up studies to explore the duration of such "cures" and their possible side effects. What kind of heterosexual sex life does a "cured" homosexual enjoy after undergoing this routine? Does the homosexual who has been conditioned to fear and dislike the nude male body develop an aversion to his own naked body and genitals, perhaps to sex in general? Would such treatment be effective in "curing" deviant political orientations?

It is not surprising that aversion therapy seems to work—drastic measures can be expected to have drastic results, whether the elimination of a particular sexual orientation or something else. The human body and the human brain can only stand so much, and undoubtedly the same procedure could be used to "cure" a heterosexual of his or her sexual orientation were that a socially approved goal.

Even more esoteric cures have been proposed for homosexuality. Some mail-order cults will send the devout a special "prayer cloth" guaranteed to protect them against sexual sins—for a fee. One wealthy European physician claimed a high degree of success in curing homosexuals by injecting pulverized lamb's embryos into his patients' bloodstream.

All the preceding does not mean that there has never been a scientifically conducted investigation of homosexuality* or that an unbiased appraisal of evidence is impossible. While studies have failed to unearth any concrete evidence one way or the other as to possible genetic predispositions toward homosexuality, such research will undoubtedly continue. Hormonal and biochemical studies have proved fruitless in the past, but this is no guarantee that some sort of correlation may not be discovered, perhaps attributable to the homosexual life-style in an anti-homosexual society. As our knowledge of sexuality in general increases, it may well be that we will isolate a constellation of factors which contribute to a homosexual predisposition.

But one of the most crucial determinants of our success in gaining a better understanding of homosexuality will be the reason for which we undertake research. If we want to know more about homosexuals because they are one type of human being and we want to know more about ourselves as a species, it is possible that we will be able to set aside our social biases and arrive at some objective facts. If, on the other hand, we study homosexuality in order to eliminate homosexuals, we may very well succeed someday in eliminating homosexuals, but we will not have gained much real understanding of homosexuality—or of humanity, for that matter.

At a time when both Kinsey and Freud have become part of our general culture, the enormous complexity of human sexual identity, orientation, and behavior should be perfectly clear. Much of what is defined as perversion and aberration in our society is really quite common among both heterosexuals and homosexuals. Many forms of sexual behavior that are taboo in our culture are considered prerequisites for normalcy in others. The whole concept of perversion is culturally specific and socially defined.

It would be simplistic to say that we live in a sexually sick society. While most people will agree that this is true, the statement is of little value since we can neither point to nor describe a society which we can be certain has a healthy attitude toward sexuality. We simply do not know that much about sexuality.

Until we know a great deal more about our sexuality, it seems unrealistic to define sexual normalcy or health in terms of sexual conformity. A more sensible measure of sickness and health would be the effect of his own sexuality on each individual. Where a person is happy with his sex life and finds

*A number of such investigations are listed as suggested readings at the end of this book.

it fulfilling there is little reason to be concerned about it one way or another. Where a person is uncomfortable with his sex life—no matter how conventional it may be—or finds that it does not fulfill his emotional needs, there is some justification for trying to help him come to terms with it or suggesting alternatives.

It may be that in a truly healthy society some of the sexual practices we encounter today would not exist or would appear in a different form. Perhaps new forms of sexuality would develop. But we are unlikely to move any closer to a healthy society if we continue to enforce conformity to sexual standards that have clearly been damaging to many heterosexuals and homosexuals in the past.

We do not know what sex would be like in an ideal society, but we can at least make some judgments about our own society as we come to see it more clearly. The process of becoming aware may not be an easy one, but when our unexpressed values are made explicit, we can compare them with the principles we hold to be most important.

Where our existing sexual standards deny many people the right to happiness, freedom, and love, we would do better to change our standards than to try to change our fellow human beings.

# Are Some of Your Best Friends Gay?

About a year ago I visited a straight couple for a weekend in the country. Jill had been a close friend of mine from early childhood, and when she married, her husband David welcomed me as a family friend.

Before I came out openly as a homosexual, there had been nothing out of the ordinary about our friendship. I would visit them for dinner every couple of months or so, we'd talk, play cards, and usually manage to drink just enough to regret it the next morning. I didn't go out of my way to disguise my homosexuality, but I did nothing to call attention to it. I had no idea whether they suspected I was gay or not.

When I did finally come out of the closet three years ago, it meant a great deal that these friends did not seem put off by it. I no longer avoided mentioning the details of the gay side of my life, what went on in the bars, whom I was currently having an affair with, how my family was reacting to my open homosexuality. I had few close gay friends at the time, so the chance to talk about some of these things with understanding friends was important to me.

On the surface, Jill and David seemed to be completely at ease with me and my homosexuality. Our relationship seemed even better than it had in the past, because I no longer felt the need to hold anything back.

There were a few strains involved, however. While Jill, an intelligent and delightfully eccentric woman, showed virtually no change in her attitude toward me, I could sense a slight discomfort on the part of her husband. He did not know quite what to make of me. I could understand his feelings. Few straight people know what to expect from an open homosexual. They've heard so many stories, so many myths about homosexual behavior, that they're often unsure whether they can take a gay person at face value. But David kept his doubts to himself and treated me just as he might have treated any straight friend.

On this particular weekend, we were staying at a gracious old summer home, tucked into the side of a hill above a lake, and we spent the better

113

part of the day down by the water, sunbathing and swimming. It was a glorious day, and we decided that we'd go skinny dipping by moonlight that night.

That evening we were up at the house, pleasantly tired out from the day's activities. Since I manage to get away from the city so seldom, I was determined to take full advantage of the country air no matter how comfortable it was to sit around the house. Although it had gotten chillier, I reminded my friends of our plans for an evening swim.

Jill said she'd had it for the day, but David seemed to have his heart set on one more dip. He tried to convince her to join us, but she could not be persuaded.

I sensed David's uneasiness, although he said nothing. I thought that it might be more tactful of me to suggest we forget about the swim, but on the other hand I felt that this would be equivalent to accepting the notion that there was some valid reason for a straight man to be uncomfortable about skinny dipping with a homosexual. I knew I would be hurt and our friendship would suffer if David were to make his nervousness explicit. We were both on the line.

I decided to go ahead with the swim and see what happened. We went down to the lake, took our clothes off, and had a swim, without incident. I could still sense some nervousness on David's part, but I was pleased that he had gone ahead with the swim in spite of it.

Later that evening, I had a few words alone with Jill and told her I had been aware that David had felt rather awkward about the situation. I said I thought he had handled it quite well.

She admitted that he had not felt completely at ease. While I had gone to look for towels before the swim, he had said to her rather sheepishly, "I know it's silly of me, and I know that Peter would never dream of doing anything, but I just can't help worrying about what to do if . . ."

## GAY FRIENDS

Most straight people do find it somewhat difficult to have gay friends. Wherever lines are drawn that set people apart and define them as different, it is likely to be at least slightly more difficult to communicate than where no such lines exist.

Black people and white people, gay people and straight people, live in different worlds, no matter how much we sometimes try to disguise the fact. We do not, by any means, live in an integrated society. The divisions within our society promote different life-styles and different subcultures, and sexual distinctions are a good deal less easily bridged than religious or racial distinctions. Few straight people are completely comfortable with homosexuals.

There are several reasons why it is particularly difficult to have a homosexual for a friend, more so than to have a friend of a different race or ethnic background. For one thing, when racial differences are involved, you know where you stand from the start. Homosexuals, on the other hand, are not so easily identified. You may have a gay friend for years without ever realizing that he is gay.

Furthermore, people are likely to alter their attitudes about you if they discover you have a gay friend. The white person with a black friend is not likely to be suspected of being black himself, but the straight person with a gay friend may raise a few eyebrows.

Minor homosexual experiences are so common that most people have at least one friend who has had some sort of gay experience but will never mention it. Many people have a close friend who identifies himself as a homosexual but who keeps his homosexuality so secret that they will never be aware that he is gay.

It's incredibly easy to pass for straight, perhaps too easy. Many gay people maintain a straight façade because to come out openly as homosexual may involve difficulties they would prefer to avoid.

There is no way to identify a friend as gay unless you happen to catch him in a compromising situation. It's not difficult to maintain a straight fiction, for the last thing that most people want to find out is that a close friend is homosexual. Most people fail to notice obvious clues or to hear revealing slips of the tongue, simply because they would prefer not to know. Even where it is impossible to ignore a dead giveaway, people often come up with rationalizations.

Few people want to know that a friend is gay, because it puts them on the spot themselves. What do you say to a close friend you have just discovered is gay? How do you reevaluate your past relationship? What can you expect from your friend in the future? Can things go on as they always were, or will the relationship have to be altered or even terminated?

Part of the discomfort involved in discovering that a friend is gay is based on simple confusion about how to relate to a homosexual, and part of it is based on fear.

The fear can sometimes be traced to the popular notion that sex is a dominating force in homosexuals' lives. Many people believe that everything a gay person does has a sexual motivation, that every act and every word is part of a careful plan to get someone else into bed. Homosexuals are viewed as calculating and devious, people who should never be taken at their face value. The possibility that homosexuals might have anything but sex on their minds is seldom entertained.

This myth, and the narrow view of homosexuals it encourages, sometimes leads straight people to reevaluate their relationship with a friend who they discover is gay. Looking back, simple and innocent expressions of friendship on the part of the homosexual are suddenly viewed as attempts at seduction. The homosexual can never have had "honorable" intentions, his friendship can never have been disinterested.

Needless to say, this kind of reaction can be devastating to the homosexual involved. His integrity, the value of his friendship, his worth as a person, are cast in the mud.

Some people base their reaction to a friend's admission of homosexuality on the myth that homosexuals are completely unable to keep their hands off anybody of the same sex, regardless of whether or not the person is interested in any sexual involvement. They may not call the value of the past friendship into question, but they think it perfectly obvious that the friendship can have no future and must be terminated. They will explain that of course they could never feel the same about their old friend again.

Part of the reason that many people find homosexuals threatening is that for any person, man or woman, straight or gay, the currents of sexuality are occasionally stronger and closer to the surface than it is customary to admit.

Close friendships between men and women, whether single, married, or divorced, may involve no conscious element of sexual attraction whatsoever, and yet from time to time they may find themselves in situations in which one or both wonder in a mild sort of way, "What if . . .?"

Some people, however, find themselves uncomfortable with homosexuals—and especially with friends whom they know to be gay—because "What if . . . ?" becomes threatening in a homosexual context. They are concerned that these feelings, innocuous and inconsequential in a heterosexual context, may indicate homosexual tendencies in themselves which they are afraid to face.

Actually, such feelings may very well indicate homosexual tendencies, since the average person is able to respond occasionally to both sexes. But because homosexuality is viewed in our society as an all-or-nothing phenomenon—and a highly unacceptable one at that—some people fear that the slightest trace of homosexual inclinations within themselves may mean that they are in danger of becoming full-fledged homosexuals. Ill at ease about their own sexual identity, such people often find it necessary to bring a friendship with a gay person to an abrupt halt.

Many homosexuals who have not come out into the open maintain long-term friendships with straight people of their own sex without ever feeling the slightest sexual interest in them. Straight men who assume that simply because they are male they will be irresistibly attractive to all male homosexuals never stop to consider that for both straights and gays, tastes in friends may have nothing at all to do with tastes in sex partners.

Nevertheless, most gay people are just as susceptible as straight people to idle sexual speculation from time to time and attribute just about as much importance to it. Occasionally, a gay person will find that he is strongly attracted to a straight friend sexually, or even that he has fallen in love with him.

This sort of situation arises most frequently with gay people who are struggling with their homosexuality or attempting to repress it. People who identify themselves as gay but are avoiding any involvement in the gay world have few emotional outlets for their homosexual feelings. Unable to bring themselves to enter the gay world, they have little opportunity to find sex partners or meet other gay people. In such cases, they may find that carrying a torch for an unsuspecting straight friend may answer some of their needs.

This is particularly common among younger gays who have not yet come to terms with their homosexuality and may not even be aware that a gay world exists. Adolescent crushes often have a strong homosexual component. Indeed, it is the intensity of the love felt for a special friend that may lead an adolescent to suspect that he is homosexual, even when no conscious feelings of sexual attraction are involved.

I had had a few crushes and a few sexual experiences during junior high school, but it had not really occurred to me to think of myself as homosexual. During high school one friend became so important to me that he formed the center of my life. We were together a great deal and our friendship grew stronger and deeper each year. He was the only person I felt I could really talk to, and we would get into soul-searching conversations that lasted into the small hours of the morning. Sometimes we would even discuss the extent of our friendship and how much we would be prepared to sacrifice for one another.

We couldn't have been much closer, and yet there was never any visible hint of homosexuality in our relationship—I knew that he had a hearty interest in girls. I dreamed of him, thought of him constantly, and was happy only when I was with him. I found him very good-looking, and yet was not aware of any sexual feelings for him. I saw my love for him as essentially platonic, but so overpowering that I began to ask myself: "Could I possibly be a homosexual?"

Finally I had to tell him how I felt or come completely apart at the seams. One night, as we were taking a walk around the neighborhood, I told him I loved him.

"Oh," he said, "that's disgusting—I couldn't get involved in anything like that."

The ground opened up beneath me. I quickly tried to qualify my words. I loved him like a brother, I said, like a friend. Nothing more than that.

The incident passed, but things were never quite the same between us again. We drifted apart. I still thought of him as the best friend I'd ever had or ever would have, but we seldom saw each other after we both went off to college, and when we did, we found the conversation strained. A few years later I heard that he had married, but he never wrote to me about it and I haven't heard from him since.

But from the moment that I told him I loved him, I knew that I was a homosexual and never seriously questioned that fact again, in spite of the years it took me to accept myself. I had been told that the love I felt was shameful and foul, and it took me a long time to realize that it was not so. It also took a long time before I could open myself up to another human being and say, "I love you."

Why do so many straight people react with anger or revulsion when they discover that a homosexual feels love or sexual attraction for them? To tell a person that he is loved is not to insult him.

Most straight people become angry and repelled when they learn that a homosexual has feelings for them, because they assume that this means he believes them to be homosexual themselves. Labeling him, they assume that he must label them as well. Men tend to be particularly sensitive in such situations, because they assume that they are being viewed as women, that some sign of effeminacy attributed to homosexuals has been found in them.

There is no reason why a person who does not share the feelings that another feels for him cannot be gracious in explaining that such feelings are not shared and in providing an easy way for the other person to disengage. Gay men and women are expected to do so when they become the object of heterosexual attentions.

The real rub here is that very few straight people are honestly indifferent to the possibility that they themselves might be mistaken for homosexuals, and those who have acknowledged homosexual friends are often placed under suspicion of being gay themselves. Because of the strong feelings against homosexuals in this country, the average person can see no reason for associating with homosexuals unless one has homosexual inclinations oneself. Even married men and women are not beyond suspicion. They may be considered peculiar, immoral, or simply lacking in good taste and judgment.

Nor are the possible repercussions limited to social relations. The man who has a homosexual friend may be unable to get a security clearance required for his job. The couple with an adopted child may be threatened with loss of their child if they are judged to be an unfavorable moral influence because they have maintained a friendship with a homosexual. The person whose employer holds particularly strong antihomosexual attitudes may find himself passed up for promotion or even fired for the company he keeps if the word gets around.

Prejudice against homosexuals remains so widespread that the straight person who associates with homosexuals may find himself subject to some of the forms of discrimination gay people are familiar with.

Straight people who really wish to have gay people for friends may be called upon to make a strong commitment to the principle that sexual orientation is no ground for bias. It is not always easy.

## STRAIGHT FRIENDS

Gay people who really wish to have straight people for friends may be called upon to make a strong commitment to the principle that sexual orientation is no ground for bias. It is not always easy.

Many straight people today are trying to gain a better understanding of gay people and honestly wish to treat homosexuals just as they would anybody else. Some succeed, but many encounter major difficulties.

Some straights have an intellectual commitment to sexual equality, but find it difficult to deal with the uneasiness they feel in a situation where they must meet and interact with gay people. They have a lifetime of acquired feelings and expectations about homosexuals which they are unable to eradicate overnight.

Because straight people usually know so little about homosexuals and the gay world, they often make mistakes in dealing with homosexuals that no gay person would make. They may be unintentionally insulting, patronizing, or overly inquisitive. They may be just a shade too sympathetic, too concerned with discounting the stereotypes, to actually treat the homosexual as an ordinary human being.

On the other hand, they may get in over their head. Trying to be as tolerant as possible, they may suddenly encounter a situation which is more than they can handle and become so visibly uncomfortable that it is impossible to feel at ease with them. They may find that they can deal with a gay person only in very neutral terms. When the conversation turns to the details of the homosexual's life or his relations with other homosexuals, they are unable to be anything but shocked.

Many homosexuals find these difficulties too much to bother with. Gay people may find it difficult to enjoy themselves with straight people under these circumstances—they feel they must be on their "best behavior" when they would prefer to simply be themselves.

Some gay people have experienced so much hostility in the straight world that they don't want to have anything to do with straight people at all. They have developed a stereotype of straight people just as rigid and unappealing as the straight stereotypes regarding gays. Others simply believe that the distance between the straight and gay worlds is unbridgeable, no matter how good the intentions on both sides. Attempts at communication and understanding will ultimately fail, as far as they are concerned, so why waste the time trying?

The gay people who want to have nothing to do with straights are far outnumbered by those who do. Most gay people come into contact with straights on a regular basis where they work and where they live. Many who are not openly gay have a circle of straight friends whom they value, and even many of those who are openly gay have a few straight friends with whom they are completely comfortable.

As the liberation movement has spread and increasing numbers of gays have come out of the closet, many have found that the straight reaction to their open homosexuality is not as negative or hostile as they had feared it would be. On the other hand, the more they adopt an openly gay life, the more heterosexual society cramps their style. Many straight people are tolerant, but tolerance is a far cry from acceptance. All too often straights are willing to accept gays only if the gays are careful to make their homosexuality as unobtrusive as possible.

When they find that they are expected to be homosexuals in name only, many gay people who have come out publicly become disenchanted with straight society and see little reason to maintain straight friendships. They see less and less of their straight friends without really intending to do so. They find themselves entering into new friendships with gay people, and fewer and fewer with straights. Soon they are surprised and not particularly disturbed to find that they have few remaining ties to the straight world.

Gay people who feel that there is value in preserving friendships with straights often have to work at it. They may have to hold themselves back somewhat until old straight friends have gotten used to them in their new role as homosexuals. They may have to make allowances for their friends' lack of understanding or misinformation about gay people and the gay world, as well as for occasional unintentionally offensive remarks.

Last year a young straight college student asked my lover and me if we would come to one of his classes to answer questions when he presented a report on homosexuality. His intentions were good, I suppose, but his information was somewhat limited: he kept assuring us that he believed that "queers" were entitled to equal rights. We agreed to come to his class.

When we got there and the class had started, the student went to the blackboard and wrote: DEAN SMITH IS A COCKSUCKING FAGGOT. When he began his talk, he said that this was his way of confronting the other students with their bigotry—how many of them used terms like this for homosexuals? My lover and I sat there like zoo specimens.

There are some straight people who use many of the various offensive slang terms for homosexuals without realizing they are put-downs. Embarrassment about homosexuality is still so common that some people cannot bring themselves to use the word "homosexual"—they find it distastefully clinical. Instead they will refer to homos, queers, queens, fairies, faggots, pansies, and—where gay women are concerned—dykes and lezzies, not really realizing that gay people find these terms insulting and demeaning.

Some people who would never dream of referring to blacks as niggers or Jews as kikes will use derogatory terms for gay people casually. Some don't realize this is in poor taste; others don't think it matters.

People who use "nigger" usually will have the sense not to do so in front of black people. It's not difficult to maintain this minimum courtesy, because there is seldom any problem in identifying blacks. But most gay people are invisible, and straights are often unaware that some of their friends are gay. Gay people who are still in the closet often hear people whom they consider friends refer to homosexuals as queers and faggots or tell antihomosexual jokes. This experience is hardly likely to make a gay person feel that he will be well received if he ceases to be secretive about his homosexuality.

Many gay people find the idea of coming out quite terrifying. Aside from the difficulties they can expect to have with their families, they fear that their straight friends will turn against them and no longer want to have anything to do with them. If somebody is a real friend, an admission of homosexuality won't change his or her feelings in the slightest, but many gay people find it difficult to put this to the test.

When gay people tell straight friends they are gay, various stock responses are encountered over and over. "But you don't look gay"—as though all homosexuals could be expected to look alike. Some straight people will say that they would have preferred not to know. After all, if the person was able to keep his homosexuality a secret so successfully, why make such a big isssue of it now? Nobody really wants to know. The emotional cost of a secret life is enormous.

Another common response is "I'm sorry" or "What a shame." After all, some people will say, everyone has his problems, and you just have to learn to live with them. But not many homosexuals enjoy being treated as though they were handicapped or emotionally crippled.

The situation is an awkward one. Given the fact that a friend may have felt it necessary to hide his homosexuality for years, it is hard to know how to respond to it in positive terms when it is finally revealed. About the only thing you can say is "Right on!"

Once a gay person has made his homosexuality known, even his most sympathetic friends may find it difficult to treat him as he would like to be treated. Who knows how homosexuals like to be treated anyway?

It's a lot easier to figure out how gay people do *not* like to be treated, for this requires only a little common sense.

The homosexual who has left the closet does not want to be treated like an invalid with an unmentionable disease—he does not want to be treated like a tragic victim of circumstances beyond his control. Things can be bad enough for gay people in our society so that they would prefer not to be constantly reminded of how bad they are, no matter how sympathetic the intentions. It is too easy for a sympathetic attitude to come across as patronizing or condescending. Besides, after a while gay people get thoroughly tired of talking about the problems they encounter as gay people.

Straight people sometimes wonder how they should introduce a gay friend to other acquaintances. Do you say that he is gay, and thereby make an issue out of it, or do you avoid mentioning it, thereby creating an impression that his homosexuality is an embarrassment to you? The best thing for a straight person in this position to do is ask his gay friend what he would prefer. Most gay people see no point in making an issue about the matter with every stranger they meet. They have told their friends about their homosexuality because their friends are important to them. Unless there is some particular reason for introducing someone as a gay friend, what difference does it make?

The problem most frequently encountered by gay people who have left the closet is being expected to be on "good" behavior. The "good" homosexual is the gay equivalent of an Uncle Tom. He is supposed to be serious and reticent about his homosexuality. If it comes up as a topic of discussion, he is expected to deal with it in intellectual rather than emotional terms, speak in a sociological vein about the many problems faced by homosexuals. He should be understanding about the hostility he encounters from many straights—after all, they really can't help it, you know, they were brought up that way and they don't know any better. He should never reveal the measure of the anger he sometimes feels.

The "good" homosexual is a heterosexual homosexual. He may wear a sign around his neck stating "I am a homosexual," but he should look, act, think, and feel no differently than a straight person would. He should not be an embarrassment. His straight friends should never have to feel uncomfortable about introducing him to people whose respect they want to keep. He should be a tribute to their liberalism, not to their unconventionality.

Actually, the "good" homosexual should not even really be a heterosexual homosexual. Heterosexuals are all too open about their sexuality, and the "good" homosexual should avoid giving any hint that he has a sex life. He must be sexually neutral.

The "good" homosexual does not mention the affairs he has from time to time or the men he is seeing. If he falls in love, he does not make others uncomfortable by trying to share his joy with them. If an affair comes to a sudden end, he does not embarrass his straight friends by telling them of his unhappiness. He should not mention having sex with other men, because most straight people find the whole idea distasteful. If he has a lover, the two of them should behave like gentlemen—straight gentlemen—in front of other people. This is particularly noticeable when it comes to displays of affection.

My lover Marc and I found this to be the case the first time we visited my family as a couple. It had taken a good deal of courage for my parents to even invite us together in the first place. They were anything but pleased about my homosexuality, and it was difficult for them to be confronted with living proof of that homosexuality in the form of my lover. It was an awkward situation for all of us, and yet a vital step in attempting to understand one another better.

We sat around having a drink and chatting. Without thinking anything of it, I rested my arm on Marc's shoulder while we talked. Later, my parents told me privately that it had made them very uncomfortable to watch us "making love" right before their eyes. Making love? The same thing happened when we visited Marc's relatives. He happened to put his hand on my knee and was later told how embarrassing it had been to watch us "making out and petting."

I could understand and sympathize with our families' reactions. In straight society, men are not supposed to touch. Nor are they supposed to be homosexuals.

Many straight people will say "Right on" when it's a matter of leaving the closet, admitting that we are gay, and being ourselves after years of hiding and secrecy. But when we try to really be ourselves, live full and happy lives, search for love, and enjoy it when we find it—they tell us we are going too far. It is all right for us to be homosexuals in name, but we must leave our love in the closet.

This is too much to ask.

## INTEGRATION

Are gay people so different from straight people that there is no way we can live together comfortably with mutual respect?

Perhaps. Some of my friends in the gay movement feel that no *rapprochement* between gays and straights is possible, or even desirable.

On the other hand, my lover and I have several straight friends we wouldn't part with for the world, people who like us as we are, not as we might behave to make others more comfortable.

But what about the rest of the world?

The majority of straight people in our society do not like gay people. Some despise us and believe that we should be eliminated. There are many straight people, however, who have no strong feelings one way or the other. They don't understand gay people, they find us peculiar, but they don't bear us any particular ill will.

This is one of the things that many gay people find so surprising when they finally decide to leave the closet. For years they have believed that they were universally despised, that if they came out publicly it would be all they could do to survive. If they were recognized as homosexuals, they would be attacked and beaten on the street. If they held hands in public they would be arrested or harassed. If their homosexuality were known, they would lose their jobs on the spot.

But they come out and they find that their fears were exaggerated. They are more likely to be called a name than to be physically attacked. They hold hands, and they find that while a few people glare at them or make remarks, raise their eyebrows and quickly look away, most people don't seem to notice. Some gay people do lose their jobs when they come out, but this doesn't happen as often as they expect.

In the city, most people are too harried and pressed to bother paying much attention to the people around them. If they don't like homosexuals, fine, they don't like them, but few are prepared to do anything about it. Urban life oppresses almost everybody, and people seldom have the energy or time to devote to deliberately making things more oppressive for others.

In New York City, it's not all that difficult to be gay. Homosexuals elsewhere face more problems and find it much less easy to come out. It is only in the largest American cities that gay people can lead anything like normal lives. In smaller cities, suburbs, rural areas, the whole vast sweep of Middle America, any sort of real integration, mutual acceptance, and respect seems very unlikely in the near future.

The younger generation attach a good deal less importance to sexual conformity than their parents do. Fewer young people today accept the notion that any one person or group of people has the right to determine standards of sexual morality for others. Love and sex are matters of individual choice, and society has no business interfering.

It is the older generation today that clings most strongly to antihomosexual sentiments, and this fact has an enormous impact, not only on homosexuals, but on their parents as well.

Today, most homosexuals' parents were brought up at a time when homosexuality was virtually unmentionable—many were not even aware that such a thing as "homosexuality" existed until they were well into their adult lives. When the existence of homosexuality was acknowledged, it was depicted as bizarre and unnatural. Many older people heard of homosexuality only in the context of sin and damnation. The fact that most churches are today redefining their attitudes toward homosexuals has little effect on these people.

The parental generation also grew up in the heyday of Freudian psychology and parlor psychiatry. Encouraged to find causes for their own emotional problems in the way their parents treated them, they were also told that the fate of their own children lay directly in their hands. There has probably never been—and hopefully will never again be—a generation so painfully self-conscious about raising its children. Nothing they could do could fail to influence their children in crucial ways, and there were no easy answers or guides for the right way to assure that one's child would grow up to be a happy and healthy adult.

The parents of homosexuals have been led to believe that they must blame themselves for the homosexuality of their children, as though they had placed some dreadful and unforgivable curse upon them. Unable to accept the guilt they believe is t...irs, many have been unable to accept their children as homosexuals.

Finally, today's parents have been called upon to accommodate themselves to more radical changes in the nature of society and its values than have taken place for any other generation of parents in history. Their children were born into the electronic era, the age of open racial conflict, psychedelic drugs, sexual revolution, and a sweeping, harshly critical reexamination of America's values and her role in the world. The young are growing up in this milieu—their parents can only hope to cope with it. They are required to accept new ways of looking at so many things that for some accepting homosexuality is the straw that breaks the camel's back. They simply can't do it.

Those parents who do make an effort to understand and accept their children as homosexuals have not merely their own attitudes, fears, and misconceptions to deal with, but those of their friends, neighbors, and employers. Many fear that they will lose their friends and that their family reputation will be ruined.

Again, the same issue is raised: to what extent should a homosexual today restrict his self-expression because of straight society's discomfort about homosexuality?

Should I not have written this book because it will be embarrassing to most of my family and relatives? Should my lover and I pretend not to be lovers because many straight people will find our affection for one another offensive? When I hear someone make a vicious remark about homosexuals, should I keep silent because to speak out will only aggravate the situation? Should I ever have left the closet?

Each gay person has to draw the line for himself.

Integration is not around the corner. There are straights who are hostile to gays and those who are indifferent. There are also many straights today who are sympathetic to gays. But sympathy cannot guarantee understanding, nor can an intellectual commitment to a principle guarantee that its practice will come easily or without continuing effort.

If increased integration and improved understanding between gay people and straight people are our goals, a good deal of effort will be required on both sides.

It is never easy to cross the lines which society draws between people, but in crossing them we inevitably learn much about ourselves. It may require a special effort for gay people and straight people to get to know one another and to overcome their mutual discomfort and misunderstanding, but it is probably well worth it. The time to start is now.

# Can a Homosexual Get a Fair Trial?

I am a criminal.

That in itself is not enough to upset me.

In America today, more and more average citizens are becoming criminals every day—and many of them don't think they're doing anything wrong. A lot of people smoke pot. Many men become criminals when they pay for sex. Many very ordinary husbands and wives break the law when they have a particularly uninhibited tumble in bed.

Most of the people who do these things never get arrested. In New York, my chances of getting arrested for consensual sodomy are minimal so long as I exercise a reasonable amount of discretion.

But there are some things that bother me about my legal status. I don't mind the fact of being a criminal per se, but I resent the fact that the government assumes it has the right to define my love as a crime. I resent the fact that when the laws on the books are occasionally enforced, they are more likely to be enforced against me than against a heterosexual. I resent the fact that if somebody commits a crime against me, I am less likely to get help from the police or justice in court than a heterosexual in a similar situation.

Within reasonable limits, I can live as I please in New York, and my lover and I don't really give a second thought to the law when we sleep together and make love. There are some parts of town where we wouldn't feel safe walking down the street together holding hands, but on many of those streets nobody feels safe these days. We don't have it so bad.

The city may be one of the few places in America where we can live together comfortably and openly as gay people, but that doesn't mean we like city life. We try to get out of the city whenever we can, and one of these years we'd like to rent a car for the summer and drive across the country to see America.

But it will probably be quite a while before we take that trip. In spite of the fact that this is our country too, we don't feel very welcome in it.

Almost everywhere in the United States, two gay people can be arrested

127

for lewd and indecent behavior if somebody catches them holding hands or kissing. If we were to stop at a motel for the night and make love, we would be subject to arrest in all but five states, even though we are both adults and our sexual relations were conducted in private. Sentences for consensual sodomy run as high as life imprisonment, but even a two-year sentence is more than I'm prepared to face.

But it isn't just the law that makes me feel unwelcome in America, there's no need to go cross-country to find violence and ugliness. As close to home as Long Island, New Jersey, and Connecticut, I know of many instances in which gay people have been attacked and beaten, sometimes by the police themselves. There is no recourse to law when the police don't like your looks. Gay people have been hauled in "on suspicion of drug possession" in New Jersey and given a "rectal search" for drugs with a cop's billy club. It's an experience I can live without.

There are few places in America today where homosexuals have any reason to feel welcome or safe. It's not surprising that the vast majority of gay people still make every effort to avoid discovery.

Of course, Marc and I could probably pass for straight with little difficulty, dress conservatively, put an "HONOR POLICE HEROES" sticker on the bumper of our rented car, and make our trip without major problems. But that is not the way I want to see America.

Nor is it the way America should want to be seen.


## THE LAW

In only a few nations in the world—among them the People's Republic of China, the Soviet Union, Cuba, and a few of the other communist satellite nations—are the penalties for engaging in homosexual relations more stringent than those found in the United States. Because we so often contrast our form of government with that found in these other countries, it may seem peculiar that our legal approach to homosexuality is so similar to theirs and so at odds with that of the rest of the Free World. In order to account for this, it is necessary to take a brief look at the history of antihomosexual legislation.

Antihomosexuality has been a characteristic of the Judeo-Christian tradition for more than 2,500 years. Mosaic law decreed that homosexual relations be punished with death by stoning. The antihomosexual-relations attitudes of the Hebrews were adopted by the early Christians, elaborated and intensified by St. Paul, and have been retained in the religious tradition of Western civilization through the present.

Early Roman law did not punish homosexual relations, but under the first Christian emperors sodomy was officially defined as a capital offense, punishable by decapitation, and in later years public burning at the stake. Homosexuality, equated with heresy and witchcraft, was considered beyond the realm of ordinary sin, a monstrosity for which no redemption was possible. In Europe during the Middle Ages, homosexuals continued to be burned at the stake, and in France this practice was not brought to a halt until the middle of the eighteenth century.

In English law, which served as the basis for American law, sodomy was punishable by death until the middle of the nineteenth century, at which time a Victorian statute reduced the penalty to life imprisonment. A generation later, the sentence was reduced to two years at hard labor.

Napoleon eliminated private homosexual relations between consenting adults from the French penal code at the beginning of the nineteenth century, and the French example set the pattern for most of Western Europe, with the exception of the Anglo-Saxon nations and Germany, which only recently repealed her laws against consensual sodomy.

In Britain, the report of the Wolfenden Committee led to repeal of the laws against consensual sodomy in 1967, but in the United States only five states have repealed their prohibitions against consensual sodomy between adults to date: Illinois, Connecticut, Colorado, Idaho, and Oregon. Even in these states other laws directed primarily against homosexuals are still on the books and the legal situation of the average homosexual has not improved much. In spite of the increasing visibility of homosexuals in states which have retained their sodomy laws and the growth of the gay liberation movement, there is little evidence that sodomy repeal can be expected across the nation in the near future.

Why does America cling so fiercely to her medieval antihomosexual legislation? For one thing, it must be remembered that the colonization of this country was accomplished in large part by religious dissidents whose Puritan morality made them unwelcome in their own homeland. The anti-sexual ethos is part of the American tradition, and one which has had an enormous influence on all of us, as has the American propensity for attempting to legislate private morality, from Prohibition to abortion.

In addition, the exaggerated narrowness of the masculine role in American society requires strong social and legal sanctions against homosexuality. Numerous factors in American politics also operate against legal reform where homosexuals are concerned, but these will be discussed elsewhere.

Many people are not quite sure what "sodomy" means. Various state laws define it as an unspeakable crime against nature, an unmentionable crime against man and beast, deviant sexual relations, sexual perversion, and a whole string of other notably inspecific terms.

Sodomy has been viewed as such a major embarrassment that neither the legislators who framed the laws nor the judges who have applied them have been able to bring themselves to speak about it very plainly. In simple terms, sodomy means anal intercourse, and in most states has been broadened by statute to include fellatio, whether practiced by individuals of the same sex or of different sexes. Most state laws also prohibit sodomy with animals, but animals seldom file charges.

Sodomy laws are a hodgepodge of sexual puritanism and self-righteous vengeance. In most states, they apply to married and unmarried heterosexuals as well as homosexuals; nobody should have the right to decide for himself which private sexual acts are moral and which are not. In practice, the laws are applied almost exclusively to homosexuals. The Texas sodomy law was recently ruled unconstitutional on the ground that it infringed upon the rights of married persons, but the solution was to revise the laws so that they covered only homosexuals, rather than to remove them from the books.

Penalties are vengeful and vicious. In some states they are comparable to sentences usually handed down for manslaughter and murder. Three states provide maximum sentences of life imprisonment—in Georgia, a life sentence is mandatory unless clemency is recommended. North Carolina judiciously limited itself to a maximum sentence of sixty years in prison, but drastically reduced the penalties three years ago when an unfortunate homosexual actually received such a sentence and even the state legislature felt that the punishment was cruel and unusual. Nevertheless, nearly three quarters of the states in the Union still consider it reasonable to imprison two men who make love together for maximum terms of between ten and twenty years. A handful of states have reduced sodomy to a misdemeanor, punishable by fine or imprisonment, while a few others have decided to remove it from the books altogether. By crossing state lines, a homosexual can make himself vulnerable to sentences of whatever severity he prefers.

The maximum sentences are not always—or even frequently—imposed for convictions of sodomy. In some states, judges are at liberty to hand down suspended sentences and offer a lengthy probation period if the defendant commits himself to undertake psychiatric treatment to "change" him into a heterosexual.

Several of our states, including California and Pennsylvania, have enacted so-called sexual psychopath laws which permit the courts a great deal of leeway as far as the constitutional rights of homosexuals and other sexual "deviants" are concerned. Under these laws, a homosexual may be made a ward of the court and sentenced to an indefinite period of "treatment" at the court's discretion—usually in a state mental hospital, where he may be forced to undergo aversion therapy designed to alter his sexual orientation. Such sentences do not require a trial by jury and may remain in force until the criminal is "cured" of his sexual aberration. It is up to the court, of course, to determine what constitutes a satisfactory cure.

The homosexual who is convicted and imprisoned for breaking one of the laws against homosexual relations finds himself in a grim situation. In spite of the enormous amount of homosexual activity that goes on in prison, those who are convicted on homosexual charges or who look "obviously" homosexual receive especially severe treatment.

Homosexuals in prison are frequently raped by one or more other prisoners or guards. Treatment for injury resulting from gang rapes and beatings is minimal. "Known" homosexuals will often be segregated in a special section of the prison, where they will be severely punished if they engage in any homosexual activities. Solitary confinement in "the pit" without a bed or toilet facilities is a common punishment. Unofficial beatings by guards are anything but rare. Those imprisoned for homosexual offenses are extremely unlikely to be paroled before serving their full sentence.

How much does the average homosexual have to worry about being prosecuted under sodomy and "sexual psychopath" laws? Hardly at all. These laws are seldom enforced and convictions are difficult to obtain. When they are applied, they are applied selectively and usually with a purpose. A homosexual who does not play along with the police when charged with a lesser offense, for example, may find himself charged with sodomy.

The laws are sometimes used as a warning or to set an example if the gay life in a particular city begins to become too open for the taste of the police department or City Hall. Occasionally arrests are made as a demonstration of police power or an expression of personal antipathy toward homosexuals.

The sodomy laws are morally indefensible even if only a handful of homosexuals are arrested under them, but they are of far greater significance when viewed in a larger legal context. If homosexual relations are a crime, then so are many related possibilities: loitering with intent to commit sodomy, attempted sodomy, solicitation to engage in sodomy, conspiracy to commit sodomy, etc. As if this were insufficient, vaguely worded state laws against outrageous or disorderly conduct, lewd or lascivious behavior and conduct offensive to public morality broaden the powers of the police even further. Some people consider homosexuals outrageous, lewd, and offensive simply because they are homosexuals. Not the sodomy laws, but the broad range of these other laws whose interpretation is left to the discretion of the police, accounts for the numerous homosexuals with arrest records.

How do these laws work in practice? If the charges are not dropped at the precinct station, the majority of these cases are thrown out of court for lack of evidence. Even though convictions are seldom obtained, these arrests are anything but a harmless exercise in police harassment. The record of arrest is retained on file, regardless of whether or not the accused was convicted, and few states have any provisions for expungement. The homosexual who is arrested on any charge that fails to stick carries an arrest record with him for the rest of his life, a fact that he is legally required to enter on all government forms, employment applications, insurance questionnaires, and the like.

Even where sodomy laws have been repealed, homosexuals are sometimes subject to legal harassment which leaves them with arrest records. Both Connecticut and Illinois have repealed their sodomy and solicitation laws, but homosexuals in Chicago complain that the police have started to use statutes that predated these laws against them. Thus, a Chicago police decoy may pass himself off as a homosexual, get picked up, and ask his victim to buy him a cup of coffee on the way home. As soon as the money is on the counter, the homosexual can be arrested for attempting to hire a prostitute.

The Chicago police have also taken advantage of another venerable statute which makes it illegal to frequent a "disorderly" house, defined as an establishment in which any sort of physical contact of a sexual nature takes place. A police decoy can enter a crowded bar, make a pickup, and lead his victim on until he attempts some sort of physical contact—a hand on the cop's knee, for example. Immediately the bar qualifies legally as a disorderly house, and not just the homosexual who played "kneesies" with the decoy, but every homosexual in the place is subject to arrest for frequenting an illegal establishment. Where the police can convince their victims to reveal their places of employment, the employers are called and informed of the arrests. Although the charges are likely to be dropped, the sex criminals are then free to go home and contemplate their new arrest records and possible loss of their jobs.

Some people are unimpressed by the injustice of this. They assume that the only homosexuals who ever get arrested on these charges are those who have sex in public or who make a practice of annoying nonhomosexuals with unwelcome propositions.

There seems to be some confusion about what is meant by "in public." Few homosexuals are foolish enough to have sex on the sidewalk or anywhere, for that matter, where one could expect to attract the attention of straight people or the police. I have heard of a few homosexuals who will take a chance on an uncrowded theater balcony if it's dark enough, but I suspect that this is more common among heterosexuals. Similarly, some gay people will have sex in a car if they can find a secluded place to park, but whereas the homosexual who gets caught in such a situation is likely to be arrested, the heterosexual on lover's lane is usually simply told to move along.

There are many gay people who will have sex in a semipublic place if they believe that they are likely to encounter only other gay people or if they think they can count on enough advance warning to get out of a compromising situation. At gay beaches many gay people will wander off into the dunes or shrubbery where they can find some privacy, and in public parks with particular areas which are considered to be gay much the same thing is likely to occur. Gays and straights who favor the tea-room scene probably run a greater risk of being caught in the act by police or straights who are not devotees of the scene, but it is certainly not their *intent* to be discovered in a public place.

Not only is it illegal to be caught having sex in a public or semipublic place, however; it is also illegal to proposition, solicit, or discuss the possibility of having homosexual relations. Here again it depends on how one defines "public." Most people would agree that if you are in any public place where other people are present who can overhear you and are offended by what you are suggesting, this should count as public. But what if you are sitting on a park bench talking with another person and there is nobody else around who could possibly hear you—is this public? Or suppose you're in a gay bar where nobody cares whom you proposition or how—is this public?

The notion that gay people are frequently arrested for making unwelcome advances toward straights is rather farfetched. The whole purpose of cruising is to locate people who are interested in homosexual relations. Even if a homosexual does get his signals crossed and propositions a straight person who is not interested in sex, a complaint to the police and a subsequent arrest are hardly likely. The straight may ignore the homosexual, he may tell him to go to hell or call him a nasty name, he may punch him in the nose, but he's not likely to take the time to call the police, hang around to press charges, and possibly have to appear in court simply because he was propositioned.

Just how is it that homosexuals do get arrested?

A great deal of vigilance is required of the police. They must patrol the beaches, parks, back roads, tea rooms, and other places where homosexuals might conceivably have sex. But this is hardly enough, for there are many places where homosexuals might think to proposition one another even if they would not risk having sex. This means, for example, that it is important to patrol gay bars to make sure no one is saying anything he shouldn't. But outside of the bars, out in the open where visibility is better, few other minority groups compare with gay people in their ability to spot an approaching uniform at a distance and compose themselves with lightning speed. Few policemen are quick enough to get to the scene of the crime in time to overhear a lewd suggestion.

Several effective methods of detecting and preventing homosexual crimes have been developed. Electronic surveillance has proved particularly useful. In some cities, park benches and other public areas where homosexuals might proposition one another are wired for sound by the police. This saves a great deal of labor, because numerous private conversations can be monitored at once from the precinct station or the squad car.

Similarly, closed-circuit television cameras are often strategically deployed in places of particular interest, such as public rest rooms in transportation facilities, hotels, and popular department stores—you may have noticed them yourself.

But a machine cannot always be trusted to do a man's job, and success in uncovering homosexual crime ultimately rests with the undercover cop. Not just anyone can be a police decoy. One must be young and attractive enough to interest the average homosexual. Intensive training is sometimes required. The successful decoy must learn how to dress in ways that are attractive to gay people, and how to carry himself like a homosexual and speak the slang of the gay world. Finally—and most important—he must learn how to cruise like a homosexual so that others will know that he is interested in them. Actually, in order to be an effective decoy, a police officer must be indistinguishable from a homosexual.

All too few police have a real aptitude for this calling, and police departments in some cities find it necessary to recruit civilian help. The most effective recruitment program involves underage boys who are caught loitering around tea rooms. Teen-agers in this position usually prefer police work to having their hobby revealed to their parents. As police informers—and witnesses in a pinch—they are useful fighting crime in the local tea rooms. Some of them are even paid for their work.

Police enticement and entrapment of homosexuals are still common in many American cities and account for the vast majority of the homosexual arrests made every year. Usually it is the word of the arresting officer against that of the accused—without any further witnesses, because it is hard to do effective decoy work in teams. In order to have sufficient grounds for arrest, the solitary decoy must attract the attention of a homosexual, engage him in conversation, and—with the aid of appropriate leading or suggestive remarks —get him to make some sort of sexual proposition or suggestion, anything that can be taken as evidence of a desire to commit sodomy. Some eager beavers go further than this, forcing themselves to allow the homosexual to perform criminal fellatio on them before arresting him.

It is a tragic commentary on the decline of law and order in our society that so many of our law enforcement specialists must devote themselves to the thankless—and often distasteful—task of ferreting out homosexuals who attempt to hide their criminal behavior from the public. It is difficult for the average person to grasp the extent of the sacrifice many of these officers make. The average citizen never sees the criminal acts these men must witness, never hears the shocking conversations they must overhear. But their job is not completely without reward.

The laws against homosexual acts are selectively enforced—certainly not nearly all the homosexuals who engage in the proscribed acts are arrested, and virtually no heterosexuals are arrested for them. The problem with the selective application and enforcement of any law is that it encourages police corruption. This not only means that the police may choose to enforce the law against individuals whom they dislike or enforce them on grounds other than those covered by the statute in question—political affiliation, length of hair, or color of skin. It also means that there is a constant temptation for blackmail and extortion by the police.

It makes very little difference whether an individual threatened with arrest is actually charged with a crime and placed under arrest when others committing the same crime are quite obviously getting away with it. The temptation to pick a wealthy-looking victim and shake him down for a bribe is not irresistible, but a surprising number of policemen seem to find it so. Shakedowns by the police are such a common and well-known phenomenon in the gay world that petty criminals often pose as undercover cops, flash a phony badge, and cash in on the well-established game.

The more deeply one becomes involved in a discussion of the laws which affect the lives and rights of homosexuals, the more inevitably one is drawn into a discussion of the manner in which they are enforced. The laws themselves are archaic and unenforceable in any but the most arbitrary manner. They are of less significance in a legal context than they are in a social context. No matter what the original intent behind these laws, they have unforeseen results today.

## THE POLICE

Except in a few states, every time a homosexual makes love, he breaks the law. While it is not strictly illegal to *be* a homosexual, virtually every homosexual must be technically considered a criminal unless he is willing to lead a life of complete celibacy. For this reason, it is no surprise that relations between homosexuals and the police are generally poor. In larger cities where a recognizable gay ghetto exists, the relations between the police and the gay community are often not just poor but openly hostile.

The laws against sodomy and solicitation, and those related to them which are used against homosexuals are clearly unenforceable. What enforcement does take place is quite visibly selective and arbitrary. The laws themselves are patently unconstitutional—or at least many homosexuals consider them to be. Insult is added to injury when they become a major source of graft and corruption within many police departments.

Finally, the laws are deeply offensive. By their very existence, they tell all homosexuals that no matter how decent and moral a life they try to lead, society considers them criminals and undesirables, second-class citizens with limited rights. No homosexual can respect these laws, and some gay people find it difficult to maintain respect for the political system which created them, the society which continues to allow them to exist, and those who choose to enforce them on a discriminatory basis.

If many gay people have come to mistrust or dislike the police, the feeling is certainly mutual. Antihomosexual sentiment seems to run particularly high among those who enter police work in comparison to other occupations. A number of factors contribute to this problem.

Sweeping generalizations cannot be made about the police any more than they can about homosexuals. There are dedicated and admirable police officers to be found on every police force, men and women who devote themselves to the unpleasant job of protecting others and sometimes lose their lives in the process. No matter how inflammatory the rhetoric or how often some people call the police "pigs," most people will admit that there are some occasions when they are relieved to see an approaching patrol car or a cop on the beat. It would be equally unrealistic, however, to assume that all police can be or ought to be viewed in such a positive light.

Some men enter police work for other than the most admirable motives. Some are attracted to the role and the rights it confers, rather than to the concepts of protection and law enforcement. Others see themselves as the guardians of morality, rather than of the laws and the people they are intended to protect. A few enter police work because it provides an acceptable way for them to vent their hostility and treat others brutally under the cover of law.

Not all the individuals who join the police have a strong bias against homosexuals, but many do. Even those who don't may acquire antihomosexual attitudes, because these are institutionalized in police training procedures and the daily operation of the average precinct.

The average police trainee is unlikely to receive a highly theoretical introduction to the law and law enforcement. Such concepts as crimes without victims, unenforceable laws, selective enforcement, civil liberties, and priorities in law enforcement are unlikely to be emphasized when one of the main goals is to instill a deep commitment to existing laws and their enforcement. The average policeman who has completed training may already have picked up hints of prevailing police attitudes toward homosexuals, for gay people are the one group which is still acceptable as the butt of snide humor for anecdotes or illustrative examples. "Fairies" and "queers" are fair game, while "niggers" are not—there are likely to be blacks on any urban police force today, but you would certainly not expect to find any recognizable homosexuals.

Once the new policeman is assigned to a precinct, he acquires a great deal of information about the unofficial aspects of law enforcement. Some precincts have explicit programs of harassment of gay people. In at least one

New York City precinct, a sign is posted in a prominent place advising patrolmen to be especially on the lookout for drug addicts, thieves, and homosexuals. The new recruit may be told by more experienced men that homosexuals are particularly useful for filling arrest quotas when the department needs to polish its image to counteract bad publicity or scandal—the public always laps up a dramatic raid on a place where homosexuals and other undesirables congregate. A more experienced buddy may even tell him off the record that homosexuals are usually good for a shakedown and that gay bars can usually be harassed into making payoffs.

The policeman who receives special training for assignment to the vice squad is likely to find even more reason to abuse homosexuals, for in no other place is antihomosexuality so thoroughly institutionalized. Standard texts on criminology and vice control usually present the most distorted and biased views on homosexuals to be found in print anywhere. Trainees are frequently encouraged to equate homosexuals with all other types of sex offenders: child molesters, exhibitionists, voyeurs, etc.

*Vice Control in California,* a text widely used in the training of police in that state, contains the following warning, for example: "Many do-gooders and other misinformed people have been asking for more social and official tolerance for homosexuals. Their arguments are usually to the effect that a person's private sex life is none of the law's business and 'When a homosexual makes love to another homosexual, they aren't hurting anybody else.' The truth of the matter is that these 'Hollywood and Greenwich Village cannibals' are constantly on the lookout for new stuff, persons who are not homosexuals. If this were not so, it would be an utter impossibility for any vice investigator to even make an arrest. Homosexuals are constantly seeking recruits and prefer young boys and young men to older queers. The contaminating influence they exert can be reduced to a minimum by tough, relentless law enforcement."

When interviewed by a reporter from the Los Angeles *Advocate,* America's most prestigious homosexual newspaper, Dr. John B. Williams, the author of the text, was glad to explain his reasons for the inclusion of the passage above: "Now, the reason for this statement is that—and I didn't put it in just because it wasn't pertinent to just outsiders, just for police—but the reason for the statement is because, when the guys are young, they call themselves queens and belles. Now when they get older, they switch to what homosexuals call 'aunties.' Now, these aunties are 35, 40, and older. Now, they cannot attract other homosexuals. So, then, these people prey on what we call recruiting. Young, good-looking guys, or, when they can't get them, they'll then attack small children, as one guy did the other day and raped a 1½-year-old girl and killed her." Dr. Williams, who has a degree in anesthesiology, served as head of the Los Angeles Police Department's Administrative Vice Division. Now at work on another book on the same subject, he is an associate professor of police science at California State College, Los Angeles.

Even where institutionalized hostility toward homosexuals is minimal, the nature of police work encourages police with personal prejudices against gays to put them into action. Homosexuals are especially vulnerable to police harassment and brutality—most of them wish to avoid any publicity about their sexual orientation since it may cost them their jobs. Police can and often do pick up a homosexual without charging him with anything, beat him, call him derogatory names, and then tell him to get lost or they'll arrest him for loitering or soliciting, thereby assuring that he will at least acquire an arrest record. The homosexual is in no position to complain about the matter to the department or a review board. Homosexual transvestites are particularly susceptible to this sort of treatment.

Homosexuals are often victims of the law, but discrimination frequently means that they do not even enjoy its protection in matters totally unrelated to their sexual conduct. Fearing publicity and exposure should they have to appear in court, many homosexuals do not dare to report instances of assault, robbery, or blackmail. When they do report such crimes they stand much less chance of cooperation or action on the part of the police than a heterosexual. In New York's Greenwich Village, for example, patrolmen have repeatedly refused to take action against straight gangs which beat and rob homosexuals, even when these individuals remain present at the scene of the crime and their victims are willing and anxious to press charges.

Lack of police protection for homosexuals is a problem encountered not only in large cities. In Bridgeport, Connecticut, nine homosexuals were recently attacked by a band of fifty or sixty young toughs and beaten with rocks, tire irons, chains, and planks torn up from park benches. Police in the area made no move to intervene. When one of the gay women, drenched in blood and visibly injured, approached an on-duty cop stationed in the picnic area where the gays had been watching an Independence Day fireworks display prior to the attack, he refused to help her. Although her armed assailants were in plain sight, he told her to move on. Such incidents are seldom reported in the press because they are considered of minimal interest to the straight public.

In various parts of the country organized crime has found it profitable to maintain control of the establishments catering to homosexuals, such as the bars and the baths. Ways are found to discourage legitimate businessmen from competing, and friendly relations between the Syndicate and the police sometimes facilitate this. While the Los Angeles Police Department is infamous in the gay world for its brutality toward homosexuals and its campaigns of enticement, entrapment, and surveillance, no other department in the nation has a better reputation for collusion with the Mafia than the New York Police Department.

In New York City, the mob has an iron grip on the gay community, controlling virtually all the bars, baths, and after-hours clubs which cater to gays. Many of these establishments operate without adequate licenses or safety standards. They flourish because they are just as profitable for the police as they are for the Syndicate.

An elaborate system of payoffs structures the relationship between the police and the Mafia. For years, the liquor laws of New York State were applied so as to deny licenses to bars catering to homosexuals and to revoke the licenses of those known to have a homosexual clientele on the ground that homosexuals were immoral and could not be permitted to congregate.

The fact that gay bars were illegal meant that police complicity was required in order to keep them open. By the time homosexuals were officially granted their constitutional right of association by the State Supreme Court, and the bars became quasi-legal, the Mafia had such extensive control of the gay community, and the system of payoffs to the police was so firmly established, that there was little likelihood of an end to the widespread corruption. The police could always find some technical ground for closing bars which failed to follow through with the payoffs demanded—inadequate wiring, fire hazards, suspicion of this or that criminal activity.

A delicate balance of move and countermove by the police and the Mafia evolved, with the two forces sometimes working together, sometimes at odds with each other. If a particular establishment failed to pay off or if the police wished to increase the amount of the payoffs, they would bring pressure to bear on the Mafia by either closing the bars or harassing their gay clientele. Raids were not uncommon in which the entire clientele of the bar would be detained, threatened, abused, and many arrested and taken to the local precinct. No matter how the system worked, the homosexuals were caught in the middle and were the only ones to really suffer.

Gay people had no alternative to the Mafia-controlled bars. Prohibited by law from meeting in public, unwelcome in straight establishments, they had no other place where they could conveniently meet each other. Legitimate businessmen had no way of opening establishments that could serve as alternatives to the Syndicate bars. Either the mob would raid a new bar, smash its facilities and rough up its employees, or goon squads would harass and attack the new establishment's clientele. The police worked hand in glove with the Mafia in discouraging legitimate businesses which would not prove profitable to them. They could be paid to provide additional harassment of the bar's patrons, and close the establishment on a technicality until the owners were willing to come to terms with the Mafia.

It was a police raid that ignited the Stonewall riots in 1969, and led to the renaissance of the gay movement in a new, far more militant form, but violence frequently followed on the heels of such raids. In 1970, a raid on a popular Greenwich Village bar, the Snake Pit, resulted in the arrest of 167 people, who were taken to the Sixth Precinct for interrogation and verbal abuse. This would not have been much out of the ordinary had not a twenty-three-year-old Argentinian visiting the United States on a visa attempted to escape by leaping from a second-story window—and impaled himself on a spiked fence below. The attempt at escape was motivated by the fear that he would be deported. Federal law provides that any noncitizen may be deported simply for being a homosexual.

The situation has hardly improved since then. The increasing popularity of the Syndicate after-hours clubs, especially those with orgy rooms in back, has meant that gay people have found themselves in the middle even more frequently. Numerous after-hours clubs have been raided over the past year, their sound systems and bar facilities smashed beyond repair by the police, their customers mistreated.

Speculation has attributed this wave of harassment to several factors. Lower-echelon policemen who have not been sufficiently cut in on the payoffs have been accused of making unofficial raids on their own, out of uniform, and armed with shotguns. The standard procedure has been to confiscate the bar's entire supply of liquor, presumably for resale elsewhere. Rival factions within organized crime syndicates are also suspected of having staged raids into each other's territory.

These events are seldom reported in the press. Homosexuals are criminals and the police are expected to maintain a certain level of public decency where they congregate. In July 1971, however, a massive move against "organized crime and illegal after-hours establishments" did receive widespread publicity at a time when accusations of police corruption had left the NYPD with a particularly tarnished image. Out of more than five hundred illegally operated after-hours establishments in New York City, nine were raided and closed, all but one of them in the Greenwich Village area. Eight of them catered to homosexuals. Before the week was out, at least one of these bars had reopened under the same management.

The laws concerning homosexuals are not the only unenforceable laws on the books, nor are they the only ones involving victimless crimes. Many other laws are selectively and arbitrarily applied, and other minority groups besides homosexuals have reason to complain of mistreatment by the police.

One of the tenets of American democracy holds that when all else fails, the aggrieved may turn to the courts and the judiciary for redress. How do homosexuals fare in court?

# WITH LIBERTY AND JUSTICE FOR ALL

It is not technically illegal to be a homosexual, but it is illegal almost everywhere in the United States to engage in any form of behavior which would justify a person's being classified as a homosexual. Thus it is legal to call oneself a homosexual, but illegal to be a homosexual in fact. Very few people voluntarily choose a life of complete celibacy. Homosexuals, however, must do so if they do not wish to become criminals.

The Ninth Amendment declares that American citizens have unenumerated rights, and that the failure of the Constitution to specify a particular behavior as a right does not constitute evidence that it is not a right. The Constitution makes no specific mention of the right to engage in heterosexual intercourse, but denial of this right would not be tolerated for a moment. Consensual sexual relations fall under the category of unenumerated rights.

The Constitution guarantees the right to protection against unreasonable search and seizure and the right of association. Nevertheless, laws against consensual homosexual relations are used to justify surveillance, enticement, and entrapment techniques used against homosexuals, as well as attempts to force them to register as homosexuals with the police in some states. Records are maintained by various departments of the federal and state governments and law-enforcement agencies at all levels of individuals known to be homosexual, suspected of being homosexual, or known to have associated with homosexuals.

Numerous other constitutional guarantees appear to be violated by state laws directed against homosexuals. The penalties in many states for sodomy and other homosexual "crimes" constitute cruel and unusual punishment by most people's standards. The "sexual psychopath" legislation adopted in several states does little to guarantee due process of law. Many of the statutes concerning homosexual relations have been criticized as the enactment of religious doctrine into law. The fact that all these state laws concern crimes without victims, are clearly unenforceable, and are applied arbitrarily suggests violation of the constitutional guarantee of equal protection under the law.

Numerous attempts have been made to test the constitutionality of the laws relating to homosexual conduct. Success has been minimal.

Why?

One explanation is that regardless of how these laws affect the lives of homosexuals, they have practically no effect on the heterosexual majority; consequently, there is minimal public interest in whether or not they are sensible, just, or constitutional. The Supreme Court moves with the shifting tides of public opinion over the years, interpreting the Constitution in the light of changing circumstances and public reaction. The majority of Americans have little interest in homosexuals or the laws that affect them. Many would rather not hear about them at all.

Another explanation for the continued existence of these laws is based on the view that the rights of homosexual citizens were never intended to be protected by the Constitution.

Under certain circumstances, the rights guaranteed by the Constitution may be suspended. This happens most commonly in the case of convicted criminals, many of whose rights—that of association, for example—may be abridged. While there is no law which specifically states that it is a crime to *be* a homosexual, some judges have determined this to be the case *de facto*. The reasoning is as follows: by admitting himself to *be* a homosexual, an individual admits to having engaged in homosexual acts, intending to engage in them, or seriously contemplating such actions. Since homosexual acts are a crime, an admitted homosexual is convicted by his own admission of criminal status, justifying suspension of his constitutional rights.

The most recent instance of this denial of constitutional protection to homosexuals involved an application for a certificate of incorporation under the laws of the state of New York by the Gay Activists Alliance, a militant, nonviolent homosexual civil rights organization. New York's Secretary of State, John P. Lomenzo, turned down the application on the grounds that the word "gay" was obscene and improper for inclusion in the title of a certified corporation and that he believed GAA "sought to promote activities contrary to the public policy of the state and specific provisions of the penal law." The decision was appealed to the State Supreme Court where Justice T. Paul Kane upheld it on the ground that to be homosexual implied criminal status. This latter decision is also being appealed, but there is no guarantee that the appeal will be accepted and heard.

The fate of past appeals to higher courts on matters involving the rights of homosexuals provides little basis for optimism as far as achieving legal reform through court action is concerned.* Many carefully documented test cases have been brought to the Supreme Court because a favorable ruling could invalidate *all* state laws against sodomy as unconstitutional in a single sweep. Numerous appeals have been turned down by the Supreme Court in recent years on the ground that they were not serious enough to merit con-

---

*On September 13, 1971, a U.S. District Court judge ruled in three test cases brought by the American Civil Liberties Union that the Government cannot ask "probing personal questions" about the sex lives of homosexuals, nor withhold security clearances for refusal to answer such questions. Security clearances cannot be denied on the basis of information acquired about sexual practices unless the Government can demonstrate a clear connection—a "nexus"—between these practices and an individual's reliability or vulnerability to blackmail. This potentially important ruling is likely to be appealed to the U.S. Circuit Court of Appeals by the Department of Defense, which in any case remains free to deny homosexuals security clearances under other administrative regulations.

sideration at present. Many patently discriminatory rulings of lower courts have been allowed to stand. Until the High Court decides to take action on homosexual civil rights, legal reform must be sought through costly and time-consuming attempts to achieve repeal in individual state legislatures.

In the lower courts, the situation is not much better. When charges involving illegal homosexual acts are not dismissed for lack of evidence, the homosexual who is brought to court is not likely to fare well. Many homosexuals, fearing publicity which may cost them their jobs, waive their right to a trial by jury and hope for the best. Even when a homosexual does insist upon a jury trial, he has little reason to assume that the jurors will be impartial regarding his homosexuality.

Gay people are usually tried by straight juries. Even straights who have had a few homosexual experiences are seldom sympathetic toward "real" homosexuals. The right to peremptory challenge ensures that the prosecution can remove any juror easily identified as homosexual who might be expected to understand the case from the homosexual point of view. (Public-opinion surveys have shown that not a few straight people consider murder the only crime more serious than homosexual relations. This raises some question as to how fair a trial a homosexual can expect from a straight jury.)

The procedures which have been established for testing potential jurors for signs of bias toward racial and ethnic minorities, and removing for cause those jurors whose personal bias might prejudice fair judgment, have not been applied in any of our courts to assure that homosexuals get a fair trial. As long as homosexuals are defined as *de facto* criminals, there is no reason why a juror should be expected to be less prejudiced against homosexuals than against any other criminal.

Nor is there any guarantee that a judge trying a homosexual will be free of prejudice. In the case of other minority groups, most justices will at least refrain from making directly derogatory remarks while presiding or in presenting their opinions. When homosexuals are involved, a surprising number of directly discriminatory remarks can be found in the court record of many cases.

In a recent case, currently under appeal, the judge asked the defendant whether he was a homosexual. The defense attorney objected on the grounds that the question was of no relevance to the facts of the case, which did not involve homosexual charges. The judge agreed, but overruled the objection on the ground that homosexuality *did* have a bearing on the defendant's credibility as a witness. In other words, a man's honesty may be questioned on the ground that he is a homosexual.

When homosexuals do bring charges against those who have assaulted or robbed them, the possibility for successful prosecution is greatly decreased if their homosexuality becomes known. The victim's homosexuality is often viewed as an extenuating circumstance which decreases the importance of the crime committed against him. If a homosexual has been beaten or robbed by someone he has picked up, the defense will sometimes base its case on the notion that a sexual invitation from a homosexual was so disturbing to the defendant that he was driven to assault and robbery out of revulsion.

Such a defense would hardly succeed if a heterosexual were involved, but juries have so frequently accepted this line of argument and failed to convict defendants—even when serious crimes are involved—that the prosecutor or the judge generally counsels the victim to press charges for a much lesser offense.

Such cases indicate not so much bias on the part of the prosecution as a realistic appraisal of how the average jury will react and the desire to obtain at least some sort of conviction. For example, two young homosexuals in a car picked up a pair of hitchhikers who indicated they were interested in sexual relations. To facilitate further discussion of the matter, one of the homosexuals sat in back with one of the hitchhikers, while the other took a seat in front next to the driver. The hitchhikers held the two homosexuals up and forced them to stop the car, beat them severely, and pushed the car over a cliff with the homosexuals still inside. Both were critically injured. After a lengthy hospitalization, they attempted to press charges. Under normal circumstances, the charges would have included attempted murder, assault, and several other possible felonies. The matter was tossed around the prosecutor's office for weeks and the defendants were finally allowed to plead guilty on a charge of simple assault, a misdemeanor punishable by a six-month sentence.

Homosexuals appear in court for many reasons totally unconnected with their homosexuality and sometimes receive as fair treatment as anyone else. But whether we are talking about the laws, their enforcement, police protection, or judicial proceedings, the person identified as a homosexual cannot realistically expect equal treatment under the law with heterosexuals. Constitutional guarantees notwithstanding, the homosexual is a second-class citizen.

# Should You Hire a Homosexual?

"You don't know me—right? You don't fuck with me—right? Don't fuck with me, 'cause I'm going for ass here. You're messing with private files here."

"You're messing with private lives!" cried a seventeen-year-old activist.

The employee of Fidelifacts Inc. struck the young man and pushed him to the floor. A camera team from a local television station filmed the scene, while more gays angrily pushed their way into the crowded office of the private investigatory agency.

GAA had "zapped" Fidelifacts for contributing to employment discrimination against homosexuals. For a modest sum—as low as $12.50—the agency would investigate the private life of a prospective employee for any company wishing to pay for the service.

Many private businesses today will go to great lengths to make sure that they do not hire a homosexual by mistake. Fidelifacts and other detective agencies across the country specialize in prying into people's private lives for any signs of unconventional sex.

This is not a malicious business, of course. Fidelifacts, for example, has no personal grudge against homosexuals as people, merely as employees. As a service to prospective customers, the agency sends out a flyer about the undesirability of hiring homosexuals.

Vincent Gillen, president of Fidelifacts, is quoted in the agency's literature: "The problem of homosexuality seems to be increasing. Frankly, it's a difficult thing to establish. I like to go on the rule of thumb that if one looks like a duck, walks like a duck, associates only with ducks, and quacks like a duck, he probably is a duck."

How do the detectives discover whether somebody is a probable duck? They solicit hearsay and personal opinions from neighbors and acquaintances. They check mailboxes. In some cases, they will even put a tail on the bird to see whether he frequents bars or associates with known ducks.

Because of the labor involved, a thorough investigation like this generally costs a good deal more than $12.50. It is usually simpler and cheaper to purchase illegal information from the police regarding records of arrest on homosexual charges, whether they were dropped or not. In New York and probably many other cities, some police and employees in other government agencies are perfectly willing to make this information available for a small fee.

Armed with rubber squeegie ducks and the wrath of the just, the Gay Activists Alliance stormed noisily into the Fidelifacts office in Manhattan on a cold January afternoon and tried to commission an investigation of the company's president, Vincent Gillen, who had locked himself in the men's room at the first sign of the homosexuals' arrival. "We don't handle *your* business," they were told by the next ranking executive, who quickly placed a call to the police. There was some problem in maintaining law and order that day, for the city police were in the midst of a euphemistic "job action"—an illegal police strike.

I had been on many "zaps" before, most of them directed at candidates in the 1970 elections or at Mayor Lindsay. This was the first zap of the new year and—aside from the takeover of *Harper's* magazine—the first of a long series of actions against private companies.

I had always had a tendency to show undue deference to authority, and used a courteous, though loud, approach to politicians. But when I saw the thin, red-headed seventeen-year-old punched and knocked to the floor, my pent-up anger was suddenly released. I found myself cursing as I'd never cursed, shaking my fist in the employee's face in an ecstasy of indignation.

The whole atmosphere of the agency's offices added to the mood. If it had been a computerized operation, with sleek aluminum consoles and stacks of IBM cards, there would have been a protective aura of technological legitimacy about the place: we're not dealing with people, we're dealing with numbers and facts. But the place was dingy and unprofessional—lives were scattered on the desks and spilled out of open file drawers. The tables were covered with stacks of tabloid newspapers from which clippings had been carefully removed. The desks were littered with office debris: torn envelopes, crumpled bits of paper with cryptic messages, yellow pads with lists of figures—from bank statements, credit agencies?

Everything about the place and the people in it was contemptible. When we had entered they had been hunched over their desks examining their files like unattractive little boys sniggering over adult smut collected without their parents' knowledge. I felt a cold disgust at the thought of these men pawing through the evidence they had collected about innocent people: this one was a homosexual, that one had a mistress, this one was behind in his payments on a loan, that one had been arrested for stealing hubcaps when he was a teen-ager.

When two clean-cut, loyal cops who had remained on the job finally arrived and suggested that we leave the offices or face arrest, they were like a breath of fresh air.

A week later *The New York Times* reported that four less loyal members of the NYPD, a court clerk, and a clerk at the Department of Motor Vehicles, had been indicted on charges of taking money in exchange for the release of confidential information to Fidelifacts, Pinkerton's, Burns International Detective Agency, several other private investigatory companies, and two airlines: American Airlines and TransCaribbean Airways, Inc. Bribery is a felony punishable by up to seven years' imprisonment, but Gillen and the executives from the other companies involved were permitted to plead guilty to the misdemeanor charge of giving an unlawful gratuity to a public servant. The decision to accept the lesser plea, punishable by fine or a maximum of one year's imprisonment, was reportedly based on "the time and cost of drawn-out litigation."

Just this moment, nine months later, I went to the bedroom, checked the phone book, and placed a call to find out if Gillen and his friends were still doing their dirty work.

"Good morning, Fidelifacts."


## PRIVATE LIVES

Straight people often believe that if gay people kept their homosexuality private they would rarely encounter discrimination. If it is true, they say, that most homosexuals are indistinguishable from heterosexuals, how can there possibly be all this discrimination that you complain about?

Discrimination is so institutionalized in our society that it—like homosexuals—is often virtually invisible. The whole pattern of employment practices is structured so as to deny homosexuals the right to protect their private lives. It could hardly have been done consciously.

This systematic discrimination is too complex and effective to have been deliberately planned. It is the natural outgrowth of antihomosexuality in America, but it is so deeply ingrained in everyday life that few straight people are aware of it at all. Laws, regulations, and standard procedures which seldom affect the lives of heterosexuals can have an enormous impact on homosexuals.

Gay people do not have a right to a private life. Every male homosexual is forced to either admit his homosexuality or perjure himself. If he lies, he must go on lying and be increasingly careful to avoid discovery. If he admits to being homosexual, the admission becomes public information that will follow him throughout his life.

A known homosexual can, of course, get a job, but many areas of employment are closed to him and he will be subject to discrimination in every area of his life in which the law permits distinctions to be made between heterosexuals and homosexuals. This is not the end of the world. Other minority groups face similar problems, even when their rights are theoretically protected by law. If the laws against homosexuality were repealed today, we would not see the end of discrimination for many years.

How are homosexuals forced to expose their private lives?

Army regulation 635-89 states that homosexuality "appreciably limits the ability of an individual to function effectively in a military environment." The homosexual is "unfit for military service and impairs the morale and discipline of the Army." The other branches of the military have similar policies.

Every male citizen of the United States is required to register for the draft. When called for a preinduction physical, every young man is required to state whether or not he has homosexual tendencies, on pain of court martial or dishonorable discharge should he be discovered to have lied.

The item specifying homosexual tendencies has recently been removed from the preinduction questionnaire, and homosexuality is now covered under the blanket category of any physical or mental condition which in the individual's opinion disqualifies him from military service. Since most young homosexuals know that homosexuality is still grounds for an "unsuitable" discharge in all branches of the service, they should, by law, indicate their sexual orientation.

Most homosexuals lie and refuse to admit their homosexuality. Of those who pass for straight and do end up in the service, most "function effectively in a military environment," avoid discovery, and receive honorable discharges.

If a homosexual decides to comply with the law and admits his sexual orientation, this becomes a permanent part of his draft record even if he does not serve. But not all those who admit their homosexuality are exempted from the service.

Until recent years an admission of homosexuality usually guaranteed exemption, but the unpopularity of the Vietnam war and the new mood of gay liberation have changed all that. Over the past years more and more homosexuals have been willing to admit their homosexuality, and some non-homosexuals have claimed to be gay in order to beat the draft.

When the regulations were set, the military did not expect to lose more than about 1 percent of those subject to the draft, but suddenly the percentage of self-admitted homosexuals began to increase dramatically.

Although the military refuses to admit that it has changed its views in the slightest, there is no way to disguise the change in policy toward homosexuals. It is no longer enough to state that you are homosexual. Everyone

is assumed straight until proven otherwise. The homosexual must prove that
he is gay in order to avoid induction that will immediately subject him to
discharge.

For a while, some young men tried to prove their homosexuality by
showing up for their physical in drag, by lisping and adopting a stereotyped
image of effeminacy. The authorities soon suspected that a few straights
were dodging the draft with these tactics and tightened up the regulations.
Anyone who comes on as a stereotyped homosexual today is more likely to
be suspected of faking it than the average-looking person who claims to
be gay.

How can you prove that you are gay without breaking the laws against
lewd or indecent public behavior? You must get a letter from a psychiatrist
certifying your homosexuality. If you do not have a letter or your letter is
not quite convincing, you must be certified by three civilian psychiatrists
attached to the induction center. These people are not always infallible or
disinterested, so some young men who claim to be homosexuals are drafted
anyway.

Anyone who is inducted into the service in spite of an admission of
homosexuality is in an unenviable position. Even if he tries to walk the
straight and narrow, his military records follow him from base to base informing his commanding officers of his admission. He will sometimes be
harassed and mistreated out of dislike for homosexuals. Other times, he will
get especially rough treatment as those responsible for his training try to
"make a man out of him."

Some homosexuals in this position seek a discharge at the start of basic
training by again claiming to be homosexual. Even this does not always work.

Drafted in spite of his admitted homosexuality, one young soldier immediately went to the base psychiatrist at boot camp, who saw no reason to
doubt him. Military intelligence then asked for the names of all the civilians
with whom he had had sex prior to induction. They would verify his claim by
questioning these persons, who would, of course, be subject to prosecution
for violation of the sodomy laws. When the fellow refused, he received orders
for duty in Vietnam. Finally, he was fortunate enough to be granted an
"unsuitable" discharge.

Many men in the service attempt to hide their homosexuality because
they wish to serve or because a military career offers benefits that they might
not be able to obtain elsewhere: The G.I. bill, G.I. insurance and loans, and
numerous veterans' benefits. If they are discovered to be homosexual, they
will not necessarily receive "unsuitable" discharges.

A "general discharge under honorable conditions" is sometimes used
in cases of homosexuality. Future employers may still wish to know why the
discharge was "general" rather than "honorable," but not all the veteran's

benefits are stripped from him. In the case of an "unsuitable" discharge, however, all veterans' benefits are denied, regardless of length of service. With a dishonorable discharge, the ex-soldier also loses many citizenship rights.

Career men who are close to retirement have sometimes been bounced out of the military with nothing to show for their years of service but an undesirable discharge, which will make it particularly hard for them to find a new job. While noting that the majority of homosexuals in the military go undetected, the Indiana Institute for Sex Research recently estimated that between two and three thousand servicemen receive less than honorable discharges on the ground of homosexuality *per year*.

If one man in the armed services is discovered to be homosexual, it seldom stops there: military intelligence usually takes over. The soldier may be told that he will be allowed to remain in the service or will be given a general instead of an "unsuitable" discharge if he gives the names of his sex partners and all those whom he suspects of being gay.

One Air Force sergeant with a particularly fine memory managed to come up with close to two hundred and fifty names, many of them civilians he had met before entering the service or who lived near his base. No direct action could be taken against the civilians, of course, but accusations of homosexuality are usually passed on to the FBI and the Federal Civil Service Commission in such cases. Where the information may go from there is anybody's guess.

While I was in the Air Force I witnessed one of these military witch-hunts. A woman in the WAF squadron was accused of homosexuality, and before long a number of WAFs had been called in for questioning. The accusations spread in an ever widening circle throughout the squadron, and the prime suspects were constantly followed on and off base by agents of the Office of Special Investigations. A number of discharges were finally forthcoming, along with several nervous breakdowns and one successful suicide. Women in the military are just as vulnerable as men.

Military records are confidential by law, although they may be passed on to other government agencies for inclusion in dossiers on private citizens. When a person with homosexuality on his record goes in search of civilian employment he need not make any mention of the circumstances of his separation from the military if he does not choose to do so. Most prospective employers, however, are reluctant to hire anyone with other than an honorable discharge and become suspicious if a job applicant shows any reluctance to discuss his draft record.

Some employers will insist that the applicant sign an official waiver permitting the release of his records to them for examination. Many large corporations insist upon this as a matter of policy and require prospective employees to sign such a release on the job application form. So do most branches of the federal and state civil service, although this information is available to them through other channels.

Not every employer considers homosexuality a bar to employment. Small businesses rarely go through such careful investigations before hiring someone. But when the fact of homosexuality does come out, most employers will choose a nonhomosexual over a homosexual to fill a position. For low-paying positions, the details of an applicant's private life are often of little importance, but for a prestigious job with a high salary the matter is seldom left to chance. In choosing between different individuals to fill an executive position, many major corporations commission a private investigation of their backgrounds and private lives through a detective agency, such as Fidelifacts.

Some areas of employment are completely closed to anyone with a record of homosexuality. Security clearances are required for work with companies handling defense contracts, even where the applicant will not be working directly on classified projects. Homosexuals are barred from most civil service employment, although in some areas they will be permitted to hold low-rated jobs that are not of a "sensitive" nature. Individuals with a record of homosexuality are very unlikely to get licenses to teach, but they have almost as much difficulty in many far less controversial types of employment.

In order to get a license to drive a cab in New York a homosexual must get a written statement from a psychiatrist to the effect that his homosexuality is not serious enough to pose a threat to passengers. (In Connecticut this past year a bill was introduced in the state legislature to deny driver's licenses to homosexuals on the ground that they were unfit to drive, but it failed to pass.) In Albany the Chamber of Commerce became distraught at the notion that gay people might be hired as firemen. The Telephone Company is notorious for its dislike of homosexuals.

Not all homosexuals are on record as homosexuals. Although many gay people have acquired arrest records for homosexual activities, the vast majority have not. Even though increasing numbers of people admit to homosexuality at preinduction examinations, the majority of homosexuals have perjured themselves in order to maintain their privacy, and most of those who have served their country have not been discovered.

These people are in the clear as far as employment goes, so long as they are able to continue avoiding discovery. To do so, they are forced to perjure themselves again and again. Employment is not the only area in which homosexuality is considered to be of vital interest, and an admission of homosexuality under any circumstances may eventually lead to loss of a job or difficulty in finding one.

Some insurance companies, for example, refuse to insure homosexuals. Others will insure gay people at a higher rate than straights. Household Finance and some other loan companies and banks have been accused of asking leading questions in the attempt to ascertain whether applicants for loans are homosexual. These companies are said to have unofficial policies against lending to homosexuals, and it is not uncommon for personal history or credit information to be released to private investigatory agencies.

If a homosexual is a victim of job discrimination by the federal government, this may make it difficult to find employment elsewhere. Whether or not he has given any visible indications of homosexuality, civil service policies instituted in 1950 make it possible to require any federal employee suspected of homosexuality to undergo a medical and psychiatric examination as well as investigation by the FBI. If evidence of homosexuality is discovered, the employee can be fired without notice. It is stipulated that the precise reason for dismissal be entered upon each individual's record and forwarded to the Civil Service Commission, which can make this information available to other prospective employers.

When a homosexual goes hunting for a job, there are obviously many ways in which his homosexuality may become known. As a service to regular customers, such as large corporations, some employment agencies will note in their referrals that a job applicant is believed to be homosexual if he looks "obviously" gay—whether or not the potential employer has requested this information. One New York employment agency uses the code letters "HCF": high-class fairy.

When a homosexual goes for a job interview with a major company, any number of means are likely to be used in the attempt to discover indications of homosexuality. He may be asked why he is not married. In interviews conducted at IBM, for example, the following approach has been used:

> Do you plan to get married?
> Do you have a girl friend?
> Exactly where do you socialize?
> Are you a homosexual?

The application forms used by many large corporations and those for most federal, state, and city civil service positions specifically inquire about "homosexual tendencies." Even where the question is not put directly, there are numerous other ways in which the dread secret can come to light. "Were you ever barred or disqualified from appointment to a city, state, or federal position? If 'yes,' give details....Have you ever been refused a security clearance? Have you ever been refused insurance or denied a loan? Have you ever been arrested? If so, give details...."

Many application forms today include a waiver entitling the prospective employer to inspect military or civil service records. Virtually all ask for the names and addresses of previous employers and the circumstances under which employment was terminated. Give details. Anyone who has gone on record as a homosexual or has been fired for being gay is unlikely to be able to disguise the fact, even through extensive lying.

The average heterosexual is completely unaware of these problems. He does not face them himself, for it is not a crime to be heterosexual. What seems like a lot of red tape and pointless paperwork to the heterosexual applying for a job often determines whether or not a homosexual will be able to find employment commensurate with his qualifications.

## PUBLIC LIVES

Just what's wrong with homosexuals, anyhow?

The elaborate precautions taken to assure that even the most discreet and unnoticeable of homosexuals not be employed might suggest that they are invariably carriers of some highly virulent plague.

Is a homosexual an employment risk?

The standard explanation for the federal government's discriminatory policies is that homosexuals are particularly vulnerable to blackmail. If homosexuals did not have to worry about being fired when discovered, their homosexuality would not make them any more susceptible to blackmail than anyone else. Even so, no evidence exists that homosexuals have been black- mailed more often than heterosexuals who wish to keep details of their private lives secret.

In a recent study of several hundred cases in which classified informa- tion fell into the hands of foreign powers, only two involved the blackmailing of homosexuals. Either gay people have learned to be more adept at hiding their private lives than straights, or our "enemies" have as great a reluctance as the United States to deal with homosexuals.

The blackmail myth is exposed by the barring of open, self-admitted homosexuals from federal employment. Even when there is no possibility of blackmail, homosexuals are simply not acceptable.

These policies are usually justified on the ground that homosexuals damage the morale and efficiency of those who are forced to work with them. No trial period, no attempt to test this notion: the belief is unques- tioned.

There are some people today whose efficiency is impaired if they are compelled to work with members of other races or religions, but civil rights law does not accept this as a valid excuse for employment discrimination. If some whites don't like blacks, that's too bad for them. They can quit their jobs and look for work elsewhere, but they cannot expect a reputable employer to refuse to hire Negroes. This principle clearly does not apply to homosexuals today.

Do homosexuals actually impair morale and efficiency where they work? Since most homosexuals have managed to find jobs and lead productive lives in spite of discrimination against them, it would seem difficult to demonstrate this. Considering their comparative numbers in the population, there are probably ten times as many heterosexuals as homosexuals who cause friction on the job. I've certainly known a number of them.

It is not the way a homosexual behaves but merely the fact of his being a homosexual that usually gets him into trouble with his boss or coworkers. If homosexuals are so disruptive, why is it that they only get fired when somebody finds out that they are homosexual? Are they mysteriously transformed from good employees to bad ones overnight?

A gay man or woman may work in close cooperation with others for years without difficulty or discomfort on anybody's part. Suddenly the truth comes out and the homosexual's presence is intolerable. No matter what rationalizations are drummed up, this is bigotry pure and simple.

Some people are willing to concede that homosexuals have as much right to work as anyone else, but hasten to add that there are some types of employment for which they are unsuited. These qualifications are usually based upon the stereotypes about homosexuals that are prevalent in American society.

All homosexuals are effeminate—they are not fit for men's work. Gay people are not supposed to be able to serve with distinction or even scrape by in the armed forces, police work, or other occupations usually reserved for men in our society. Women who enter these professions which are thought to be incompatible with the feminine role are often assumed to be lesbians. Believed to be unable to defend themselves, male homosexuals are considered incapable of defending or protecting others.

The Greeks had quite a different attitude: "An army of lovers cannot lose." To the embarrassment of many modern gays, homosexuality has been a prominent and sometimes undisguised feature of the military throughout history. In America, homosexuality has flourished in many of the occupations which are considered to be most masculine. Athletes, lumberjacks, truck drivers, forest rangers, construction workers, cattlemen—any profession where men have little contact with women both encourages homosexuality and attracts homosexuals.

Another popular myth insists that homosexuals are unable to restrain their sexual desires as others do and are constantly and offensively on the make, often forcing their attentions on heterosexuals under the most inappropriate circumstances. For this reason, it is sometimes said, homosexuals are not suited for any line of work which will bring them into regular contact with the general public. Gay people should not be hired as salespeople, receptionists, bank tellers, bus drivers, waiters or waitresses, stewards or stewardesses, and especially not for any job that will bring them into contact with children. Certainly they have the right to work—stick them in a back room somewhere. A closet perhaps?

Some people used to believe that a black face would offend public sensibilities. This argument holds no more water when applied to gay people than to any other group. Either you treat all human beings as equals or you don't—you can't have it both ways.

No matter how many precautions they take, some gay people are discovered and fired.

More discoveries of homosexuality can be traced to arrests for engaging in homosexual activities than to any other source. The police in many cities will make a point of informing a homosexual's employer of his arrest if at all possible, even when they know that the charges will be dropped or thrown out of court.

Although arrest records are supposed to be confidential in New York, in many other states there is no legal bar to dissemination of arrest information by the police. Even in areas where this is prohibited, the police may sidestep the law by claiming that an employer must be contacted for purposes of identification: we just arrested this guy on a morals charge and we want to know if he works for you.

In New York, other methods of circumventing the law have been devised. Investigatory agencies maintain contacts with police departments in New Jersey, where the release of information is not illegal. For a gratuity, New Jersey cops are often willing to request details of New York arrests from the computerized banks of information on private citizens maintained by the FBI and by police departments in other states.

Most gay people live in dread of being arrested and take great pains to avoid it. Often believing that the police are above the law, many have never bothered to familiarize themselves with their rights and do not know that they are entitled to withhold information about their employment. Even those who *do* know their rights are often cowed into revealing more than the required name and address by threats of more serious criminal charges or misleading reassurance that it is all just a formality.

If a homosexual does stand up for his rights he may end up in hot water anyway. I know several gays who have been threatened with arrest simply for demanding the badge number of a cop who is harassing them. When gay people contest the charges brought against them, they may be hard put to explain the reason for a day in court to their employers, even though the arresting officer seldom shows up and the charges are dropped.

Rivalries on the job may also bring a person's homosexuality into the light when rumors become part of business politics. The man or woman who shares an apartment with someone of the same sex may become the topic of office gossip if there is something to be gained from it. Being spotted entering a gay bar or being seen in public with an "obvious" homosexual may be enough to start the rumor mill grinding. Not all people who are fired for homosexuality are actually homosexuals.

Most commonly it is homosexuals with well-paid positions of responsibility who have the most to fear in terms of discovery. If they lose their jobs they lose many of the benefits that went along with them and are likely to have to start again at the beginning. Requests for information on the reasons for terminating previous employment may make it impossible for them to get anywhere near as good a job as they had. It is not surprising that the most successful homosexuals tend to be the most closeted as well.

As a general rule, the higher one's position and the greater one's authority, the less likely one is to be accepted as an open homosexual. Many companies fear for their corporate image today should a homosexual hold a high executive position. These are probably the same companies who will be looking for a token homosexual five years from now and put him in an office next to the house black or female member of the board. Wait and see.

There are exceptions to the rule, of course, especially today, when homosexuality is finally beginning to be viewed in the context of civil rights. I know a number of very successful homosexuals who decided to leave the closet and were surprised to find that their employers didn't care about their sexual orientation and even admired them for being frank about it.

Some gay people have come out in public because they had reason to believe that their union would protect their jobs. Marc, for example, felt more secure in revealing his homosexuality after the United Federation of Teachers adopted an unofficial policy of protecting the rights of homosexual teachers in the New York City school system. On a national scale, it seems likely that homosexuals will receive the greatest protection against discrimination from forward-looking unions and professional associations rather than government in the near future.

Homosexuals are sometimes tolerated—even welcomed—outside the various professions that are usually considered to be especially "gay": bookkeeping, dress design, window display, hairdressing, interior decoration, art, music, acting, radio work, religious service, nursing, and social work. In some offices an open homosexual will be accepted as one of the gang by his coworkers, while in others he will be treated like a leper and made so uncomfortable that he may decide to look for work elsewhere. His reception depends on the quality of the people he is working with and for.

As the influence of the gay liberation movement has spread, some homosexuals have decided to come out as a matter of principle, regardless of the consequences.

When Marc was invited to participate in a discussion of homosexuality on the David Susskind Show, we spent an agonized evening together while he tried to decide whether or not to accept. He had been out of the closet in most respects, but he never told his parents or his co-workers. He was uncertain of his parents' reaction and expected the worst. He knew that the UFT would probably try to protect his teaching position, but he realized that enormous pressures could be brought to bear on the school administration to find some way to get rid of him.

It was one thing to come out among friends, in the movement, and in public places where he was unlikely to be recognized, but to do it on national television was another.

Marc decided to go ahead with the show and things turned out better than he had dared to hope. Although a few people at school became noticeably cooler after the broadcast, most responded with support and congratulations. He was told that the school would stand behind him if there was any pressure for his removal. "So how come you were the only one with long hair?" his mother asked.

Not everybody is this fortunate.

A friend in Connecticut who worked as a counselor in a school for the deaf appeared on television and received a letter of dismissal from the headmaster soon after:

I have received a phone call from a very disturbed parent who saw you on Channel 24 on Tuesday night, Dec. 22. She concluded from your statements made on television that you have an abnormal problem that would make your employment as a counselor questionable. She has a boy in the school, which naturally makes her very concerned. It will take time to research this whole thing out, and in the meantime, it would not be wise for you to return to work. I therefore must suspend you without pay until I can investigate this report.

Overnight: from a respected employee to a child molester.

Even heterosexuals occasionally become victims of antihomosexual prejudice. A straight high school teacher was fired after honoring his students' request for a forum on homosexuality by inviting members of the University of Iowa Gay Liberation Front to address his class in sex education. It was perfectly all right to mention homosexuality as a disease, but to balance this viewpoint by allowing homosexuals to speak for themselves was irresponsible and immoral. Education can only go so far.

Some heterosexuals lose their jobs because they are suspected of being homosexuals or because they do not show sufficient intolerance for homosexuality. Security clearances are sometimes denied on the ground that an individual has associated with persons suspected of being homosexual. Many straights who have no personal bias toward homosexuals find it necessary to act as though they did: you are known by the company you keep.

Homosexuals who successfully pass for straight may still encounter problems which the majority of heterosexuals do not face. Although he may not necessarily be suspected of homosexuality, the unmarried man in our society is considered to be less responsible, less stable, and more of a risk than the married man with children. Like the homosexual, the confirmed bachelor has failed to meet society's expectations of him, and both are likely to be considered a little peculiar. When opportunities for advancement materialize, a married man with a respectable public image stands a better chance of being promoted than an equally qualified bachelor.

There are various ways in which homosexuals share forms of discrimination with other single men and women, and these biases derive from the same source: the demand for conformity to sexual roles.

Employment is not the only area in which homosexuals face discrimination, of course. Restaurants, bars, and other public accommodations often refuse to serve individuals suspected of being homosexual. Even in Greenwich Village you see a few signs in the windows of restaurants or bars which read "If you're gay—stay away" or "No faggots." At present, New York City regulations governing cabarets, dance halls, and food-catering establishments prohibit the serving or hiring of homosexuals. Any such business frequented by homosexuals can lose its license to operate. Under the existing regulations gay people do not have the right to drink, dance, or eat in public.

Many hotels and motels will refuse accommodations to two men suspected of being homosexual, while it is common practice to allow unmarried heterosexual couples to register under false names, often without any pretense at all. Housing developments and apartment complexes often adopt a "no singles" policy in order to bar homosexuals from finding residence there. In some places, one unmarried person can rent an apartment while two single individuals will not be permitted to do so.

When it comes to employment, housing, public accommodations, and public services, gay people are treated like pariahs and there's no disguising the fact. They don't like this sort of treatment any better than anyone else would. Many today are prepared to do something about it.

## DISCRIMINATION

When I was first becoming involved in the movement, it took me a few months to become comfortable with the techniques involved in zaps. I was not accustomed to shouting at people. I had never stood up to a cop and risked arrest. I was not used to calling attention to myself in public.

I remember trying to give a speech in public one day to raise support for a demonstration. We had set up a table with leaflets on the corner of

Sheridan Square in Greenwich Village, and several of us were supposed to take turns standing on a chair and addressing the passing crowd through a bullhorn. Climbing onto the shaky chair, I felt enormously foolish. I was so embarrassed that I could hardly stand, much less speak coherently. I was not used to soap-box oratory.

As the months went by it became easier and easier to speak out in public. With familiarity, I acquired a taste for zapping. Zaps were adventures. There was the feeling of being a small band of brave men and women, facing a hostile world together. It was right out of Hollywood, a half-real fantasy mission into the dangers of straight society. Will the police move in? Will the straights attack? Tune in next week.

I sometimes like to imagine that we were continuing a tradition of homosexual courage that had been underground for centuries. An army of lovers cannot fail.

Confrontation politics became second nature, but the glamour began to wear thin in time. I had been to so many demonstrations, spoken to so many straight people, and seen so little real change.

It was one thing to go zapping with a band of friends, but the longer Marc and I were together the less enjoyable I found confrontations. When I had been alone, I had little to lose. With my lover at my side, I was risking everything I had in life.

Sometimes on the night before a zap or on the way to a heavy confrontation I would become anxious. What if Marc and I were arrested, separated, and put in different cells? What if he should be injured by the police or attacked by the crowd? What if something were to happen to me and he were left alone to try to make a new start in life?

I felt that if anything were to happen to Marc there would be no question of making a new start myself. I had found the person I loved and if I lost him I would be ready to kill. There is no restraint when you have nothing left to lose. Frustration bred anger, but having to put my love on the line stirred far stronger feelings.

Why go on with it? Why not say to hell with straight society and try to find some way to lead a quiet, inconspicuous, comfortable life with my love?

I knew that many straight people thought we were all deranged: why are those crazy queers always complaining and making such a fuss in public? Some people thought we were neurotics in search of a cause, that if it weren't gay rights it would be vivisection or the end of the world we were screaming about. Some thought we were dupes of foreign powers. Why go on with the uphill struggle? Where was it really getting us, what was it really accomplishing?

Naïvely, I felt that since it was justice we were seeking, straight society would *have* to see it eventually and do something about it.

The people in the movement who had given up all hope had long since

dropped out of sight, some to communes, others to who knows where—
someplace they could plan in secret. But there we were, time after time,
taking it all to the public and expecting something to happen. In spite of
Vietnam, Kent, Jackson, Attica, we could not really believe that America
was deaf or blind or cruel. Perhaps we were waiting for martyrs of our own.

The movement had been primarily a white middle-class phenomenon
and few of us had managed to completely erase our white middle-class values
and optimistic faith in the system. A dear friend, one of the most radical
figures in the activist movement, believes quite firmly that the police are an
army of occupation and that a new wave of repression against homosexuals
is likely to develop in America quite soon, a backlash that will make the
Middle Ages seem enlightened in comparison.

Arthur says he has no faith in the system, and yet he's at the front of
the group every time, whether it's City Hall, the State Capitol, the D.A.'s
office, or wherever. He speaks with passion about freedom and democracy—
I will never forget him being dragged off by the police in front of City Hall,
raising a clenched fist, and crying "Justice for homosexuals!"

It sounds funny. "Justice for homosexuals!" To use the word "homosexual" in this context always makes a few bystanders smirk. Homosexuals
are not people.

Why do we go on?

Arthur calls for justice and equality but says that we would be foolish to
expect them in this country. Yet when bystanders jeer or the police lead him
away, he seems shocked. Behind his rhetoric, he still has a basic faith in
America and her people, I think. It is a faith from which most of us suffer.

The activists in the movement are quixotic—dreamers perhaps. No
matter how cynical we become, we have an enormous vulnerability because
we still believe. The words of the Constitution, the Declaration of Independence, the mottoes carved into public buildings, the pursuit of happiness,
equality under the law: Christ, we cannot rid ourselves of the idea that people really care. Sometimes I believe that gay liberation is the Children's
Crusade of the twentieth century, the march of innocence into indifference.

In January 1971 the Gay Activists Alliance managed to get a bill introduced in the New York City Council to extend the protection of city human
rights legislation to homosexuals. The basic rights of all other minorities are
protected. Existing laws forbid discrimination on the grounds of race, color,
creed, national origin, ancestry, age, sex, and physical handicap. "Sex" is
defined as gender, and does not cover homosexuals.

The gay bill would extend protection against discrimination in employment, housing, and public accommodations on the ground of "sexual orientation"—the gender of one's sex partner. It seems little to ask. The principle of
protection of minority rights has been recognized and accepted across the

United States at all levels of government. Do we not have the same rights as others?

It was not enough simply to get the bill introduced. We knew that it would die in committee if we could not bring political pressure to bear on several key politicians. We lobbied for months, finally gaining the promised support of a majority of the City Council. We tried to draw the mass media's attention to the bill and encourage popular support for it. We tried to raise public awareness about discrimination against gay people: we petitioned and demonstrated and zapped and worked like demons. We got the Mayor's support. We organized the formation of a citizens' committee of prominent nonhomosexuals in support of gay civil rights. No movement on the bill.

The internal politics of the City Council were our major stumbling block: none of the key councilmen had any intention of publicly associating themselves with the issue of homosexuality. The chairman of the committee in which the bill had languished for nine months had no real intention of doing anything at all to promote its passage. The bill could not come to a vote in the full Council without first being scheduled for hearings in committee. It became perfectly obvious that the bill would be allowed to die without ever having hearings, in spite of the support we had lined up for it.

Time after time we were promised that a date for hearings would be set, but they never materialized. We became familiar with more delaying tactics than we had ever dreamed existed. When we felt that we had exhausted every conceivable form of lobbying, GAA sent a letter to the sponsors of the bill, the chairman of the committee in which it had been buried, the majority leader of the Council, and the Mayor. It read, in part:

We have tried, through the use of peaceful, reasonable, "approved" techniques, to petition the government. The denial of our rights and needs by a portion of the government of that same city that profits so greatly through our participation in its economic, cultural, social, and political fabric has moved us to the point where we are willing to take the full power of our anger and frustration into the streets. The responsibility for the results of these actions will lie firmly on the hearts and heads of those elected representatives who have ignored our call for civil rights protection for homosexuals.

One thing we had learned in the past is that you have to be willing to back up threats in order to maintain your credibility. In the letter we had set a deadline for the announcement of hearings, and we had to be prepared to take to the streets if the deadline passed.

A meeting was held to plan the actions which would be taken if the deadline was not met. I was at home working on this book, trying to meet a deadline of my own. Marc got home at one in the morning with the details of the planned actions. I found them somewhat hair-raising: they were the most highly coordinated and militant steps GAA had ever considered taking.

Everything was planned in detail. Marc and I were to avoid arrest the first night, but were to attempt to break through the police lines we expected to encounter at the second and more volatile demonstration later in the week. We still believed that the public conscience could be moved.

The deadline was Thursday, September 30. When no announcement of hearings was forthcoming, the GAA meeting that night broke up early and a hundred of us marched over to the apartment house where the chairman of the committee lived. Some entered the lobby of the building, while others remained outside demonstrating. Soon the police arrived, and we agreed to leave, serving notice that we would be back Saturday night in far greater numbers if there was no motion on the bill before then.

Nothing happened Friday, and we began to make our final preparations for the action Saturday night. We planned to enter the building and sit in until arrested, but we knew that the police were expecting us and that there might be difficulty gaining entrance. We drew up several different contingency plans for entering, depending on where the police set up their barricades.

The situation was volatile. We planned to end the Saturday night dance at the GAA Firehouse at 1 A.M. and lead everyone over to the demonstration. We were worried about violence breaking out, for many of the people who would participate were not GAA members and had had no experience in demonstrating before. Expecting provocateurs to join the march, we trained marshals to keep the crowd under control. We made one last effort to get Mayor Lindsay to intervene, stating quite honestly that we were afraid a riot might develop if the police were not carefully controlled. The Mayor could not be bothered.

The level of tension in the Firehouse rose to unprecedented heights. People were afraid of the demonstration, yet determined to participate in it. As the time approached on Saturday night, our "undercover agents" at the site of the demonstration informed us that police barricades had been set up, paddy wagons were parked along the street, and a busload of TPF—the Tactical Police Force, the city's most brutal cops—had already arrived, armed to the hilt as usual. At 12:45 the dance was brought to a halt, Marc gave a rousing speech, and we moved out en masse at 1:00, a thousand strong. Marc and I held hands the whole way, wondering where we would be and whether we would be together an hour or two later.

When we reached the apartment building, an ugly scene confronted us. Lines of TPF were massed behind the barricades, playing with their clubs, contempt and hatred written on their faces. During earlier discussions with police officials we had come to an agreement that six of us would be allowed to enter the building to verify whether our councilman was present. The TPF were not inclined to honor the agreement and seemed to operate outside of the regular chain of command of the Police Department. When Marc and I attempted to move past the barricades according to plan, the TPF came boiling out, clubs flying.

It was the most nightmarish scene I had ever witnessed: long, brutal clubs smashing left and right, landing on people's heads, the crowd panicking, pushing first toward the barricades and then falling back. The glare of the TV lights made the whole thing unreal, and doubly frightening.

Dragging one demonstrator off to be arrested, the TPF withdrew behind the barricades: The District Chief for Manhattan South invited Marc and me behind the lines to discuss the situation. He finally permitted six of us to enter the building, where we immediately stated that we would not leave until we had seen our councilman. A half hour later we were arrested by officers from our local precinct—very decent sorts—handcuffed together, led out through the rear entrance, and taken off in a paddy wagon. For us, the confrontation was over.

Back at the apartment building, however, the worst was yet to come. The TPF began taunting the crowd, daring them to cross the police lines, insulting them for being homosexuals. When the demonstration was called to a close and the crowd began to disperse, the TPF again burst forth from behind the barricades, separated a group of the demonstrators from the mass of the crowd, herded them behind the building away from the TV cameras with their clubs, and began to beat them savagely. Two were sufficiently injured before they escaped to require immediate hospitalization that night on suspicion of having received concussions.

Five days later hearings for our bill were scheduled for October 18, 1971, a tribute to democracy in action.

Children's Crusade?

Children, in fact, have been the basic problem with the bill. Nothing terrifies the average parent more than the idea that his or her child might come into contact with a homosexual. The reason the bill has been such a politically sensitive issue is that it would protect the rights of homosexual teachers to teach. Civil rights is one thing, but homosexual teachers are another.

The subject of gay teachers inspires some of the most virulent expressions of antihomosexual sentiment. A recent mass mailing from an unspecified source, billed as a public service warning to "all civil libertarians" had this to say:

HOMOSEXUAL CHILD-MOLESTERS TO BECOME SCHOOL TEACHERS

ARE YOU AWARE that the organized homosexual movement of America is conspiring to *force* the schools of New York City to hire homosexual child-molesters to teach *your* children?

There is, at present, a bill before the New York City Council known as the Clingan-Burden Bill, which would force the schools to hire homosexuals as teachers. In addition, the Gay Activists Alliance, a totalitarian political organization dedicated to the advancement of homosexuality, *and the suppression of normal sexuality,* has been publicly demanding that the Board of Education hire homosexuals to teach in the public school system. . . .

Unless you write or call your State Senators, State Assemblymen, and City Councilmen, the organized homosexuals will succeed, at the expense of your children, in their plans to increase the numbers of homosexuals. For your children's sake, take action before it is too late.

Is it already too late?

# What Does a Gay Teacher
# Teach Your Child?

One Saturday several weeks ago Marc stormed into our apartment in a rage after spending the afternoon with some gay friends petitioning for the Clingan-Burden bill.

It had been a successful afternoon: Marc and the others had collected more than seven hundred signatures in support of the bill. Most of these had come from straight people, who were surprisingly sympathetic about the need for employment protection for gays. Public attitudes seemed to be changing: a year ago when we had first tried petitioning in public we had encountered a good deal of hostility and mockery.

Marc had enjoyed the afternoon, but as he rode home on the subway he began to dwell on one incident that had only mildly irritated him earlier in the day. By the time he reached home he was furious. He had spent fifteen minutes trying to convince one homosexual to sign in support of legislation that would have extended civil rights protection to him.

The fellow had identified himself as gay, listened to an explanation of the petition, and then said that he couldn't sign it. Most homosexuals enjoyed molesting children. Most gay people did not deserve to have their right to work protected, especially not if they were teachers.

Marc pointed out that he taught young children and had never had the slightest urge to molest any of them. He asked the fellow whether he had had any gay teachers when he was in school. Yes, there were several he thought had probably been gay. Had they molested him? No. Or anyone else? No. Did he know of any child who had been molested by a homosexual? No. Did any of the homosexuals he had ever known take a sexual interest in children? No.

Why did he think, then, that homosexuals were child molesters? No reason, but *everybody* knew they were. He walked off without signing.

Some homosexuals have the most bizarre notions of what all gay people —except themselves—are like. The anti-Semitic Jew. The Negro who doesn't like blacks. Now the homosexual who can't stand gay people.

Outside of the gay world it is not surprising to encounter the myth that homosexuals are child molesters. Many straight people believe it.

I have never known anybody who claimed to have been molested by a homosexual during childhood. I have never known a homosexual who expressed the slightest interest in molesting children. I know that children do get molested by somebody from time to time, because there are criminal statistics to prove it. I do know that many people assume that it is homosexuals who are responsible for the majority of these cases, because many straight people have told me so.

Who really wants to have sex with a child?

## CHILDREN

Children have certain basic sexual rights. Among these are the right not to be involuntarily exposed to the sexual activities of others and the right not to be forced or coerced into engaging in sexual acts against their will.

We recognize how stimulating sexual activity can be, regardless of whether or not one is personally involved in it: sex in public is forbidden because it forces others to become involved without their consent, if only as witnesses. In the case of children, this principle is considered particularly important because children are believed to be especially impressionable.

Protection from involuntary sexual involvement is not restricted to cases involving the use of force. Threats, bribery, and the misuse of a position of authority are also considered to be forms of coercion. For this reason, it is considered improper for an employer to have sexual relations with an employee or a teacher to have sexual relations with a student. In both cases, the person in the subordinate position may feel compelled by extenuating circumstances to play along when he or she would not otherwise choose to do so.

The principle of free choice in sexual matters poses some problems with regard to children. Consent is the most basic principle of sexual morality, but below a certain age children are not considered competent to make a decision when sex is involved. Fear or misplaced respect may lead them to permit inappropriate sexual liberties. Ignorance may lead them to consent to things they would never agree to do if they knew the consequences. When does a child become competent to make decisions about his or her own sex life?

A wide variety of laws has been passed to protect the sexual rights of the young. During the years between adolescence and marriage, for example, nearly all heterosexual acts are technically illegal, under statutes concerning fornication, juvenile delinquency, indecent behavior, and acts corrupting the morals of a minor.

One problem is that it is difficult to say when childhood ends. Although we do not grant full adult status to young men and women in our society until they reach the age of eighteen or twenty-one, many other societies consider puberty the beginning of adulthood and encourage marriage during the mid-teens.

In our society, there seems to be a belief that until a certain age children are not ready for sex and know next to nothing about it. Kinsey and his associates found, however, that sexual activity, even prior to puberty, was common—70 percent of the men and 50 percent of the women interviewed—although adults tended to forget many of their early experiences. Adolescents recalled many more early sexual experiences, so the researchers suggested that their findings represent a bare minimum of childhood sexual activity.

Most of this sexual activity is kept secret from parents, for even at this early age the message has been clearly received: sex is taboo.

The young are certainly capable of sex long before the legal age of consent and many seek it out frequently without any apparent harm. Nevertheless, our laws forbid them to engage in sexual relations until they are well into sexual maturity, and often past the peak of their sexual desire. Presumably this is justified on the basis that they are not yet psychologically mature or that their moral training is incomplete.

In many other societies, young people marry, raise families, and adopt full adult responsibility in their mid-teens, so Western ideas about psychological maturity can well be questioned.

Regardless of the laws, it seems reasonable to follow the Indiana Institute for Sex Research in calling young men and women sixteen and over "adults," young people between twelve and sixteen "minors," and reserving the term "children" for those under twelve who are unlikely to have reached puberty.

There is some question as to whether the existing laws actually protect or infringe on the sexual rights of young people. Should a sixteen-year-old boy be subject to arrest for sleeping with a fifteen-year-old girl? Should a twenty-one-year-old "man" be subject to imprisonment for having sex with a consenting "boy" twenty years old? Does the government have the right to regulate sex in whatever way it chooses?

Some people will agree that adults have the right to engage in any sort of sexual relations that does not infringe upon the rights of others. Clearly such a right would be violated by the majority of legislation in this country regulating sexual activity, even for married individuals.

Although most of the sexual activity that goes on during childhood involves children of approximately the same ages, instances of "child molestation" do occur. In the vast majority of cases, the adult involved is male.

A quarter of the women Kinsey interviewed said that sexual advances had been made toward them by adult men before they entered adolescence.

Most often these advances involved exhibition of the male genitals, fondling, masturbation, and the like—actual coitus was rare. Twenty percent of the cases were incestuous.

In a recent study of child molestation by the American Humane Association it was found that there were ten to twelve times as many cases of heterosexual molestation as homosexual molestation. Female homosexual molestation was so rare as to be insignificant. The men who molested children were found to be known to the child or parents in 75 percent of the cases. In 60 percent of the cases the child was coerced by the direct use of force or the threat of bodily harm.

In studying sex crimes, homosexual molestation involved coercion so seldom that the investigators at the Indiana Institute for Sex Research* eliminated the category of "homosexual aggression" from their list of sex offenses, while finding it quite necessary to retain the category of "heterosexual aggression." Their data also indicated that heterosexual offenders tended to pick younger children than homosexual offenders picked.

What kind of man molests a child? The largest category of offenders was labeled "pedophiles," although the researchers pointed out that this did not always indicate a sexual preference for children, but simply that many of these people considered children acceptable sex partners.

Another category of child molesters was labeled "socio-sexually underdeveloped." These were individuals, usually with a puritanical upbringing, who preferred adults as sexual partners but were unsuccessful in establishing adult relationships due to fear, guilt, or ineptitude. They seemed to be continuing a pattern of preadolescent sexual behavior with children because they could not find other sex partners and had failed to mature psychologically themselves.

Amoral delinquents—sociopaths—represented another type of offender. These individuals seemed to feel no moral restraints with regard to sex: it made little difference to them whether their sex partner was an adult or a child, female, male, or even animal.

A large number of those engaging in sexual relations with children were found to be mentally defective. Alcohol was often involved in cases of molestation—especially where violence was employed—but use of other drugs seemed to have little or no role in sex crimes.

According to the Institute for Sex Research, the younger the victim, the less strongly the molester was oriented toward homosexuality. Of those arrested for homosexual molestation of children, 75 percent had had sexual intercourse with women prior to their offense and about half were married at the time of the offense. Furthermore, those who had engaged in homo-

*Sex Offenders, by Gebhard, Gagnon, Pomeroy, and Christenson. See bibliography.

sexual molestation of children had often engaged in heterosexual molestation of children.

These findings imply that a sexual interest in children—pedophilia—is not rigidly divided along lines of sexual orientation: those who like children tend to be interested in both sexes. It must be remembered that "homosexual" molestation means that the two individuals involved were of the same sex, not necessarily that either or both of them were homosexuals.

Of those convicted of homosexual molestation, half were judged to be pedophiles, a tenth mentally defective, and a tenth drunk. The rest of the cases were attributed to amoral delinquency, situational factors, and the like.

Violence was almost never a factor in "homosexual" offenses, and most of the time it appeared that the "victim" was not unwilling. Naturally, many of those accused of sex crimes claim that their victims sought out the experiences or encouraged them. Only where these claims coincided with the prison record of the facts of the case did the sex researchers accept these claims as true—it is not unlikely that some "innocent" convicts were excluded for this reason. In 70 percent of the cases involving children, both the convicts and the records agreed that the boy was either receptive or encouraging. This was found to be true in more than 80 percent of the cases involving minors and 90 percent of the cases involving adults, age sixteen and over.

These findings are not particularly surprising. Homosexual activity is awfully common, and the strong male sex drive during adolescence—when heterosexual activities are often restricted—helps to explain why many boys are not averse to homosexual experiences with older men.

From this study of homosexual child molestation a pattern emerges. Interest in children is comparatively rare and usually appears to be a form of pedophilia in which *both* heterosexual and homosexual interests are common. In cases where the homosexual orientation is stronger, the preferred sex object is sometimes an adolescent, but more often a young adult sixteen or over. In many cases where minors are involved, situational factors are important—the adult in question has been unable to find a more desirable partner close to his age and has had a costly lapse in judgment. In other cases, psychological immaturity or a strict sexual upbringing has made adult relations impossible, and the individual appears to be continuing an earlier pattern of adolescent homosexual activity which he found less threatening.

It should not be denied that the facts do indicate that a small minority of the male homosexual population does prefer boys in their mid-teens or early adult years as sexual partners. How concerned should we be about this?

Some people will be concerned and outraged no matter what While they may consider a heterosexual experience with a sixteen-year-old girl an indication of poor judgment and irresponsibility, a homosexual experience with a sixteen-year-old boy indicates the most monstrous depravity. These attitudes reflect our cultural biases. If the law and public opinion were based on the fact that a young man is biologically an adult at this age, there would be less justification for concern.

There may well be a basic biological tendency, which is suppressed in our society, for homosexual relationships to form between older and younger males. Although this pattern appears in other mammals and in other societies past and present, it is surprisingly uncommon in our own. In ancient Greece, a young man was expected to take an adolescent boy for his lover and provide him with a moral education and training in athletic and military skills.

In the gay world of America, homosexual relationships between adolescent boys and adults are quite uncommon—a good deal less common than comparable heterosexual relationships. Adult homosexual relationships tend to form between individuals of roughly the same age, as is the case for homosexual relationships in earlier years. But this may be a matter of social conditioning, convenience, and shared interests. A fair percentage of young homosexuals find older men especially attractive, and some of the most stable relationships are found between individuals who are several years apart in age.

When I began to look outside of my circle of high school friends for homosexual relationships, I found myself much more attracted to men a good deal older than I was. When I began to frequent the bars I usually entered relationships with men in their twenties or early thirties, because they were the ones I preferred. I did not have a relationship with a man younger than myself until I was twenty-five.

There are a number of psychological factors which make some gay men prefer partners who are younger or older than themselves. For the young homosexual, an older man is more sexually experienced, stable, and less likely to be promiscuous. For the older homosexual, a young man may be more affectionate, more easily aroused, and less likely to compare his partner's sexual performance with that of others. To some extent, elements of a father-son relationship may also enter the picture: the older homosexual may be more protective and provide emotional support for his younger companion.

Although few adult homosexuals will risk involvement with an underage boy, there are some places where adolescents who are interested in homosexual relations can be found. Many hustlers and most runaways are still in their teens and often have a basically homosexual orientation. Some young boys frequent the tea rooms in search of older sex partners. In some public parks there are particular areas where young boys who wish to be picked up will congregate.

If a young man does not actively seek out sex with an older homosexual, he is unlikely to ever be approached. Two thirds of the cases of "homosexual molestation" which were studied involved older friends or family acquaint-ances, not the lurking strangers of our myths. Nor are those who become in-volved with adolescents usually "dirty old men." The average age is about thirty—an age that I, at least, found appealing when I was an adolescent. For many adolescent gays, involvement with older homosexuals often seems less risky than involvement with their peers; fewer tales are likely to be told.

Actually, it is not so surprising that adolescent boys have a tendency to become involved with older men. Although we seldom recognize the fact, such relationships are institutionalized in our society. Think of the comic books, adventure movies, and TV programs directed at adolescent boys. So many heroes have younger sidekicks, so many boys have older buddies: Batman and Robin, Superman and Jimmy Olsen, Buck Rogers and Buddy—the list could go on and on, and most of the super he-men have curiously platonic relationships with adult women.

The issue of sexual relations with children is likely to draw increasing attention as reforms in sex legislation are considered. The important role of alcohol, rather than other drugs, and the influence of a puritanical rather than "permissive" or simply informative sex education, provide food for thought. The time may come when the age of consent for both homosexual and hetero-sexual relations may be made more realistic. At present, however, hetero-sexuals constitute a far greater "threat" to children and adolescents than homosexuals do.

## GAY TEACHERS

Teaching is one of the professions in which the highest percentage of homosexuals is to be found—more than twice the incidence of homosexuality in the population at large in some cities.

Homosexuals are just as likely as heterosexuals to like children and to want to help them grow and learn, yet homosexuals are much less likely to have children of their own. For gays who want to work with children, teach-ing is a reasonable solution.

In spite of the generally low salaries, teaching is a profession held in high esteem. For gays of either sex who realize that society considers a homo-sexual orientation inferior, teaching may provide a source of the self-esteem and social recognition that may be important for happiness.

Denied the opportunity to live their lives as they choose with any degree of safety, many gay people restrict their sex life and compensate for it by a greater devotion to learning. Most gays do not become actively involved in the gay world until they have finished high school or college, and they often end up spending nights studying rather than dating or searching for a marital partner. It is not surprising, then, that they are often drawn to academic life. Gay teachers sometimes bring more knowledge to the classroom simply because they have devoted more time to acquiring it.

We have a long tradition of acceptance of unmarried teachers. Until recent years, only unmarried persons were considered suitable as teachers in many parts of the country. Teaching is one of those few professions which provide a certain guarantee against suspicion of homosexuality.

Because an unmarried teacher is assumed to be devoting his or her life to children, some of the onus for not marrying and raising a family is removed. The teacher was not attractive enough to find a husband or wife, it is said, or was simply unfortunate in never meeting the right person. Even though he may have no children of his own the educator is held in high regard for contributing to the well-being of the coming generation.

Lacking children of his own, the homosexual may take comfort from the idea that if he passes on the knowledge that he has acquired, to the children he teaches, he survives in them in a sense. Only in this way does he gain any sort of personal immortality.

Often it is the unmarried, childless teacher who is best able to relate to his students because he has no other, conflicting demands upon his attention or interest. He does not carry anger at his own children over into the classroom. He is better able to compartmentalize his life. Off work, he has no need to concern himself with children; on the job, he is better able to give them his full attention.

How many of us look back with special fondness to an "old maid" teacher who played an especially important role in shaping our intellectual development, or to a dedicated, unmarried man who inspired us because of his devotion to his field of study? How many ever stop to wonder whether these teachers were homosexual?

To the homosexual, for whom family life and friendship in a heterosexual society can be sparse, the school may provide a surrogate family and social circle which receives all the devotion and loyalty that others would direct elsewhere. The teaching staff works together, shares confidences, and will often join as a team to help a problem child make a more satisfactory adjustment. Some homosexuals find the companionship in teaching that they have been unable to find elsewhere and respond by investing their love in their work.

Should a teacher be discovered to be homosexual, he will very likely lose his job. A heterosexual may lead a wild sex life outside of working hours, may be unfaithful in marriage or break other sexual taboos, but his private sexual life is seldom considered to have any bearing on his ability or right to teach. Heterosexuals, by and large, have a right to their own private sex life—homosexuals do not.

Because of the danger of being discovered, some homosexual teachers severely limit their private lives, avoiding homosexual contacts, and in the process, miss the opportunity to meet someone with whom to share a fulfilling relationship. While not completely curtailing their sex lives, others feel they must take special pains to cover their tracks, traveling to other cities in search of sex or love, and living in constant fear of discovery and loss of job and pension. The homosexual has little security in the school system, regardless of how fine a teacher he may be or how discreet his private sex life. In most places, a whisper can wreck a career.

A gay teacher—or a straight one—may be accused of homosexuality, even when he has never given any indication of it in school. All it takes is one student who dislikes him sufficiently to start the rumors flying. Time and again teachers have been dismissed on the basis of charges that they have made homosexual advances to students, although there is no proof that they have done so. These cases seldom come to court where the charges might be put to the test. The school board doesn't want to tie its hands with legal technicalities and the victim seldom wants further publicity.

An accusation of homosexuality is usually considered sufficient grounds to subject a teacher to an investigation of his private life that he has been careful to keep secret. Such investigations, often handled through private detective agencies, are sometimes initiated for other reasons—political differences between the teacher in question and the school board, for example. If homosexuality is discovered, it provides a handy excuse to sack a good teacher for spurious reasons.

Gay teachers in New York have faced a new problem in recent years with respect to the issue of community control over local schools. Teachers who are of different race or ethnic background from the majority of the community may be charged with homosexuality in order to provide grounds for replacing them. In several school districts this became such a recurring problem that the United Federation of Teachers was finally forced to protect the rights of homosexual teachers.

Although it is now difficult in New York City to get a teacher fired on the ground that his private life involves homosexuality, gay teachers still face discrimination. The City Board of Examiners, which controls the licensing of teachers, conducts investigations into the backgrounds and private lives of teaching applicants and considers "homosexual tendencies" to disqualify anyone from teaching. In its generosity, the board will make a few exceptions: if a prospective teacher will agree to undergo compulsory "aversion therapy" in order to be "changed" into a heterosexual, the board will consider hiring him—if the therapy is "successful."

But can a child ever really be safe with a homosexual teacher, even one who has been "cured"?

As a matter of fact, a child is a good deal safer with a homosexual teacher than with a heterosexual teacher. In the last forty years of the New York City school system, for example, only one case of homosexual molestation has been brought to court, while many heterosexual teachers have been officially charged with improper sexual involvement with their pupils.

Are children safe with heterosexual teachers?

## PROPAGANDA

What would happen if discrimination against homosexual teachers were made illegal? Many straight people fear that homosexuals would proselytize among their students.

Some say that if a child identified with a homosexual teacher he would turn out to be homosexual himself. Others believe that gay teachers would argue in favor of homosexuality at the first opportunity, trying to convince their students that it was glamorous, something worth experiencing no matter what the risks.

It is said that if we were to actually permit homosexual "perverts" to lead their lives freely and openly, increasing numbers of people would decide to become homosexual and the human race would eventually die out. It is perplexing that homosexuality can be portrayed as so grossly unnatural and yet so infinitely appealing in the same breath. Perhaps those who rely on this argument find homosexuality more attractive than they would like to admit.

The argument that to permit is to condone or encourage is a specious one. The law allows individuals to adopt the religion and political philosophy of their choice, but this is seldom interpreted as promoting any particular religion or political affiliation. Homosexuality is not an ideology or a creed in the first place—it is not something that can effectively be taught or preached.

The whole suspicion that to permit homosexuality would be to encourage it probably rests with unconscious recognition of the way in which heterosexuality—permitted—is promoted in every conceivable way. Homosexuals are often accused of flaunting their sexuality, of forcing it upon others, and of making it the most important fact of their lives. These accusations would seem far more just if directed at heterosexuals.

Heterosexual propaganda begins in the school from the very start. All the primers have nice little girls and boys, but you don't find close, affectionate relationships that might be interpreted as homosexual. If you encountered anybody who by the furthest stretch of the imagination might have been homosexual, it was probably in the form of a warning against taking candy from strangers. There are no gay couples in reading texts—all adults are heterosexual, and most are married.

In later school years, as students encounter literature written by homosexuals, or history concerning individuals who were homosexual, this aspect, is completely obscured.

How many people knew Walt Whitman was gay when they first encountered his poems in high school? Explicitly homosexual passages—"Many a soldier's kiss dwells on these bearded lips..."—might occasionally have been treated as metaphorical rather than literal, but questionable poems were more commonly omitted from collections of poetry. Who found out that Tchaikovsky was gay in music appreciation or heard about Michelangelo's sexual orientation in fine arts?

The whole concept of "platonic" love had to be invented in our society—not in Plato's—to explain why that kindly old fellow Socrates took such an interest in beautiful young men. Do you remember going over the Socratic dialogues in school and having it tediously explained to you why they didn't mean what they seemed to mean? Any indication of homosexuality and especially of the beauty of homosexual love is carefully excised from all the material young students receive. Lovers are presented as friends, if at all. Sex in general is shrouded in romanticism, and homosexual sex is nonexistent.

History is written from a strictly heterosexual viewpoint. Achilles and Patroclus were the best of friends. Alexander loved his horse Bucephalus, rather than Hephaestion. Caesar's *wife* was beyond suspicion, but who knew that "the 'mistress' of every man in Rome" was not? Frederick the Great was said to use men as tools and to show little sign of human warmth: who knew that his father had executed his lover before his eyes? Dag Hammarskjöld is remembered as a man of peace, but not as a homosexual statesman. By default, every single important figure in the arts or in history was apparently heterosexual.

In high school, any student who is suspected of having homosexual tendencies is likely to be sent for "guidance" or compelled to undergo psychiatric treatment. In some parts of the country students believed to be homosexual can be expelled and forced to continue their education in trade schools—if they still wish further education, that is. Apparently the risk that these young people might contaminate those around them is deemed sufficient justification for suspending any and all of their rights. Apparently those already enrolled in trade schools are not considered important enough to merit such "protection."

In those forward-looking schools where sex-education courses are available, few take even a neutral stance on the subject of homosexuality. On the contrary, homosexuality is usually presented along with venereal disease as a dangerous sickness to be avoided at all costs by walking the sexual straight and narrow. Most parents shudder at the possibility that a homosexual might teach a course in sex education.

In spite of the deluge of heterosexual propaganda, in spite of the cruel treatment of young people who are found out to have homosexual interests, homosexuality continues to appear at the same rate in each new generation. If this much propaganda cannot sway a young person from a homosexual orientation, it seems highly unlikely that even an equivalent amount of gay propaganda could convert a basically heterosexual youth. Sexual orientation is not a matter of persuasion—it runs far deeper than that.

Do homosexual teachers proselytize at all? The opportunities to do so are certainly limited.

In most parts of the country, any teacher who lets it be known that he is gay, much less advocates a homosexual life-style for his students, will lose his job, regardless of his teaching qualifications. Although it is expected that straight teachers make their heterosexuality perfectly obvious and encourage it in their students, it is intolerable for a homosexual teacher even to be known to be gay. Rather than proselytize, the gay teacher must make every effort to conceal his homosexuality.

In many towns and cities the gay teacher must hide his homosexuality simply to protect himself against his students. Harassment of teachers who are suspected of being homosexual is not uncommon—some parents condone or encourage such attacks. In some circles, beating up "queers" is a proof of manhood, evidence that a teen-age gang, for example, is held together by the youthful *machismo* of its members, rather than "latent" homosexual feelings for one another.

What constitutes propaganda? Many people assume that a homosexual would be unfit to teach a course in sex education because he would proselytize for homosexuality. It seems absurd to imagine that any gay teacher would be foolish enough to actually do so. But if he were to present the various current opinions about homosexuality, ranging from sin to sickness to acceptability, he would be accused of propagandizing, while the straight teacher who presented only the most medieval view of homosexuality would be viewed as perfectly fair. For a known homosexual to even appear to be living a happy life would strike some people as propaganda: everyone knows homosexuals are wretchedly unhappy. A straight teacher cannot risk presenting a balanced view of homosexuality today—it is much less likely that a gay teacher would be allowed to.

It should be clear that a gay teacher is in no position to proselytize, and if he were and wished to he wouldn't succeed. Unfortunately, in some instances it would be highly advantageous if a gay teacher *were* free to be open about his homosexuality.

Speaking from my own experience and that of many gay friends, high school can be hell for a young homosexual. Young men or women who are first becoming aware that they are homosexual are placed under an enormous emotional strain. Why are they different from everyone else? Why do people hate homosexuals so much? How can they hide the truth from family, friends, and school authorities?

How many high school students are troubled by inner conflicts over homosexuality which they dare not express to anyone? How many "inexplicable" youthful suicides can be traced to the isolation and fear imposed on young homosexuals? Just as a student who is a member of any other minority group can benefit from the opportunity to talk to a teacher who shares his minority status, the chance for gay students to talk about their problems with a gay teacher would be of enormous value. Members of other minority groups can at least turn to family and friends; the young homosexual cannot.

What would a gay teacher say to a gay student who approached him with problems in coming to grips with his homosexuality? Hopefully, he would point out both the positive and negative sides of the issue. The student should feel no shame or guilt: homosexual love is as valid and valuable as any other form of love. On the other hand, he should not think that the gay life will be a bed of roses, given the antihomosexual biases and discriminatory practices in America.

A gay teacher might point out, where others would not, that there is no need to decide that one is either strictly homosexual or strictly heterosexual. Openness to both heterosexual and homosexual experiences should be encouraged, for it will lead to greater freedom and happiness in the long run. The student should be reassured that he need not devote himself to a constant struggle to deny his homosexual interests, nor should he feel obliged to identify himself for once and for all as a homosexual as many young people mistakenly do. Sex should be placed in its proper context as a positive form of self-expression and self-exploration, rather than any sort of rigid commitment.

Many people argue that even if a gay teacher makes no deliberate attempt to proselytize, the very fact of his homosexuality will have a profound influence on his students. Others insist that a male homosexual cannot provide an adequate masculine image with which his male students can identify, and that a female homosexual provides a poor model for femininity.

The schools already have a disproportionate number of homosexual teachers, yet there has been no increase in homosexuality in our society. Gender and role identifications are likely to solidify in the earliest stages of childhood, and by the time a child reaches school age he or she is unlikely to undergo any significant changes in these areas.

Some people say that gay teachers are a bad moral influence on their students aside from their homosexuality. Their lives are different: they do not marry, they have sexual relations with many different people, they do not share society's values. The same attitude is not taken with regard to unmarried heterosexuals, of course, no matter how promiscuous the lives they lead. Actually, gay people tend to have the same basic values as nonhomosexuals. They were brought up in the straight world and heterosexual "morality" has been deeply ingrained in them, often to their detriment.

Gay teachers are sometimes better prepared to deal with problems of sexual identity and behavior in their students than straight teachers. Living in a heterosexual world, most homosexuals have acquired a sensitivity to the nuances of heterosexual behavior as well as having a natural familiarity with homosexuality. The straight teacher, on the other hand, is usually completely unprepared to deal with any indications of homosexuality in his students.

In a teaching program in a state hospital, for example, one teacher felt he could best help a schizophrenic adolescent boy in his care by encouraging him to form an extremely dependent relationship with him. Soon the boy became seductive toward him, displaying and seeking more and more open expressions of affection—some of them frankly sexual. His heterosexual teacher panicked, not because of the seduction itself, but because of the response to it he found in himself. Ashamed of his reactions and fearing that he was developing homosexual tendencies, he tried to keep the whole matter a secret and strongly rejected the boy, causing him a great deal of emotional damage. When the matter finally came to light, the professional staff pointed out that had the teacher been less terrified of homosexuality he could have saved the boy a painful regression.

When one of the emotionally disturbed children under Marc's care showed a similar pattern of behavior, on the other hand, Marc was able to deal with it perfectly comfortably. Well aware of the difference between the expression of affection and the expression of sexuality, he did not confuse his pupils with mixed signals and was able to read their behavior as signs of their needs, not his. He was able to express the affection they needed without feeling that his masculinity was threatened.

One boy who was particularly affectionate began to become more and more so until he bordered on being seductive. Finally one day he told Marc that he wanted to kiss him on the lips. "There's nothing wrong with kissing people," Marc said, "but it's not appropriate for children to kiss their teachers on the lips." The boy was able to accept this as a statement of fact, rather than a rejection, and his seductive behavior soon faded away.

The cherished belief that gay teachers are some sort of ravening sexual monsters seems strange when an examination of the statistics concerning incidents of child molestation shows that the overwhelming majority of cases involve *heterosexual* seduction or assault. Actually, there are many more cases of heterosexual assault of teachers by students than the reverse.

The only thing that "proselytizing" of the heterosexual or homosexual variety is likely to influence is the tolerance with which developing young-sters view those who differ from them. Here we can see that the barrage of heterosexual propaganda has had far-reaching effects: homosexuals are generally despised and treated as objects of derision rather than human beings.

An open acceptance of diversity would provide us all with greater freedom, not usher in new totalitarian sexual attitudes to replace those encouraged today.

# Does America Need a
##                                 Gay President?

As an undergraduate, I majored in political science at Columbia University. At no point did I seriously believe that I might have a career in politics or government. I was not certain either of these careers would appeal to me in the first place, but I knew that my homosexuality effectively barred me from them. It would be impossible to run for public office when I was so vulnerable to a smear campaign based on my homosexuality, and as a homosexual there was no chance of getting the security clearance necessary for government work.

I saw myself teaching political theory at a small, prestigious college, living in an ivory tower. It would not be hard to play the role of a confirmed bachelor, a slightly eccentric professor. Perhaps I would even find a lover who also taught and we would be able to share an apartment or house together without attracting too much attention. It was a pleasant enough prospect. I would be living among highly educated people who might show a slightly greater tolerance for my homosexuality, were it discovered, than the public at large. Furthermore, as a professor I would enjoy a certain amount of prestige to compensate for the lack of acceptance I experienced as a homosexual. At least, my parents would be able to speak of me with pride.

When I got my degree I went on to graduate work in political theory at Columbia. My first year was quiet and successful, but over the summer I became involved in the gay movement. Initially, I remained on the fringes, uncertain how strong a commitment I was prepared to make. But before long I found myself deeply involved. When classes started in the fall I was faced with a serious conflict over where to invest my time.

My involvement in the movement worked enormous changes in me. Until then it had never occurred to me to question the antihomosexual aspects of our society. These things were the facts of life, and I would have to accommodate myself to them—stay in the closet, hide my homosexuality,

181

and accept the fact that parts of my private emotional life might have to be sacrificed for a successful career—if I was to find any personal peace.

But I no longer saw accommodation as the answer. I had accepted many of society's stereotypes about gay people and even applied them to myself, but the more active I became in the movement, the more untenable the stereotypes became.

All homosexuals were supposed to be sick and unhappy: I had never felt more alive, self-confident, or happy in my life. For the first time I began to really respect myself. The gay people I met were bright, articulate, dynamic, creative individuals, not the self-pitying neurotics I had been led to expect. And their faces—where were the marks of tragedy, the signs of suffering? On the contrary, there was an overpowering impression of growth: nobody was standing still, everyone was reaching out, developing.

Still I was hesitant to burn my bridges behind me. I stayed on at Columbia, doing the minimum amount of work required, and devoting most of my time and energy to movement activities. As my view of myself changed, I began to see my studies in a new light.

Homosexuals were mentioned in only one of the political-science courses I had taken: political psychology. The brief mention homosexuals did receive categorized them as one among many pathological, deviant groups. A book by an esteemed political scientist at Yale suggested that no one should be permitted to run for or hold political office without first being tested for homosexuality and other forms of mental illness, which were obviously at odds with responsible politics. None of the great political theories of Western civilization concerned themselves in the slightest with homosexuals. Not a single course or text on American government made the slightest mention of the nation's gay population. We did not exist.

It began to seem rather pointless to prepare myself to teach straight political theory when I was denied any relevance or access to the political process myself. It was all well and good to sit in the library and read theoretical explanations of American democracy, but gay people were being beaten up on the streets by the police. It was fine to have a learned seminar discussion about the slow but sure justice meted out through the articulation of competing interests in the American political system, but for months the gay community had been seeking an appointment with the mayor of New York City to no avail. I became more and more convinced that political theory had little bearing on political reality. What appeared logical on paper failed to materialize in practice.

With mixed emotions, I resigned from the graduate program and became a full-time homosexual. I have yet to regret it.

Three months later I studied political theory on the steps of City Hall. I was there with a group of other gay people, attempting to get into the building to set up an appointment with a city councilman who had managed to ignore our letters, phone calls, and visits for half a year.

Police burst through the main door and pushed us down the steps of City Hall into the parking lot below, prodding us with their clubs. In coordination, mounted police appeared from both sides of the building and rode into us, trampling on us, herding us away.

For the first time in my life I felt a boiling fury at the police and deep radical disenchantment with the political system. Dodging horses, trembling with rage, I shouted: *"We are not animals—we are human beings!"*

## HOMOSEXUALS AND POLITICS

Homosexuals are effectively barred from public office everywhere in the United States today. The discovery that a political officeholder is homosexual is considered sufficient ground to demand his resignation.

Politicians must also avoid guilt by association. If an important aide is identified as a homosexual, it is almost invariably necessary to dismiss him to avoid acquiring a reputation for being "soft" on homosexuality, and subject to suspicion oneself.

The widespread intolerance toward homosexuality in politics can be traced in part to the role of the politician. Politicians are expected to be male. Our educational system presents politics as a predominantly male occupation. Even the professions from which most of the nation's politicians are drawn are predominantly male: law, the military, industrial management, and in rural areas, farming.

In some professions strict adherence to the masculine role is more important than usual, and politics is one of these. The bachelor has a limited chance for election to high public office; we expect our politicians to have proved their masculinity through marriage. The politician is expected to be competitive. No matter how well qualified, the man who does not compete will not be elected. The politician must be aggressive. He will be representing his constituents' interests and must show that he is prepared to fight for them. The candidate who never makes an opportunity to show a public display of anger, a sample of how formidable he can be in action, is usually judged colorless and uninspiring.

The successful politician must be able to stir the emotions of his public. Rhetoric must be enhanced by a sophisticated use of masculine body language: the aggressive stance, the pointing finger, the pounding fist. Even the rare female politician is expected to display various masculine gestures and personality traits. Because homosexuality is considered incompatible with the masculine role, the knowledge that a political candidate is homosexual drastically undercuts any visible demonstration of his masculinity.

Jokes about homosexuals in politics usually play on the idea that they will use sexual means in the attempt to exert their influence. The political animal is male, and men influence one another through the controlled use of aggression—power. The homosexual, denied status as a male, powerless by definition, is expected to resort to "feminine" techniques of control: seduction—the controlled use of eroticism.

The politician is also expected to demonstrate exemplary moral standards. He serves as a projection of his constituents' most cherished sentiments and beliefs. He must be the average citizen writ large: his potential voters must be able to see themselves as they would like to be reflected in him. He must be shocked at what the average citizen considers deplorable: pornography, pot smoking, homosexuality. He must be pious—few politicians fail to give evidence of strong religious sentiments, regardless of their personal beliefs. Homosexuality, viewed as both immoral and criminal, is immediately assumed to disqualify a potential political candidate from a place of moral leadership.

Because the expectations are so demanding, many segments of our population do not have a chance of being elected to office. Once elected, however, the position itself serves to protect the politician.

The role of the elected official is highly prestigious. We want to believe "our man" means everything he says. We usually attribute good motives even to those with whose policies we disagree. A politician may be wrong or even stupid, but he is seldom said to be deliberately malicious. We grant him the benefit of most doubts.

For this reason, homosexuals are not completely excluded from politics. If one can pass for heterosexual well enough to get elected, one may be able to continue to have homosexual relations in the privacy of the office.

The rules of discretion upheld by the press and political colleagues will protect the elected under most circumstances. We have had and still do have senators and congressmen who are practicing homosexuals and adulterers who have never come under fire for their private sexual relations. We are even supposed to have had at least one gay President.

When a politician is publicly exposed, however, he is likely to be more harshly judged than the average person. There is no scandal like a political scandal. The public places a special trust in its politicians, and is vengeful if that trust is discovered to have been misplaced. As a general rule, a sexual scandal is likely to be far more damaging to a political career than any other kind involving criminal activities.

While a few homosexuals manage to be elected to public office by successfuly hiding their homosexuality, it cannot be said that America's homosexual citizens enjoy open representation in the political process. On the rare occasions when legislation concerning homosexuals appears on the agenda, the secretly homosexual politician is usually the last person to display a positive or even neutral attitude toward homosexuals. He is too vulnerable to suspicion to risk calling attention to himself over the issue. Most straight politicians also fear to touch the issue of homosexuality out of concern that to do so will raise doubts about their own sexual orientation. Even as a topic for political debate, homosexuality is largely taboo.

By conservative estimates, at least 8 percent of the adult American population at any one time is leading a predominantly homosexual life. This represents a sizable number of votes. The homosexual's vote, however, is of little value to him. Until very recently no politician would dream of addressing himself to homosexual issues.

This does not mean that no politician would dare mention homosexuals, of course. Election campaigns often focus on "the public morality" when more substantive issues are avoidable or lacking. Crusades against perverts and degenerates, smut and pornography, are often substituted for realistic proposals for dealing with rising crime rates, drug addiction, racial tensions, and urban bankruptcy. These campaigns for decency are usually peppered with pious talk about the need for stronger laws and stricter enforcement against homosexuals and prostitutes.

Accusations of homosexuality can be employed against ordinary individuals to further a political career or to gain publicity. Joe McCarthy's witch-hunts revived the medieval homosexuality-treason equation. Hundreds of federal employees lost their jobs on suspicion of homosexuality during the McCarthy era.

Even politicians who are sympathetic to the plight of homosexuals rarely take any steps in public to improve their lot. Under some city administrations, hiring and firing policies concerning homosexuals are relaxed unofficially. Police programs of enticement and entrapment may be curtailed or eliminated by a private directive from City Hall. New York City is a case in point.

Promising to rid the city of perverts, Robert Wagner was elected Mayor of New York in 1954. During his "reign of terror," which many New York gays remember well, police corruption and involvement with the Mafia resulted in the closing of dozens of bars. During the last Wagner administration, there were seldom more than five or six gay bars open in the city, and the Mattachine Society of New York claimed that there were more than two hundred cases of police entrapment of homosexuals nightly in Manhattan.

Following his election in 1966, Mayor John V. Lindsay unofficially ordered an end to all enticement and entrapment activities in the city, perhaps in recognition of his debt to the gay vote. Lindsay's failure to take a public stand on the treatment of homosexuals did little damage to his popularity with New York's gay population until 1970, when he became one of the major targets of the new gay liberation movement.

Lindsay's narrow reelection and the extreme antihomosexual sentiments expressed by his opponents—one suggested federal detention centers for homosexuals—caused the activist wing of the movement great concern. In spite of the mayor's tolerant policies with regard to homosexuals, there had been no public recognition that their status had changed one whit.

No law or publicly acknowledged precedent prevented the next mayor of the city from reinstituting large-scale programs of enticement and entrapment if he chose. There was no guarantee that the reign of terror would not begin again. Confrontation tactics and politically embarrassing zaps against the mayor eventually pressured him into a public statement on homosexual civil rights, made with a minimum of fanfare and scarcely mentioned in the news media.

In spite of their potential voting power, homosexuals tended to be politically apathetic. Unable to run for office, unmentionable in public policy debate, most homosexuals had little faith in the political system and many viewed it as irrelevant. Hope for legal reform centered on the courts rather than the legislature.

The riots at the Stonewall Inn on Christopher Street in New York's Greenwich Village marked the transformation of what was then called the homophile movement and the birth pangs of the gay liberation movement. Homosexuals developed a militant interest in politics.

## THE GAY MOVEMENT

When I first entered the gay bar scene in Albany in the early sixties, I occasionally heard people speak of a super-secret society known as the Mattachine. Only later did I learn that the title meant a court jester who entertains the public while keeping his true feelings hidden.

The Mattachine was a glamorous mystery—nobody knew anything about it, but speculation was rife. According to one source, it was a political underground. According to another, it was an exclusive secret club of the wealthiest and most attractive homosexuals in the nation. Nobody knew a member, for they were believed never to reveal their identity to anyone. Membership was by invitation only; they would contact prospective members, but there was no way to seek them out oneself. The Mattachine appeared to be a highly organized homosexual secret service.

This impression was strengthened by the occasional references to the Homintern, which I encountered in some of the first straight books on homosexuality. This was supposed to be an international homosexual conspiracy to take over the world. It was suggested that the Homintern had agents in various high political offices who were using their talents to betray America to communism.

The Homintern, a sort of gay Elders of Zion, was a favorite target of the far right. Dire references to this purely mythical cabal became commonplace during the McCarthy era and are still heard occasionally.

The Mattachine, however, was not mythical. Organized in Los Angeles in 1950 as the Mattachine Foundation and reorganized as the Mattachine Society in 1953, it was the first real homosexual organization and the founder of the gay movement. During the fifties and sixties a number of other organizations appeared in the larger cities of the nation, and a pattern began to develop. The old-line homophile organizations, radical and daring for their time, served primarily as social service organizations, sponsoring social events and offering legal services. They avoided calling public attention to themselves, attempted to work behind the scenes, and had little influence on the homosexual population at large.

In the late sixties, the first signs of open political activism in the movement began to appear on the East and West Coasts. Public demonstrations were held in San Francisco and Los Angeles, picket lines appeared in Philadelphia, and the Mattachine Society of New York held a "sip-in" which led to the state's Supreme Court ruling that homosexuals had the right to congregate in public, effectively legalizing gay bars. Although the organization as a whole grew increasingly conservative, New York Mattachine spun off the Mattachine Action Committee, whose members formed the nucleus of the new Gay Liberation Front.

The Gay Liberation Front was born in July 1969, as a direct result of the "Stonewall rebellion" in New York. In the coming months, other GLF's were formed in other major cities, and it became clear that the gay movement was undergoing a renaissance. The somewhat sedate homophile movement gave birth to the militant and aggressively visible gay liberation movement. During the next two years more than two hundred new gay organizations appeared in cities and on college campuses all across America. Their numbers are still increasing at an extraordinary rate.

As the movement grew, a pattern again became evident. The evolution of the Gay Liberation Front in New York was repeated in many other cities and now shows signs of recurring as the new spirit of gay militancy has begun to surface abroad.

The younger, more militant gays viewed the older homophile organizations as conservative, even right-wing. The Gay Liberation Front began as a radical leftist alternative, and for the better part of the next year the movement had a left and right wing with very little in between.

In GLF, New Left gays declared the need for a socialist or "new" Marxist identification of gay people with other oppressed minorities and held that all forms of oppression were an outgrowth of capitalism. Beyond this, there was little ideological uniformity in the left wing, however. Some spoke of political revolution, while others considered the existing social system inevitably doomed and spoke of the need for creating an alternative society by founding communes and collectives. Between these two extremes, the majority emphasized cultural revolution, although they articulated no program of action.

If gay people were to be identified with other oppressed minorities, the question immediately arose as to what stance gay organizations should take toward nongay organizations and demonstrations centering on nongay issues. The left wing adopted the principle that minority groups must support one another and marshaled support for numerous nongay issues, such as endorsement of the Black Panther Party. Other minority groups showed little interest in supporting gay people or relating to gay issues, but it was believed that if the gay movement showed sufficient support for other radical causes, their support would eventually be forthcoming. Solidarity could be earned.

Virtually no concrete support was given by other minority groups on any gay issues. Token interest in gays was apparent from time to time, but gay issues were given the lowest priority: gay people and their demands always appeared at the end of the list; gay speakers were often denied the opportunity to speak at rallies, heckled, or mocked.

The general leftist line was that gay liberation must cede precedence to more important issues, and many gays accepted this without complaint—gay people had always been of less importance. When the war had been brought to a halt, when blacks, chicanos, third-world people, women, and all others were free, then energy could be devoted to gay issues. No one could be truly free until all were free, but the freedom of some was more important than the freedom of others. When support for gays continued to take the form of thinly disguised tokenism, disillusion with the ideal of a joint struggle began to sweep the left wing of the gay movement.

The radical left gay organizations were largely unstructured and sought to combine the more attractive features of participatory democracy and rational anarchism. There were to be no official leaders, for this smacked of elitism—the bane of the status quo. But charismatic figures tended to dominate the left-wing groups because of their gift for using ideological rhetoric to enforce political conformity.

Being nonstructured, the leftist organizations spun off cells composed of members who shared common goals, interests, and ideological preferences: Third World Gay Revolution, the Jewish Gay Revolutionary Party, Street Transvestite Action Revolutionaries. Rhetoric, ideological criticism, and revolutionary purism exacerbated the political infighting. This led to the dissolution of some leftist gay organizations, paralysis of others, and a general shift in emphasis from political action to consciousness-raising.

Consciousness-raising, borrowed to some extent from the women's liberation movement, is a process whereby gays discuss their common experiences in groups, acquire insights into the ways in which their behavior and identity are shaped by a hostile society, and develop a greater awareness of their oppression. For many, CR sessions have served as a particularly effective form of nondirective encounter group.

At its best, consciousness-raising served as the intellectual wellspring of the movement, the source of radical new interpretations of the gay world, gay relationships, and straight society. At its worst, it became a system of political indoctrination. One's consciousness was not sufficiently raised if one did not see the absolute necessity for revolution or did not embrace the ideological dictates of those who dominated the CR groups.

Consciousness-raising became a weapon in the hands of some, a justification for questioning the sincerity of those with different beliefs. Those in disagreement were frequently accused of "oppressing" other gays by holding "oppressive" attitudes; charges of false consciousness were rife. Revelations of intimate personal problems and fears were sometimes used to embarrass others politically. A great deal of emotional damage was done to some individuals.

As disenchantment with revolutionary rhetoric in the place of action, demands for ideological conformity, political infighting, and the misuse of CR sessions spread in New York's GLF, a splinter organization formed in December 1969 and adopted the name Gay Activists Alliance. The organization's success in the coming year made it a model for other new organizations across the country, and the movement began to develop a militant middle, while the left and right wings declined in strength and influence.

Gay activism rested upon several basic principles. Political ideology was viewed as irrelevant—homosexuals of diverse political beliefs must work together to effect changes in the present, rather than waste time arguing over the most desirable way to create this or that future society. More would also be accomplished if gay people devoted themselves to gay issues instead of spreading themselves thin in support of other groups which showed no interest in returning the favor.

Activism meant more action and less talk. Gay people would improve their lot in society only by becoming a powerful political force in their own right. Direct confrontation with the political system was the most effective force for change; attempts to "educate" the straight public about homosexuals had accomplished little in the past. It was irrelevant whether straights liked homosexuals or not, but they must be compelled to respect their basic human rights. This could be achieved only by building sufficient political power to protect those rights.

Confrontation tactics were the most valuable tool for creating a political power base within the system, although not necessarily at harmony with it. A handful of homosexuals could embarrass a straight politician, disrupt a government office, halt the taping of a television program, or bring business to a halt in the offices of companies which discriminated against homosexuals. Militant nonviolent confrontation could convince the establishment that it would find it in its own interests to promote change.

Confrontation tactics had the added value of being visible. Until homosexual civil rights became a public issue rather than a matter for behind-the-scenes negotiation, no significant changes could be expected. Homosexuals had to become visible in order to become a meaningful political force within society; the millions of homosexuals who were still in the closet had to be encouraged to come out if they were to wield any political influence to their own advantage.

The concept of media oppression was articulated. The mass media had contributed to the invisibility of the homosexual population by declining to acknowledge the existence of homosexuals and by treating them as curiosities when they were mentioned. The media had helped foster endless debate over whether homosexuals were or were not "sick" and had distracted attention from the basic civil rights issues at the center of gay liberation. Confrontation tactics had media appeal, emphasized the political thrust of the movement, and made it possible to reach homosexuals in the closet through media coverage.

Over the past year, gay activism has become the dominant theme of the movement. In many cities activist coalitions have been formed out of the splinter groups which became disenchanted with the problems encountered in the radical leftist organizations. Many of the old-line homophile organizations have adopted a new activist orientation. The most influential activist organizations have begun to send out field workers to help organize cities in which there has been little political activity in the gay community.

The gay movement did not develop overnight, nor has it yet reached maturity. Several new directions are already becoming evident.

To date, local politics have been the main focus of gay activism, and city and state government have been its major target. The movement is already developing a national perspective and increasing attention will probably be directed toward the federal government, which is responsible for more discrimination against homosexuals than any other institution. Within the next two years, the formation of a national coalition of activist organizations —a national gay alliance—and perhaps one or more national gay organizations is likely.

As it becomes more powerful, the movement will devote major efforts to organizing smaller cities and towns. Some of the larger gay organizations have already sent busloads of activists to demonstrate in outlying areas where incidents of violence have occurred. Gay freedom buses may become as prominent a feature of the gay movement as they once were in the black civil rights movement.

Taking a broader view, there are indications that the movement is approaching another major turning point. The direction it takes will be greatly influenced by the way in which straight society reacts to it.

Most of the homosexual population has been in the closet until recently, and straight people were seldom confronted with any visible evidence that large numbers of homosexuals lived among them. Many straights disliked homosexuals more in principle than in practice. Now, as more gay people become visible, hostile elements in straight society are beginning to react. It is as though a complacent white community in the deep South had awakened one day in the early fifties and discovered that there were black families living in every neighborhood.

In the gay movement today many people are speaking of the "straight backlash." Incidents of violence against homosexuals have increased at a frightening rate over the past year. Straight gangs roam the streets of many major U.S. cities and attack homosexuals unfortunate enough to be caught alone or in small groups. The refusal of the police in many areas to protect homosexuals encourages such open violence.

In Alpine County, California, local wits began to sell "hunting licenses" entitling the purchaser to shoot a quota of homosexuals. Incidents of police brutality are on the increase. At a peaceful demonstration on Long Island for repeal of the sodomy laws in August 1971, homosexuals were maced in public for the first time, while straights who had been taunting and harassing them received no attention from the police.

Homosexuals as a group have seldom considered themselves fighters. Statistically, homosexuals show a much lesser inclination toward violence than members of almost any other minority group. But as straight attacks on homosexuals increase and are openly encouraged by the police, many gay people have begun to consider taking steps to protect themselves. At least two gay organizations have initiated programs of training in self-defense. Statistics can change.

All the same, we are not yet witnessing a real backlash. Gay people have not yet made enough significant political gains nor managed to encroach on straight society's turf. The enormous increase in straight violence against gays can be attributed to the simple fact that there are now many more visible gays to attack.

Unless the level of violence decreases, it seems likely that the gay movement will develop in two diverging directions. On the one hand, increasing numbers of movement gays will seek to enter establishment politics; many have already begun to do so. On the other, a trend toward militant hostility directed against straights and establishment politics may develop as some gays conclude that the political system is incapable of effecting meaningful reform.

## THE GAY VOTE

When my 1970 census form arrived in the mail, I set it aside with a twinge of irritation. The government had no desire to really know anything about me.

How many men are there in America? How many women? How many are married, and how many children do they have? How many blacks and whites and Puerto Ricans and Indians and Mexican-Americans and Italian-Americans and so forth are there and where do they live and how much do they earn?

How many homosexual Americans are there? Who cares?

A few days later I opened the form and began filling in the facts the government wanted to know about me. How many rooms were there in my dwelling? How long had I lived there? What rent did I pay? What was my marital status?

The question about marital status particularly irked me. I was in the middle of a love affair at the time. Had I been heterosexual, I might well have gotten married. As far as the census form was concerned, my relationships counted for nothing and never would.

I toyed with the idea of indicating my homosexuality on the form, and —after grappling with my paranoia—finally decided that it made very little difference one way or the other. If America rounded up her homosexuals and put them in detention centers at some future date, the authorities would not have to go through the census records to catch me. I was not making any serious efforts to avoid being noticed.

In the box asking for my sex, I checked "male" and wrote "homosexual" after it. In the box inquiring about marital status, I checked "other" and wrote "homosexual lover."

I wondered how they would code this information on the IBM punch cards. Would the computer reject it, or would it be filed with the other forms that had been "incorrectly" filled out?

How many homosexuals *are* there in America?

Nobody knows. Even if the information were requested on the census form, few homosexuals today would provide it. In spite of assurances to the contrary, many people doubt that individual census information is really confidential. Few homosexuals would risk identifying themselves.

Kinsey's findings are usually interpreted to mean that at any given time roughly 10 percent of the adult male population and 6 percent of the adult female population are actively leading a predominantly homosexual life. Not all of these people actually consider themselves homosexuals, but the minority who don't are aware that they are engaging in enough homosexual activity so that most people would consider them homosexual.

Approximately 8 percent of the entire adult population of the United States, then, is actively homosexual at any given time.

As of the 1970 census, a minimum of eleven million Americans eighteen and over can be assumed to be homosexuals. There is no information on where they live, how they are employed, where they spend their money, or how they vote. The only thing we know about homosexual demography is that gay people tend to move to the larger cities of the nation. Although the homosexual population in gay ghetto districts is believed to run as high as 40 percent in a few major cities, certainly the overall gay population is not this high. It seems reasonable to estimate that 10 percent of the adult urban population and 6 percent of the adult rural population is homosexual, although the homosexual population in such gay meccas as New York, Los Angeles, San Francisco, and Chicago is probably a good deal higher.

Numerically, homosexuals can and sometimes do have an important influence on American politics, although this is seldom openly acknowledged. Politicians in larger cities do often speak about the gay vote, but the news media seldom take it into consideration. Mayors Alioto and Lindsay, for example, are believed to have benefited enormously from the gay vote in their respective cities, and Bella Abzug's victory in the New York primary and her subsequent election to Congress is said to have hinged on her strong gay support.

The new political strategy adopted by the Gay Activists Alliance in the New York 1970 elections has already been adopted by gay organizations in more than a dozen U.S. cities.

Months before the 1970 elections, GAA sent questionnaires on homosexual issues to all candidates, asking them their position on repeal of the sodomy laws, police harassment of homosexuals, etc. Those who responded were rated on the basis of how favorable their responses were. Heavy leafleting, particularly in gay areas, was done in New York City. While GAA endorsed no candidates or parties, the rated responses of the various candidates were publicized. Those who had failed to respond to the questionnaire were listed as failing to respond.

GAA also sought public statements on homosexual civil rights from the candidates for major office. None of the candidates was anxious to identify himself with the issue in public, but pressure applied through confrontation tactics finally produced favorable statements from Arthur Goldberg, Charles Goodell, Richard Ottinger, and Adam Walinsky. The statements were released to the press by GAA and the candidates themselves, but received minimal attention. *The New York Times* delayed for nearly a week and finally noted in a two-inch, single-column item in the back pages of the paper that a number of candidates had spoken about homosexuals. Added to previous instances of the *Times*'s reluctance to acknowledge the existence of homosexual New Yorkers, this led to charges that the paper had discriminatory policies toward homosexuals.

Because of the press blackout, the gay activists sought a district in which to test the effectiveness of their leafleting. They chose the 66th Assembly District, in which the incumbent Republican was expected to win by a comfortable margin. While the incumbent had refused to respond to the questionnaire or meet with representatives of the gay community, his opponent, Antonio Olivieri, had taken a strong stand in favor of gay rights. Encompassing the upper East Side, with its high homosexual population, the 66th District seemed to be a perfect test case and a massive leafleting campaign was undertaken.

Olivieri was elected to the State Assembly by a five-hundred-vote margin, a victory which he publicly attributed to the gay vote. The first Democrat to be elected from the district in fifty-six years, he introduced a package of homosexual civil rights legislation soon after the legislative session began. The success of the activists' tactics was noted by organizations across the country and it seems likely that few politicians in major cities will find it quite so easy to ignore gay civil rights in the future.

Public recognition of homosexuals and their civil rights is the key to the activist political strategy now shaping the gay movement. Public statements on gay rights are considered essential for a number of reasons. First, they increase public awareness of the homosexual population and the problems they face. Second, they alert homosexuals that their votes *are* important and can have an important influence on their lives. Movement publicity urging homosexuals to register and vote has been found necessary because of past political apathy in the gay community. Third, and most important, public statements give homosexuals rational grounds for choosing among candidates for the first time in American history.

How do homosexuals vote?

Because they have never had the opportunity to vote on gay issues, homosexuals have seldom acted as a voting bloc in the past. Only in cases like the Lindsay election, where there was reason to believe a particular candidate would take unofficial steps to improve their lot, or where an opposing candidate had taken a strong antihomosexual stand in public, have gays tended to vote together. At other times, there have been no indications that their homosexuality has influenced the political affiliations of gay people. Although homosexuals as a group are often believed to vote as liberals, wealthier homosexuals and many of the more closeted gays tend to be quite conservative.

In the 1970 New York elections a greater number of Democratic candidates responded initially to the activists' questionnaires, but as the word got around, many Republican candidates who had failed to respond at the beginning later contacted GAA for additional copies of the questionnaire or for meetings with the gays. In one closely contested race on the East Side, the Republican candidate, who had been quite hostile in refusing to respond to the questionnaire, later made several unsuccessful attempts to arrange a meeting—he seemed to have had a change of heart. When elected, he cosponsored a bill in the State Senate for repeal of sodomy laws. A number of conservative Republicans responded surprisingly favorably, basing their support on the principle that the government was overstepping the proper bounds of its authority in attempting to legislate adult sexual morality.

The gay vote seems likely to be felt most strongly in the near future in closely contested elections in which the degree of the different candidates' support for gay rights varies widely. Homosexuals are likely to be most important in urban politics, except in those states in which the urban vote is likely to swing the state in a gubernatorial, senatorial, or presidential election.

In areas with large gay populations, open homosexuals are beginning to run for office. In 1971, Franklin Kameny of the Washington Mattachine ran for congressional delegate for the District of Columbia, and gay candidates are expected to run for the New York City Council and the State Legislature in the next elections.

What do homosexuals want from politicians?

The first priority, of course, is repeal of the state sodomy laws and revision or repeal of the solicitation and other statutes used to justify police entrapment and enticement procedures. Next in importance is so-called anticloset legislation that will enable homosexuals to come out openly without fear of losing their jobs. Extension of existing state and city civil rights legislation to bar discrimination in employment, housing, and public accommodation on the basis of sexual orientation is being proposed. Bills to this effect have already been introduced at the city and state levels, and the chances are good that the New York State Legislature will approve such a bill during its 1972 session. There is increasing interest in a constitutional amendment to provide broad protection of sexual civil rights.

Homosexuals share some legislative concerns with many heterosexuals, among them procedures for expungement of arrest records and protection

against surveillance, and circulation of privileged personal data, and the inequities in the tax laws which discriminate against single individuals. At the
federal level, homosexuals are particularly interested in an end to discrimination in the military and in federal employment.

When my lover and I were lobbying in Albany for repeal of the state
sodomy law, we spent a good deal of time with a state senator from the city
of Rochester. He was courteous and interested in hearing our views on the
issues involved. As we discussed the various objections he raised, he agreed
time after time that we had effectively refuted them. Still, he said, he would
have to oppose repeal of the law. As a Catholic, he did not consider homosexuality moral, and personally, he simply did not like homosexuals and
never would.

The role of the clergy in homosexual-law reform seems to be in flux.
Most of the major Protestant sects have softened their objections to homosexuality and some have actively assisted in lobbying for repeal of the
sodomy laws. The Roman Catholic Church has been strongly opposed to
such reform until recently. After its repeal during the general revision of the
state penal code in 1965, the sodomy law was reenacted in New York at the
urging of the Roman Catholic Church in a trade-off on abortion reform.

In the most recent session of the New York State Legislature, however,
the church took an ambivalent stance. Some prominent Catholic clergymen
publicly supported the sodomy-repeal and fair-employment bills, while
others opposed it privately, but the church refrained from any active lobbying
against the bills in question.

A few virulently antihomosexual fundamentalist sects have engaged in
active lobbying against homosexual civil rights at both the city and state
levels, conducting large mailing campaigns of antihomosexual hate literature.
Although the tax laws deny tax-exempt status to organizations which engage
in political lobbying, these sects and related organizations have not lost their
tax-exempt status. Complaints filed with the Internal Revenue Service have
had no effect. Homosexual civil rights organizations, on the other hand, have
been consistently denied tax-exempt status on the basis that they are lobbying to change the laws which discriminate against gay people.

The generally favorable response from the clergy has been far surpassed
by the support of law-enforcement specialists. The cop on the beat may or
may not think much of homosexuals, but in the higher echelons of law enforcement there has been a strong call for sodomy repeal and other reforms.
Laws against homosexual relations, it is argued, concern crimes without
victims, and their sporadic and selective enforcement draws the police away
from far more important work and promotes corruption.

It might seem that the chances for homosexual-law reform are very good today. To some extent this is true: the sodomy laws of three or four states may well fall during the coming year. But in other states the hopes of legal reform in the near future are dim indeed. Even in New York, where sodomy repeal and fair-employment legislation seem imminent, one state assemblyman this year felt free to refer to homosexuals as "filth and scum" on the floor of the assembly.

The gay movement is turning its attention to the presidential election of 1972 and has already received feelers from the McGovern campaign staff. There is little doubt that major efforts will be devoted to getting the presidential candidates to address themselves publicly to the issue of gay civil rights.

We cannot expect an openly gay President today any more than we can expect a black one, but perhaps we will at least see a few steps taken to end the status of homosexuals as second-class American citizens.

# Should Your Son Marry a Homosexual?

I live just a few blocks south of the Cathedral of St. John the Divine, the largest unfinished Gothic cathedral in the world. Perched over Harlem on Morningside Heights, St. John's has held a special attraction for me since I moved into the neighborhood two and a half years ago, although I have not considered myself at all religious since adolescence.

I have always sensed something friendly about St. John's in spite of its size. I like the idea that its construction was halted because it seemed impious to devote such a great amount of money to building a cathedral while the poverty of Harlem lay stretched out at its feet.

On Sunday afternoons the cathedral offers a half-hour organ concert before the four o'clock service and occasionally a special concert of modern electronic music. The concerts do not usually draw a large crowd, but many neighborhood people have become regulars: young, conservatively dressed women, secretaries perhaps, in pairs, who always stay for the service, bearded students from Columbia, sometimes with dates, a few older black couples, and neighborhood hippies with beatific marijuana smiles or occasional acid wonder. I became a regular myself, walking up on Sundays to spend a half hour immersed in the waves of sound and stained-glass light.

I had had a few affairs before I came to New York and had a few in the city as well, some brief, a few promising to last. But they never did. Some died a mutual death, some merely vanished unnoticed, but one or two left a trace of pain when they ended that it took me months to get over, live with, and fit into my life, as necessary and treasured stops along the way. Often St. John's helped me through the weeks with its open, echoing silence, its reassuring permanence, an outgrowth of the cold Manhattan bedrock itself. It was simply there. It never spoke, it never judged. It existed for those who needed it.

I was often lonely. I was one of those people who feel a great need to find another person to depend on, to share with, to lean on, to love and be loved by. I was never able to find as much as I needed in a casual romance

199

or a brief encounter and sometimes I despaired of ever finding another person whose needs would complement my own. Once or twice I thought I had found such a person, and in the aftermath it hardly seemed possible to go on, waiting, searching, hoping that the next love would be strong enough to last.

One Sunday morning after watching the sun rise through the smoky air over Harlem, I went to St. John's as soon as its doors were open. I felt particularly alone, particularly vulnerable—I hadn't slept all night. As I sat in the chapel that had become my favorite, I could hear the echoing murmur of a priest opening the day elsewhere in the cathedral. For the first time, I picked up a prayer book and it fell open to the marriage vows:

> *...to have and to hold from this day forward, for better for worse, for richer for poorer, in sickness and in health, to love and to cherish, till death do us part...*

A year later I was up to my ears in the Gay Activists Alliance, involved as I had never been involved in anything before. I was alone, but I was too busy to notice it, and I had found friends, people with whom I was doing something I believed in. The world was changing because I saw it with new eyes.

I met Marc in GAA during the madhouse of the 1970 election activities. In the rush, excitement, and occasional righteous outrage of political confrontation, we drifted closer and closer together in the organization. We were together on the corner of Eighty-sixth and Broadway on a cold day, zapping a Democratic candidate, we were out for a beer with friends in the early morning after an interminable committee meeting. In November we found an opportunity for a date together, got stoned, and held on to each other until *2001* took us off through the universe.

A few weeks later, we sat on a loading dock in the mist of a rainy evening down near the waterfront a few blocks from the Eagle's Nest, where we had stopped for a beer together, and Marc gave me a gold wedding band that had been his grandmother's and we became lovers.

Later I gave him a simple wooden ring that held many memories for me. We didn't speak much of how long our love would last, of what things would be like together, or of where our relationship might carry us. We knew that words and promises could never really guarantee the future, that the certainty we felt in each other was beautiful but could be no more certain for being spoken.

Each day together was better than the last, each night more tender. On the twenty-third of each month we would get a bottle of champagne and some flowers for the apartment and celebrate our monthly anniversaries, counting them at first as though the simple fact of their number could reassure us both that they would go on and on. But the need for reassurance became peripheral. The twenty-third became less distinct from other days. When we had been together for almost six months, we no longer wondered whether we would manage to stay together—we knew. One afternoon we met in front of Tiffany's, wandered through the store holding hands looking at the wedding bands, and finally chose one that matched the ring Marc had given me. I bought the ring, and the saleswoman smiled when we kissed and left the store laughing, full of excitement and joy, feeling thoroughly outrageous but thoroughly right.

I held on to the ring for two days, and on the morning of the twenty-third we walked up the block to St. John's and into my chapel, which we found empty. Neither one of us felt a conventional religious awe as we stood there, but there was something deep and overpowering in the air, something in ourselves. This was a place where many other people had come in the past to join their lives, and although we had no service, no family, no friends, no blessing but our own, we were part of that spirit.

We exchanged simple vows, Marc put the ring on his finger, and we walked back out into the light of day.

## MARRIAGE

When I first came out into the gay world, I hoped that I would find someone to love who loved me and settle down together. My high school loves had been as intense as most adolescent romances tend to be. When I realized that high school held no romantic future for me as a homosexual, I assumed that the gay world would be a much easier place to find love.

I was seventeen when I first found an entrance to the gay bars in Albany, New York, with the help of some fake ID. When I told the gay people I met there that I was looking for a true and lasting love, the response was uniformly one of friendly discouragement. I was told not to count on it or I would end up that much unhappier when it didn't materialize. I was told that love had a way of not lasting in the gay world, that gay people didn't seem to find it possible to remain faithful to one another. Don't expect too much out of a relationship, I was told, you'll find that you're even fickle yourself.

My early experiences seemed to bear out this warning. No affair seemed to last more than a week or two. I was dumped from time to time, and occasionally I dumped others. I remember a big blond fellow bursting into tears at the bar when I told him I didn't want to see him again. I felt enormously guilty and cruel, but couldn't imagine what I had seen in him two weeks before. I remember waiting for phone calls that never came and the agony of hearing rumors or finding last week's lover in the bar with someone new. It wasn't long before I became cynical about the gay world and cynical about myself.

That first year, I met only one pair of lovers who had been together for any length of time—five years. They rarely showed up at the bar, and when they did, people looked at them with a strange blend of approval and incredulity.

I heard myself repeating and believing things I had heard others say and had refused to believe. It was better not to become too deeply involved, because you would only get hurt in the end. You should never really open yourself up to another person—you were too vulnerable if you did. Sex was perfectly satisfying, anyway, and there was no need to waste your time looking for love. In the gay world, you had to be independent to lead a happy life.

A few more years tempered my beliefs. I no longer believed that it was impossible to find love. Those who found it stopped hanging out in the bars and became invisible. Many who didn't brought their difficulties upon themselves, going out on the side, flirting with other people, nagging jealously at their lovers, and finally wondering what had happened to the affair. The whole atmosphere of the bars, the life-style that centered upon them, seemed to make it far more difficult to maintain a relationship than it had to be.

In Albany almost all my experience had been in one bar. Several years later in New York, I found the bar scene very different, more casual, even joyful. The bars were packed, and I seldom saw the lonely figures sitting at the bar drinking away the night. Things were moving. I didn't get the feeling that a lasting relationship was much easier to find, but at least people seemed to be happy with their lives.

Even in New York, people would say that lasting relationships were uncommon. In the gay world there was little premium on fidelity, and this put an inevitable strain on relationships. If your lover was out of town, it was expected that you'd be out at the bars every night, sleeping around. You might even fall for someone new, and that would be that. There was an enormous turnover in lovers, but nobody seemed to find anything unusual in it. The gay life was freer than the straight life—there was no need to be tied down to one person. Most people seemed to prefer things that way, in fact. I came to see myself as rather odd for wanting a lover with whom I could settle down permanently. Why should I waste my best years when there was so much going on, so many beautiful people to meet.

As time went on, I realized that many of my expectations and desires were shaped by values that were a basic part of the heterosexual world, but which were not necessarily valid in the gay world. Heterosexual marriage was expected to be permanent. Children are born, raised, clothed, fed, and provided with an education. There were many reasons why stable and permanent relationships seemed to make sense in a heterosexual context.

Heterosexual marriages were expected to be monogamous. I could easily see why monogamy might be valued, for I had seen the effect of more casual sexual relations on gay relationships. Uncertainty, insecurity, and jealousy can put an enormous strain on a relationship.

But is monogamy really as natural or desirable as it is said to be? Most heterosexuals have a number of romances before they finally marry and settle down, and many continue to have affairs after they are married. The divorce rate is high and rising all the time. Why, if monogamy is working so well?

Many people do not even expect men to be monogamous. It is considered quite natural for a man to visit a prostitute if he is out of town on business. It is not especially surprising if a man has an affair on the side while his wife is in the latter stages of pregnancy. Women are expected to be a good deal more faithful—they are mothers and the ultimate responsibility for caring for the children devolves on them. Even so, many women do become involved in extramarital affairs, and as the women's liberation movement begins to question the nature of the feminine role, some doubt is cast on the notion that women are by nature less promiscuous than men.

As changing public attitudes lead to a more frank treatment of sexuality in literature, cinema, and other forms of entertainment, social expectations regarding love and sexuality have been more explicitly portrayed. Homosexuals have begun to appear in print and on the screen for the first time, and it has become even more clear that they are expected to lead tragic and unfulfilling lives. Usually, if a homosexual appears to be happy, disaster strikes to make it perfectly clear that a happy homosexual is a fluke. *The Boys in the Band* was seen as a breakthrough by many people, but it presents a stereotyped picture of unhappy people unable to come to terms with themselves. In 1970, Gordon Merrick's novel *The Lord Won't Mind* was released and billed as the first novel about homosexuals with a happy ending. The story is so patently incredible, the emotions so unreal, that I found it far more discouraging than the most sordid and tragic portrayals of the gay world.

But novels and films about heterosexuals only lead me to wonder whether we are not *all* being sold a bill of goods. While some stories deal with happy heterosexual relationships, the vast majority of heterosexual entertainment seems to focus on the strife between men and women, the unsatisfying nature of their relationships, and the near impossibility of maintaining a happy marriage.

I had never questioned the idea that homosexual relationships were predominantly unhappy, while heterosexual ones were predominantly beautiful. But as I began to take greater notice of heterosexual couples and married men and women, I began to wonder how often everything was sweetness and light. I saw far too many people bickering and nagging, angry and unhappy, to continue believing that good relationships came much more naturally to heterosexuals than they did to homosexuals. I saw far too many older married men and women whose marriages seemed to have degenerated into little more than a matter of convenience, an unfulfilling partnership that was not worth the bother and anxiety of dissolving.

As gay liberation began to surface, more and more homosexuals sought legal marriages. I had mixed feelings. When I first came out in Albany I had heard tales of glamorous drag weddings held in private homes, which copied all the details of heterosexual weddings, but were not, of course, legally binding in any way. They struck me as little more than charades. If gay people could not marry legitimately and have their union recognized by the state—and the church, if they wished—there seemed little point in imitating the heterosexual ceremony.

Now that there were gay churches performing gay marriages out in the open, now that some states had been forced to recognize homosexual marriages because their laws fail to specify the gender of the marital partners, I was not certain what to think of it. I had always thought of myself as "monogamous," although I had come to believe that this by no means meant that everyone else was or should be. If I were to find a lover with whom I thought I could spend my life, should we marry?

There were, it seemed, some benefits to be gained: official recognition of the right of homosexuals to love and live together like anyone else, some tax benefits, and a legal recognition of the relationship between two lovers, establishing them as next of kin.

But there were also some serious drawbacks. I had no reason to believe that a legal marriage would make my family any more comfortable about my homosexuality. I also wondered how much marriage could do to increase the probability that a relationship would last. It seemed absurd to adopt the official form of heterosexual marriage only to be forced to adopt the official form of heterosexual divorce as well.

There were also personal matters of principle involved, beliefs I held which could not easily be reconciled with the fact of a legal marriage. I did not believe that the government had the right to declare that my sexual relations were criminal while those of married heterosexuals were legitimate. What else was marriage under law but the sanction of the state for a particular form of sexual relations? The institution of marriage implied that only men and women who had been duly recognized by the state as a legitimate couple had the right to sleep together and make love. The marriage laws were inseparable from all the other laws in which the government assumed the right to regulate sexual conduct: those against homosexual acts, and those against heterosexual sodomy, fornication, and adultery.

On the basis of my personal belief that the government had no business snooping in anybody's bedroom or telling them whom, when, and how they could love, there was little reason to seriously consider marriage myself. But what about other gay people?

I had seen enough of the damage done by straight society's insistence on conformity to shudder at the thought of re-creating it in the gay world. It made no difference what I thought about marriage. I had no more business saying that no gay couple should marry than anyone else would have to insist that I myself marry. I had no more right to impose on others the type of relationship that I happened to prefer than gay people who happened to prefer a more promiscuous life-style had to deny me the chance to seek love in my own way. We had all experienced straight society's attempt to make everyone fit one common mold, and the last thing I wanted to see was a repetition or compounding of that error.

Besides, the gay world was in flux. Gay people were questioning the nature of all their relationships, looking for new forms of interpersonal relations, new ways of expressing their sexuality.

In the gay world of ten or twenty years ago, stereotyped roles and expectations shaped the nature of gay relationships very nearly as much as straight society's demands shaped heterosexual relationships. Many of straight society's views about homosexuals influenced the way gay people saw themselves.

Straight society said that there could be no such thing as a happy homosexual, and sure enough, many homosexuals were wretchedly unhappy. Straight society refused to recognize or grant the slightest legitimacy to gay relationships; and sure enough, gay people found it quite difficult to hold their relationships together.

The message was often reinforced when young gays entering the bars were taught from the start not to expect love to last. Those who did find lovers and built a life together vanished from the bars. They were not there to show newcomers that other possibilities existed.

In many ways, the gay subculture became a mirror image of straight society, reflecting all the myths which the heterosexual world believed to be true of homosexuals. Perhaps this was inevitable; every homosexual was brought up in the straight world.

Some gay people assumed that all homosexual relationships must be patterned on the model of heterosexual marriage, that the casual relationships were necessarily wrong and unfulfilling. Only a permanent and exclusive relationship could lend an aura of respectability to homosexual love and sex. Failing to find this, some became cynical or embittered, while others struggled with inappropriate feelings of guilt. Entering the gay world roughly ten years ago at a time when many of these attitudes were still quite common, I was influenced by them myself. It was years before I really began to question them and attempted to define myself on my own terms.

Some gay people believed that all sexual relationships had to be divided into masculine and feminine roles. One person would have to be the "husband" and one the "wife." There was an emphasis on roles that is seldom encountered today. Many gays assumed that they must be either "butch" or "femme," instead of simply being themselves. This notion still shapes straight society's view of the homosexual, because it so neatly matches the widely accepted sexual roles of the heterosexual world. Speaking to a straight audience in a forum on homosexuality recently, Marc and I had enormous difficulty in making the absence of roles in our relationship understood. "But if you're both men, I don't understand how you manage to live together. Who does the shopping and the cooking? Who does the laundry?"

The appearance of the gay liberation movement reflects the enormous changes in attitude that have already occurred in the gay world. Few gay people today feel compelled to adopt any particular stereotype or role. Each person finds different ways to express his or her basic nature; everyone has elements of masculinity and femininity which should by no means be suppressed in order to meet the requirements of some socially approved role.

No one kind of relationship is expected to be appropriate for everyone. Each person has different emotional and sexual needs, and a wide variety of relationships and life-styles are required to fill them. Marriage cannot be proposed as an ideal relationship for most gay people, any more than it can be presented as the only viable form of relationship for heterosexuals.

In a sense, the straight world is just as victimized by the idea that marriage and monogamy are manifestations of natural law as some gay people have been.

Not everybody is temperamentally suited to marriage and children. Indeed, the movement for increased sexual freedom has led to the open appearance of various alternative forms of sexual relationships between heterosexuals: trial marriages, group marriages, mate swapping, and swinging. Straight society has slowly been adopting more of the sexual life-styles that have characterized the gay world in the past. It seems possible that the new types of relationships developing in the gay world of the liberation era will eventually gain greater currency in society at large.

## RELATIONSHIPS

Few of the myths gay people have about themselves have been more damaging to them than those concerning relationships. Borrowing the values of the straight world, many gay people searched for an ideal that had nothing to do with their real needs, while others were never quite satisfied with their relationships because these did not match their preconceptions of how relationships were supposed to be.

What were these myths? First there was the myth of the relationship itself: nobody could be happy who did not have a clearly defined relationship with another person. Neither impersonal nor casual sexual relations could lead to happiness. Only those who found a lasting and exclusive relationship could have a happy and fulfilling life.

This belief led to various stereotypes. The homosexual who sought only impersonal sexual contacts was looked upon by others as somehow inferior. Either he was neurotic or emotionally crippled, or he was struggling to deny his homosexuality, avoiding any deep relationships with other gay people because this might force him to identify himself as gay. Those who preferred the impersonal sex of the tea rooms, theater balconies, and other semipublic places had no interest in becoming involved in the gay subculture. Something must be wrong with them.

The homosexual who did enter the subculture but showed no interest in finding a permanent lover was often looked upon as overly promiscuous. He could not be expected to find happiness either.

There were numerous other stereotypes. Transvestites, the leather set, the S&M crowd, hustlers—all who did not fit the "proper" image of the homosexual were viewed as somewhat strange, and often as sick. The brand of conformity expected in the gay world was very nearly as rigid as that demanded in the straight world.

Unfortunately, many homosexuals who deviated from this expectation of a lasting and exclusive relationship still accepted it as valid. Expecting to be unhappy, they were unhappy.

The spirit of liberation in the gay world today has shattered these stereotypes, but it did not happen overnight. As homosexuals over the years began to question straight society's appraisal of them, they could not avoid questioning their own stereotypical attitudes as well. If it was not wrong to be homosexual, who was to say it was wrong to be a particular type of homosexual.

As gay people came to respect themselves, "respectability" in the gay world declined in importance. Everyone had the right to do his own thing and judge himself on the basis of how well he did it, rather than on the basis of what others did or thought should be done. The gay liberation movement and the new values it promotes could not have spread and grown with such rapidity had the attitudes of the gay subculture not been in flux for a number of years.

What does it take for a homosexual to be happy today? There is no pat answer. Because each person becomes a homosexual in his own way, each homosexual has different emotional needs to fulfill, different sexual tastes to explore, different ways to achieve happiness.

What about the person who seeks only the most impersonal sexual contacts, perhaps the person whose sex life is confined to the tea-room scene? It depends. If he is enjoying himself, this is as valid a life-style as any other. Many of the people who prefer to find a sexual outlet in the tea rooms have no interest in the gay subculture. They find the gay bars unappealing, clannish, and exploitive. Sex to them has little to do with romance or affection—it is an urgent physical need to be satisfied as simply as possible. For them, the tea-room scene is a sensible solution.

Many of the heterosexuals who frequent tea rooms do so for much the same reason. Sex is free, quick, and easy to come by. Their emotional involvements lie elsewhere. The gay people who prefer impersonal sex are not necessarily cold individuals with a limited capacity for love. Many of them have deep friendships with others—gay or straight—which mean more to them than any casual romance in a bar could. Their lives have a certain comfortable stability. They have as much sex as they please and are not as dependent upon youth or beauty for companionship as many of those who are more directly involved in gay life. In their later years, their friends will still be there.

On the other hand, not everyone finds impersonal sex satisfying. While engaging in impersonal sex, some find that it fills neither their emotional nor their sexual needs. Victims of the myth that gay people are shallow and callous, they wish there could be more warmth and affection. They have been told it is not to be found in the gay world. But they have been told wrong. It is time for them to make a change in their lives.

Those who go in for casual sex are often called promiscuous, or even compulsive. Promiscuity need not have a negative connotation. Many gay people find nothing more delightful than a wide variety of sex partners. Those who enjoy casual sex may feel that they are enjoying a marvelous opportunity to meet many diverse people, sleep with attractive and interesting individuals with a wide variety of sexual tastes and skills. Their emotional involvements may lie elsewhere—why should they consider settling down when a whole world of experience awaits them? The heterosexual parallels are obvious.

Not all gay people who enjoy casual sex, even those who sleep with someone new every night, can be considered compulsive about their sexuality. Some people's sex drive is much higher than that of others, and there is no reason to deny them satisfaction. But some gay people are compulsive about sex. Some go out night after night, occasionally have sex with several people, and yet never feel satisfied. Sex may become the only way in which they can express a deep need for affection and security, and yet their sexual experiences never seem to provide them with either. Again, if what one is doing leaves one unsatisfied and unhappy, it is time to find a way to break out.

The myth that only one kind of relationship—a permanent and exclusive relationship—could really lead to happiness has not vanished completely, but numerous different relationships that were rarely workable in the past now flourish in the gay world.

Some people find that easy involvement and comfortable disengagement meet their needs. Others feel they need something more permanent, if only for security. Not everybody is ready to limit his sexual experiences to one person merely to gain security, and there is no need to do so. Many people develop relationships in which they consider themselves lovers but continue to pursue an active sex life outside of the relationship. If both partners enjoy this sort of sexual freedom, or if the one who does not is not threatened by it, such a relationship can be remarkably stable and rewarding.

Other couples handle their desire for sexual experiences outside the relationship by drawing a third party into it from time to time. Some people even live quite comfortably and happily in *ménages* of various sizes. It is interesting to watch the development of heterosexual mate swapping and extramarital swinging. Heterosexuals still seem to have a great deal more difficulty carrying this off successfully than gay people do. While gays may lead a swinging life quite openly and never worry about a lack of acceptance by their friends, the average heterosexual swinging couple rarely feel free to swing in the open or discuss it with their friends or associates who do not share their tastes.

Things have become so freewheeling in the gay world that it may seem like a rather ideal milieu to some heterosexuals. If a wider range of acceptable options were open to straight people, it seems likely that fewer would choose monogamous marriage as the ideal.

Not all homosexuals are comfortable with so much freedom and diversity. Just as there are some gays who insist that all homosexuals ought to adopt the heterosexual form of marriage and no other type of relationship, others believe that the narrow sexual roles of straight society can only be successfully abandoned by compelling gay people to adopt new and equally rigid sexual roles.

Similarly, a few individuals are opposed to permanent and exclusive relationships of any sort on ideological grounds, seeing them as an imitation of heterosexual monogamous marriage. A dear friend, and certainly one of the keenest minds to be found in the movement, strongly disapproves of the relationship Marc and I share. He views what was once the ideal as the ultimate sellout to the straight establishment. He cringes at the thought that we expect to spend the rest of our lives together and that we have no desire to make love with anyone but each other—this is embarrassingly unliberated.

We think not. We can no more be expected to fit one common mold than can anyone else, gay or straight. Marc and I do not love as we do because it is more "respectable," but because it is what makes us happy.

## LOVE

When gay people enter into relationships based on love, they refer to themselves as "lovers." Straight people sometimes find this word awkward: for some, it conjures up visions of extramarital affairs, Don Juans playing at seduction, and star-crossed teen-agers becoming involved in romances of which their families disapprove. A few straight people have suggested that it would be better if Marc and I referred to ourselves as "friends," that this would more delicately convey the nature of our relationship to people not involved in the gay world.

While friends are a treasure in themselves, to refer to lovers as friends is not really accurate. When one begins to make love with a friend, the relationship has usually become something more than friendship.

Gay couples call themselves lovers because the word expresses the nature of their relationships. It is love that holds a gay couple together: they receive no approval or support from the state, the church, or even from their families in most cases. The way in which straight society treats gay people makes it difficult to preserve a relationship if the love upon which it is based is not especially strong.

Few gays today are willing to accept the myth that love cannot be found in the gay world. There are some forces within the gay world that make it difficult to preserve a relationship, but these are not as important as they were once believed to be.

New York, for example, has a reputation for the highest gay "divorce" rate in the nation, and Fire Island has been referred to as the one place where you dare not bring your lover unless you are absolutely sure of him. It is true that where there are many gay people and a very active gay life, a faltering relationship is put under additional strain. There are more attractive people to be met, sex is more readily available, and new romances are easier to come by. If one partner in a relationship no longer values it, there will be ample opportunity and temptation to look for something more satisfying —a realistic solution, I'd say. But love is no longer expected to hinge on fidelity. There is no reason lovers cannot have sex with whomever they please if both are comfortable with such an arrangement and their relationship is basically strong.

The wild social life of the New York gay bars and Fire Island is not typical of the gay world at large, however. Gay people in small cities and towns often have a much harder time meeting other gay people, but as a consequence they are more likely to stay together when they do. Where there are no bars and public cruising areas, people find it easier to settle down and lead a quiet life. There is less going on, fewer social attractions, and settling down with one person does not seem to involve giving up much personal freedom, as it sometimes does in the city.

In the cities, all types of relationships prevail, but those who find each other's company sufficient tend to vanish from the gay subculture itself and restrict their social activities to get-togethers with friends, rather than evenings at the bars. But no matter how quiet a life a pair of homosexual lovers may lead, they are subject to many pressures which make it more difficult for them to preserve their relationship than would be the case for a heterosexual couple.

Consider a heterosexual marriage. From the engagement through the wedding, the reception, and the honeymoon, the young couple receives the blessing of the church, the encouragement of the family, and the sanction of the state.

Contrast the experience of two homosexuals who become lovers. Their decision to live together and share their lives receives no official blessing of any sort. They are criminals in the eyes of the law, sinners from the viewpoint of many religious faiths. They can expect no public approval and congratulation. If their families know of their relationship, they are likely to see it as a source of embarrassment rather than joy.

Parents are often the most devisive factor in a homosexual relationship. Few families greet the news that their homosexual child has found a lover with any enthusiasm. Many gay people dare not tell their parents even that they are homosexual, much less that they have fallen in love and plan to spend their lives with another homosexual. If the truth does come out, many parents see the lover as evidence of their child's "abnormality" and often react to him with hostility and disapproval.

Many parents will not welcome their son's lover into their home. Forcing their son to choose between them and his lover, some parents lose the son in this way. Even if the lover is welcomed, the two may be expected to act as though they were two straight friends rather than lovers, show no affection for one another, and certainly not sleep together. The need to play this game may make family visits more an ordeal than a pleasure. Even if the relationship is well received within the family, most parents will expect the lovers to be on their best straight behavior in front of company or business acquaintances.

Even if there are no family problems, the gay couple faces other problems which a straight couple is unlikely to encounter. Some lovers are unable to live together—it is often difficult for two "single" men or women to lease an apartment together, and many standard leases specify that no additional residents are permitted.

When a man finally "settles down" and marries a woman, he is usually thought to be more stable and responsible, and will be more likely to be considered for promotion where he is employed. The man who takes a male "roommate," on the other hand, may find his chances for advancement curtailed if the fact becomes known.

Employment problems can place strains on gay relationships, but there are other financial inequities as well. Two lovers cannot file a joint tax return; both continue to pay taxes at the highest rate, that for single individuals. There is no legal provision for inheritance should one or the other die unexpectedly, so it is often necessary to keep finances separate, which is not only more complicated but also likely to be more expensive. If a gay person is seriously injured or hospitalized for any other reason, his family can effectively bar his lover from visiting him, for the two have no legal relationship as next of kin.

Marriage is a mixed blessing for almost everyone. Many of the problems faced by homosexuals are also encountered by heterosexual couples who wish to live together without marrying. Some gay people have turned to marriage for a variety of reasons, among them the belief that an official marriage will strengthen the relationship or make it more socially acceptable.

But marriage shows little sign of being the answer for most gay people. The antihomosexual attitudes of our society—many of them so deeply ingrained that they are scarcely conscious—place the greatest strain on gay relationships.

The fact that so many gay people do find love and are able to maintain various forms of fulfilling relationships says something about the quality of their relationships. When two gay people stay together it is because they love one another, not because society has encouraged them or made it easy in any way.

The beautiful thing about lovers is that they really do love.

# Is Gay Better Than
# Straight?

"But if you had really had a choice, wouldn't you have rather been straight than gay?"

This may be the ultimate question that can be put to a homosexual. Each must answer it for himself.

Until I accepted myself as a homosexual, I would have given almost anything to be straight. I assumed that I would be happier, life would be simpler, moral decisions would be easier, and I would have no problems if I were heterosexual. Many straight people probably wish that this were so.

Today, I wouldn't want to be straight for anything in the world.

In our society I may pay a certain price for being gay, but it is well worth it. I can't imagine that heterosexual sex could possibly be as enjoyable as homosexual sex. I can't imagine that heterosexual love could possibly be as deep and rewarding as homosexual love. I could never find the warmth, loyalty, and friendship among straight people that I do among gays. The straight life could never offer me as much as the gay life.

Why do I feel this way? Because I'm a homosexual. Heterosexuals find it equally difficult to imagine that anyone could really prefer a way of life and love different from their own. We all take ourselves as the measure of others.

### SEX

How can anybody really find sexual relations with someone of the opposite sex fulfilling? The differences between the two sexes inevitably impose limits on communication: heterosexual sex always involves some degree of mystery. Although some people find this mystery delightful, it is also the source of much of the crude and offensive humor about the female body that is common among men.

A woman knows a woman's body, and she knows it from the inside. A

213

man knows a man's body. He knows what it feels like to be male, and where he is most sensitive to erotic feelings. Men and women do not usually know each other's bodies all that well. Embarrassment often inhibits them from telling one another about parts of their bodies that are especially sensitive.

When two men or two women make love, they have a personal knowledge of the most intimate and intense pleasures which can be aroused in their bodies. They are more aware of the options available to them in seeking sexual fulfillment. Homosexuality certainly comes more naturally than heterosexuality, which often requires a good deal more instruction and practice before it becomes really satisfying for both partners.

Many gay people believe this to be true. They view straight sex as pedestrian and unimaginative. But what is the difference between gay and straight sex? Although heterosexuals often restrict themselves to fewer sexual practices than homosexuals do, no sexual acts are distinctly homosexual or heterosexual. Some gays believe that any act will be more enjoyable if those who engage in it are both of the same sex.

Who can prove this one way or the other? How do you measure pleasure? How do you rate an orgasm?

I say that gay sex is far better than straight sex, but I happen to prefer men to women. Somebody who has tried both and finally opted for heterosexuality no doubt finds straight sex far more enjoyable. People prefer what they prefer.

The simple matter of preference does little to explain the special fascination that homosexual relations seem to have for some heterosexuals. While there is a widespread aversion to the idea of homosexual sex, there is nevertheless a remarkable amount of curiosity about what is supposed to be a distasteful subject.

More female homosexual pornography is sold to heterosexual men than to lesbians. Many straight men have a sizable repertoire of homosexual jokes which are difficult to explain in terms of antihomosexuality alone. Much of the "homosexual" graffiti on men's-room walls is not put there by homosexuals.

Homosexual sex is often spoken of in terms of "bizarre thrills" and "weird kicks." Many seem to believe that there is something dangerously alluring about homosexuality—the glamour of the illicit pervades the subject. They suspect it involves unusual pleasures that can be almost addictive. Why else would anybody be a homosexual?

People often argue against public acceptance of homosexuality on the ground that legal reforms will lead to an enormous increase in homosexual behavior. If it were tolerated, previously straight people would try it and soon become hooked. This argument has always baffled me: if homosexuality is really unnatural, why would people rush to try it at the first opportunity?

Even if they did, would they find such "abnormal" practices so overwhelmingly fulfilling that they would lose all interest in "normal" sex?

This ambivalent fascination with homosexuality has many causes. Anything that is forbidden can be appealing. If something is so clearly unpleasant, why is there any need to forbid it at all? Perhaps it is actually quite enjoyable. When we find that many of the prohibitions in our society are unrealistic and misleading, we begin to take other prohibitions with a grain of salt.

Part of the appeal of homosexuality is due to the strict separation we make between homosexuals and heterosexuals: they are totally different types of human beings, sexual strangers to one another.

The sexual power of the stranger has been recognized in the context of racial and ethnic differences—the surprisingly powerful attraction or sexual tension sometimes encountered between blacks and whites, Jews and gentiles. This same phenomenon appears between homosexuals and heterosexuals. Some homosexuals prefer to have sex with straights who swing both ways. They consider a predominantly straight man more virile and exciting, more of a challenge. By the same token, many essentially heterosexual individuals find homosexual sex especially exciting and will sometimes undergo considerable risks to seek it out. Some straight men find homosexual men extremely virile and enjoy taking a "passive" role with them which they would find unappealing in a heterosexual context.

What makes the sexual stranger so interesting?

People who do not share our own way of life seem to be free of the inhibitions which we have acquired. Many people view the straight world and the gay world as so different that they hope to find greater freedom in the one in which they do not live. Because of the sexual diversity of the gay world, fewer gays than straights have these expectations.

Sex with somebody from a different milieu is not complicated by social obligations. There is less need to put a good face on things, maintain an aura of respectability: less pretense is involved. The heterosexual who has occasional sex with homosexuals does not have to pretend that he loves them, wants to see them again, or expects to marry them. Similarly, the homosexual who enjoys "trade" does not have to pretend that the possibility for a deeper or more lasting involvement exists, as he might with some other homosexuals.

Straights may hold homosexuals in contempt, yet feel more at ease with them. Because homosexuals are defined as sexual deviates, a heterosexual man can do things with a homosexual that he would not feel comfortable doing with his wife or another woman. He may feel guilty about asking a woman to blow him, because he views the act as degrading and contemptible. He is not required to respect a homosexual, so a blow job is of little importance.

Many straights have a secret fascination with homosexuality even though they never engage in a homosexual act. Because the average straight person cannot identify with homosexuals, he can more easily treat them as the objects of sexual fantasy. It may be easier to imagine acting out some sexual urges with a homosexual man than with a woman, because some sexual acts are considered taboo in a heterosexual context, while others are physically impossible.

Simply by engaging in homosexual relations, gay people break one of the strongest sexual taboos in our society. Having crossed the boundary, it is often easier to explore other new territory; so the individual gay person is likely to have a wider variety of sexual experiences than the average straight.

In the gay world, sex is a good deal more casual than in the straight world. Gay males tend to have sex with many more different people than straights usually do, and, of course, each new person has different sexual tastes and skills. The homosexual who sleeps around on a fairly regular basis can become quite experienced and proficient in a wide range of sexual activities.

When I first entered the gay world I was delightfully astonished at how much more experienced people seemed to be. The heterosexual relations I had experienced were incredibly tame in comparison. It was not only a matter of preferring men to women. The scope of sexuality was much broader and the pleasure greatly increased. To the extent that gay people bring more diversity into their sex life than straights, I suspect that they get more out of it.

Sexual diversity is not the exclusive prerogative of gay people. Many heterosexuals engage in the sexual acts that are usually considered to be "homosexual," but it appears that they are less likely to be completely comfortable doing so. Different varieties and combinations of oral, anal, and genital sex are common, but many straight people feel guilty or embarrassed about them because they are considered to be deviant forms of sex or "perversions." They may hesitate to suggest them to their sex partners or may regret them later. The less conventional aspects of their sex life are unmentionable.

In the gay world, nothing is unmentionable. Sex is discussed openly and with complete candor. Few gay people worry about offending the sensibilities of other gays, and few fear that others will think less of them for admitting their sexual tastes. Most gay people are sexually versatile and enjoy sex a number of ways, but those who have a particularly strong preference seldom hesitate to be frank about it with a potential sex partner.

The quantity and availability of sex is another factor which many gays consider a superior feature of the gay life. In the city, sex is generally available in one form or another whenever you want it. Outside of the city, however, homosexuals are likely to find it more difficult than heterosexuals to find sex partners safely. The belief that the gay world offers far more sex comes from the assumption that there is little sex to be had in the straight world. Some gays have a distorted picture about what is and is not available in the straight world because they take what straight society says about itself at face value.

Straight society pays lip service to a wide variety of moral principles regarding sex, but it would be naïve to imagine that public morality accurately reflects private behavior. Adultery is anything but uncommon, prostitution flourishes, and unmarried straights lead an increasingly liberated sex life these days. Sexuality is just as strong a drive in heterosexuals as it is in homosexuals.

In the Hamptons on Long Island, where many gay couples live on friendly terms with straights in these resort communities, the straight swinging singles scene has met with some local resentment. After years of hearing how offensive gay people are supposed to be with their flagrant sexuality, there is a certain amusement in hearing the complaints of the permanent residents in these towns about the hordes of summer "swingles" descending upon them, cruising the bars and the beaches. "Why can't they be more quiet and considerate like the gay people?"

In America, the permissible sexual behavior for both homosexuals and heterosexuals has been severely limited until lately. Straight people's interest in gay sexual diversity probably reflects a deeper fascination with the emerging possibilities for straight sexual diversity. When people of all sexual orientations feel free to enjoy their full range of sexuality, the notion of one type of sex being better than another will probably vanish, as, incidentally, will the rigid distinction between heterosexual and homosexual behavior.

## CREATIVITY

What do these people have in common: Tchaikovsky, Cellini, Proust, Rimbaud, Handel, Gide, Verlaine, Ravel, Caravaggio, E. M. Forster, Tennessee Williams, Jean Cocteau, Virginia Woolf, John Maynard Keynes, Langston Hughes, Benjamin Britten, Gertrude Stein, Stephen Spender, Aaron Copeland, Somerset Maugham, Noel Coward, W. H. Auden, Jean Genet, Sir John Gielgud, James Baldwin, Montgomery Clift, Michelangelo, and Truman Capote?

One of the few nice myths about gay people is that they are especially creative and gifted. There seems to be no way to prove or disprove this belief, but it is shared by many heterosexuals and homosexuals nevertheless.

In some fields of artistic expression, such as dance, it is widely assumed that homosexuals far outnumber heterosexuals. In others, such as music and literature, many of the great talents are generally believed to be homosexual.

When it is claimed that various creative geniuses of the past were homosexual, little chance for verification exists. Given the taboos surrounding homosexuality today, it is equally difficult to ascertain the sexual preference of a particular famous person. Few will admit they are gay, and those with a reputation to protect and a public to please are likely to be even more reticent than most. We do have several official "bisexuals"—Gore Vidal, for example—but even this admission can damage a career. *Sexual Politics* took a dive in sales when Kate Millett had the courage to speak freely about her homosexual experiences.

The nature of relationships between members of the same sex and the mores concerning them have undergone many changes throughout the course of history. Friendship has taken on different meanings at different times and has been expressed in different ways. To read every poem by a man about a man as a tribute to homosexual love would be as great an error as the more common practice today of interpreting all homosexual themes as evidence of platonic friendship.

We interpret the past through our present-day values, beliefs, and notions of what is significant. Because of our society's antihomosexual bias, many historical relationships have been stripped of their original homosexual content, and many works of art have been incorrectly interpreted in a heterosexual context. Greece, Rome, the Renaissance, and many other historical periods have been heterosexualized for modern consumption.

On the other hand, we sometimes overestimate the significance of the indications of homosexuality we do discover. Evidence of homosexual interests on the part of several poets and painters, for example, has led to the generally accepted belief that they were homosexual, in spite of the very active heterosexual lives they also led.

Changing interpretations of historical sources have led to long-winded controversies over the sexual orientation of this or that cultural giant. Were some of Shakespeare's love sonnets written for a homosexual lover? Even Freud's sexual orientation has been called into question. His sudden break with his friend Wilhelm Fleiss and his flight into self-analysis—"There is some piece of unruly homosexual feeling at the root of the matter"—has stirred some debate.

No method has been found to calibrate creativity or measure the influence of homosexuality on a person's life, so the connection between homosexuality and creativity is still a mystery. Still, so many of the major figures in literature, music, painting, philosophy, dance, the theater, etc., are widely considered to be or have been homosexual that it is difficult not to draw the conclusion that homosexuals are disproportionately represented in the arts.

Why?

Some say that homosexuals are are temperamentally suited to the arts and entertainment. Since there is no indication that such a thing as a generalized homosexual temperament exists—the diversity of the gay world suggests quite the contrary—such an explanation is too simplistic.

Frequently we think of art as one of the main ways of expressing powerful emotions, and some people believe that homosexuals are more inclined to be emotional than others. Whether this is true or not, the antihomosexual tradition in Western society has surely forced homosexuals to encounter situations that inspire strong emotions.

An individual's homosexuality may itself be a source of emotional struggle and turmoil—or of joy. Self-acceptance can produce as much elation as the lack of it can produce depression, and finding love after years of loneliness can make it seem that much deeper and more powerful. Different people have different ways of handling their emotions, but some deal with them by expressing them creatively.

Art can also be an affirmation of personal worth, a source of self-respect and self-esteem. Regardless of how harshly one is judged by society, one can assert one's validity through creativity. A work of art takes on an existence of its own, and society tends to judge it on its own merits. Because art, when successful, does bring public recognition, creative endeavors offer gay people a chance to win the esteem that is denied them as human beings. We will forgive our greatest artists almost anything.

Works of art also have a permanence, a life of their own, which provides a certain vicarious immortality for those who create them. Homosexuals do not typically have children, but art offers the homosexual another way to make his mark on the world. Few people like to feel that their life has had no influence on the course of events; few wish to be forgotten when they die.

These psychological factors may partially explain the high incidence of homosexual creativity. Some people have adopted a Freudian approach and suggested that homosexuals, often barred from expressing their sexuality openly, transform their libido into creative energy in order to find an acceptable outlet for it. But all of these explanations could be applied to individual instances of heterosexual creativity just as easily.

In our cultural tradition certain roles are designated for homosexuals just as they are in other cultures. For centuries, it has been more acceptable for individuals in arts and entertainment to be homosexual than for others, and certain artistic professions have been viewed as the almost exclusive province of homosexuals. Which came first: the creative role or the creative homosexual?

To ask why gay people are so often involved in the arts is to pose the same sort of question as to ask why the Jews have a history of financial success. Each culture prescribes certain roles for the minorities within it, professions which they are expected to enter, but which are not considered suitable for others. Jews were permitted and expected to be bankers and merchants—Christians were not. Homosexuals have been permitted and expected to be artistic and creative, while heterosexuals have often been discouraged from careers in the arts. The connection between homosexuality and the theater, for example, can be traced back to ancient Greece. The tenacity and longevity of cultural roles is sometimes astonishing, and they are so deeply ingrained that they are often not recognized consciously. Some parents discourage artistic interests in their sons and encourage them to become involved in sports instead.

Masculine and feminine roles are strongly involved in our notions of creativity. The artist is expected to be imaginative, intuitive, and usually subjective. These expectations run counter to the basic demands of the masculine role. Creativity tends to be viewed as a feminine trait.

Feminine inspiration is supposed to flow from intuition, imagination, and emotion. Women are expected to excel in decorative and domestic arts, although often in the pejorative sense of adding frills. They are permitted to be creative but not innovative, dabblers not artists.

Men are supposed to be practical, productive, and goal-oriented. They can't be bothered with prettifying things. They are supposed to be realistic rather than imaginative—they equate intuition with superstition. While men may be artisans, their inspiration is expected to be of a pragmatic nature. It is the function of the thing created, rather than the act of creation, that justifies and legitimates male creativity. Men seek to dominate their environment rather than harmonize with it.

A special role is set aside for the male artist in our culture. He is permitted an air of lusty, Dionysian madness, a peculiarly male form of imagination, inspiration, and intuition inappropriate in other men. The male artist is a mystical figure: the gods speak through him. He is a dreamer, but his dreams are bold and dynamic. Feminine imagination is expected to be fertile, but essentially passive. The male artist is actively attuned to the elemental forces of the universe—his insight strikes like lightning.

The role of the artist inspires awe in others. He is unpredictable, eccentric, less defined than the typical male. He combines the expected feminine sensitivity and expressiveness, but transforms them by virtue of his gender into something directive and forceful. The role of the artist is a privileged one. He is permitted a special leeway in violating the rules and taboos of his society; he is inspired and cannot be judged by normal standards. Sometimes, he's absolutely mad.

The blend of masculine and feminine in the role of the male artist and the greater freedom from social restraints have meant that homosexuals have been more tolerated in the arts than in other professions. As a result, gay people have tended to gravitate toward them.

When a young man first thinks he is gay and wonders what to do with his life, professions that are notoriously homosexual are likely to have a strong appeal. He can expect to meet other gay people, and his sexual orientation is less likely to hinder his career. One of the major reasons that we find a disproportionate number of gay people in the arts is that society decrees that this is where they belong.

Some young gays are so greatly influenced by these social expectations that they seem to doubt they can really be homosexuals unless they can find some sort of work in the arts. Some spend years at art school struggling to develop a talent they simply don't have. Many young gays try for years to break into the theater because—in the gay world—acting is considered to be the gay profession *par excellence,* as it has been for thousands of years. By the same token, some essentially heterosexual individuals adopt a homosexual life-style, and even come to think of themselves as homosexuals, because that is what society expects of people in their profession. Can you really be a hairdresser and not be a homosexual? Many people aren't sure.

It is surprising how often the straight world turns to male homosexuals for its masculine ideals. Acting, the theater, the movies, modeling—all seem to draw a disproportionate number of gays.

Outside of politics, the need to maintain a heterosexual public image is probably nowhere more strongly felt than in the fields of theater and film, yet it is in these areas that homosexuals are considered to be most numerous and influential. Actors are often groomed for the role of the ideal he-man: virile, aggressive, and highly sexed. Their success often hinges on how well the public responds to the image they create. Will their male public identify with them and seek to imitate them? Will their female public find them sexually attractive?

These things are seldom left to chance. Clothing is chosen by the impression it is expected to make, and a personality and life-style must be maintained both on the screen and off which will establish the actor as a viable commercial product. Considering the central role of *hetero*sexuality in theater and cinema, it is not surprising that homosexual actors usually feel called upon to go to extraordinary lengths to disguise their true sexual orientation. During the era of the big stars, many Hollywood marriages were little more than promotion gimmicks designed to tailor the public images of the individuals involved and serve as a cover for their preferred sexual activities.

A heterosexual image is also vital in male modeling. There is a certain wry satisfaction in spotting the gorgeous hunk who has been bowled over night after night on a TV commercial by his girl friend's sparkling teeth, lack of dandruff or detergent-soft hands—in the local gay bar. Some of the most successful men in Hollywood have risen through the ranks of hustling and modeling and occasionally turn up in vintage blue movies or back issues of gay picture books.

There is probably not one prominent actor who is not rumored to be gay, often inaccurately. Naturally not all actors or models are homosexual, but if everyone who *was* suddenly came out of the closet one day, many cherished straight illusions would be hopelessly shattered.

Another role often associated with homosexuality in other cultures is that of mystic or prophet. In some societies, homosexuals play a special role in the religious life of the community, performing rites of prediction, etc. In such cases, rather than being viewed as social outcasts, the homosexual priests or shamans are powerful and respected figures. Perhaps linked to this tradition is the expectation that homosexuals will have a deeper insight into the societies in which they live because of their separation from the mainstream of community life.

Could there be a relationship between creativity and nonconformity? Perhaps in failing to conform to our society's sexual standards the homosexual is not only put under additional social pressures that might find an outlet in creativity but also finds himself in the position of an outsider, one better able to observe and perhaps interpret the social reality of which he is less a part than the heterosexual. Straight literary critics have often attributed this distinct vantage point to homosexual writers. The same phenomenon might manifest itself in other creative endeavors by a greater freedom to break with conventional subjects and styles and initiate new trends. For better or worse, look at Andy Warhol.

The myth of homosexual creativity is abused by both gays and straights. A few gays claim that it is evidence of homosexual superiority. More often this indicates a painful lack of self-confidence rather than gay chauvinism. A few straights will attempt to discredit the artistic achievements of others by accusing them of homosexuality, as though this were necessarily a damning fact. Others will attribute their own lack of success to a homosexual conspiracy.

Some straights claim that homosexuals control the arts. They say that it is more difficult for a nonhomosexual to rise to prominence in some artistic fields. Others go further and insist that a secret homosexual elite controls the form and content of fashion, art, and music with an iron hand.

Such notions reflect fear and prejudice—and sometimes envy—rather than fact. There have been accusations that a willingness to become involved in homosexual relations is a distinct asset in the performing arts. On occasion this may be true, but no more than with the heterosexual parallels...the casting couch, the office party, etc. Most of these stories are apocryphal.

The idea that homosexuals may have an especially acute perspective on straight society also appears in a reverse form: those who have unconventional insights into society must be homosexual. Limousine liberals and effete intellectuals critical of establishment politics have been called homosexual, presumably because anyone with a different point of view must be somewhat queer.

One of the most curious ideas I have encountered was voiced by some of our less progressive political leaders when news of the gay liberation movement began to appear in the mass media. Homosexuality must be suppressed, they said, because it was becoming a fad—a fashionable thing among the hip set.

Personally, I have yet to meet anyone who has adopted a homosexual life-style because he considered it chic. Even among the most sympathetic and "right on" heterosexuals I've met, virtually all have taken exaggerated pains to make it clear that they were not gay. A lot of whites worked in the black civil rights movement, but very few straights join gay liberation. Somebody might get the wrong idea.

Occasionally homosexual creativity will be described as less worthy than heterosexual creativity. Some suggest that art by homosexuals is distorted and invalid, tainted by their "perversion." One of the more popular forms of this notion is that novels and plays written by homosexuals present gay relationships in the guise of straight ones and are therefore irrelevant to heterosexuals.

Edward Albee's *Who's Afraid of Virginia Wolf?* was attacked on these grounds. Some critics said that the play was not really about a heterosexual marriage, but about a homosexual "marriage." Who but homosexuals could treat one another like that? How could a heterosexual get anything out of the play?

These accusations of irrelevance seem to come from the idea that homosexuals do not have the same emotions as real people. Homosexuals, however, have had to make do with heterosexual plays, movies, novels, poems, songs, paintings, and soap operas all their lives, and have even found occasional relevance in them. Only in the last few years has it been possible to deal openly with homosexuality in the arts in this country, and some homosexuals are quite pleased that they no longer have to disguise their work beneath a heterosexual veneer in order to avoid having it ruled obscene.

Some gay people will embrace any hint that an important person may be homosexual simply because it challenges the prevailing low opinion of homosexuals. A certain amount of the glory rubs off, and an insecure gay may try to raise his self-esteem by identifying with or imitating a public figure who is rumored to be homosexual.

There are probably more rumors circulating than there are famous homosexuals, but it is difficult to separate fact from fancy. Let's face it: any prominent person who is considered sexually attractive will be suspected of being gay simply because it would certainly be nice if he or she were.

Nobody believes that all homosexuals are creative or that all homosexuals are more creative than heterosexuals, but isn't it great that so many gay people are talented and artistic? The world would be a less colorful place without us.

## THE "NEW" HOMOSEXUAL

The new homosexual is a bearded, beaded, long-haired graduate student in classical philosophy who believes that America is no longer a free nation.

The new homosexual is a brave young lesbian who went on saying "yes" when a young tough kept hitting her on the head with a tire iron and asking her whether she was still proud to be gay—while a cop looked on with disinterest.

The new homosexual is a barefoot Ayn Rand libertarian radical for capitalism in his early fifties who recalls that when he recited a few lines of amorous poetry to a policeman at a gay demonstration the officer "could scarce hide his blushes."

The new homosexual is a quiet little man who is a member of the Catholic Workers' Party, neither smokes nor drinks, and who hasn't missed a single GAA meeting in almost two years.

The new homosexual is a transvestite with a switchblade and high heels standing on the steps of the State Capitol with a megaphone in her hand telling the crowd that revolution is around the corner while her gold bracelets gleam in the sun and her eyes shine.

The new homosexual is an ex-priest on a picket line and a Protestant cleric confronting the police.

The new homosexual is the boy and the girl and the man and the woman next door.

The new homosexual is a grade-school teacher, a doctor, a lawyer, a plumber, a carpenter, a secretary, a gym teacher, a sportscaster, a sky diver, a former inmate of a mental hospital, a psychiatrist, an ex-convict, a policeman, a CIA agent, a peace marcher, a Young Republican, a business executive, an accountant, a mechanic, and a hairdresser.

The new homosexual is a nice Jewish boy in leather who couldn't housebreak his dog because he couldn't bring himself to spank it, and who wants to buy some land as far from the city as possible, build a home, raise vegetables and marijuana, and live happily ever after—and he will, because I'll be there with him.

The "new" homosexual isn't really new at all—he has been around for years, but you never saw him before.

The era of liberation has brought many changes to the gay world, changed many gay lives and many gay heads. What is happening among gay people today is truly revolutionary, but the spirit of liberation has not suddenly given birth to a "new" type of homosexual, as the mass media are inclined to suggest. They would have you believe that homosexuals used to be sick, unhappy, self-defeating creatures who have only suddenly become healthy, stable, delightful human beings.

Straight society has ignored the existence and value of one whole segment of the population, and has missed knowing many fine, warm, fascinating individuals living quiet lives—in order to be able to live at all. Early leaders of the movement spoke out in public when it was not nearly as easy as it is today. Older gays befriended young homosexuals when they first entered the gay world, lonely and unsure of themselves. Many gay men and women gave others hope by living fine, productive lives in spite of the difficulties imposed on them by society at large.

Perhaps there were fewer happy homosexuals in earlier years, but many showed remarkable dignity and strength regardless of their personal unhappiness. Many continue to do so today. Adversity can sometimes lead people to heights that others never dream exist.

These people have made the world a better place simply for being alive. They are sisters and brothers to me in a way that crosses all boundaries of age, sex, appearance, and life-style: without them I could not be myself.

Like other minority groups, gays have a solidarity less common among the more privileged. Fewer racial, ethnic, or economic barriers are encountered in the gay world than in the straight world. If there have been prejudices between gays with different life-styles or sexual tastes, these are minimal in comparison to the vast gap that society has decreed between heterosexuals and homosexuals.

Gays tend to think of other homosexuals as nicer people than heterosexuals. Gays seldom see straights at their best. Straights are interested in straights. It is with others of their kind that they show the better side of their nature. Every social group finds itself most congenial, most understanding and sympathetic.

Gays understand and respect one another. There has always been a sense of community in the gay world. The spirit of gay community is based on shared experiences of hostility from the straight world and some of the difficulties inherent in the gay life. The experience of oppression and sometimes of personal suffering has made gay people particularly sympathetic to the feelings and needs of others. They often protect and care for one another like brothers and sisters: everyone needs to have someone to turn to.

The impression that a "new" homosexual has appeared in America is a result of the sudden new visibility of the homosexuals who were there all along. The "new" gay life-style is the fruition of the trends toward freedom which have been growing in the gay world for decades. The pot has been simmering for years and has suddenly come to a boil. Gay people have been questioning themselves, their lives, and their place in the world since before there was any movement at all. Gay liberation is a grass-roots revolution in self-image and self-esteem.

As the gay liberation movement came into being, it served as a magnet for homosexuals of all ages and from all walks of life. Unlike the homophile movement of earlier years, it was aggressively visible and influenced a far wider segment of the gay population. The number of gays who have become actively involved in the movement is still comparatively small, but has already had a major influence on the gay world in general.

In the last two years, the movement has served as the focus of change in the gay population. Movement gays go back to the bars and are damned if somebody's going to tell them they can't express affection in public. They stand up for themselves and the new ideas spread. The atmosphere in the bars has already changed a great deal.

The movement has an inevitable effect upon the homosexual who is still in the closet. Never before has he seen gay people walking around town holding hands, leafleting on street corners, demonstrating in public. Never before has he seen homosexuals on television, or in the press; instead of being apologetic, they seem to be defiantly proud of themselves.

The closeted homosexual may not leave the closet, he may not even approve of the movement, but the facts register on him whether he likes it or not: homosexuals do not always get beaten up when they come out in the open—some will defend themselves; not all homosexuals are embarrassed or ashamed about themselves; politicians will actually speak to homosexuals and court their votes; the police are not entirely beyond the law. The homosexual in the closet may never come out, but the way he sees himself and the way he feels about himself slowly changes.

The gay subculture differs from most others in that nobody is born into it. Its traditions are passed on from generation to generation, but they are not so deeply ingrained—they have not been taught since birth. This means that the individual gay is more easily influenced as his environment changes; he is more open to the effects of new experience. The gay subculture is changing at a far more rapid rate than is possible for a more firmly rooted tradition.

The gay world of today will not be the gay world of tomorrow. The new spirit of liberation will transform it in ways that are unpredictable. It may be possible to get a hint of the new directions the gay life will take by focusing on the major center of change, the gay liberation movement, but we will only encounter clues there—the movement itself is evolving.

Gay liberation is revolutionary in impact. It means far more than a simple acceptance of one's homosexuality. It is a sweeping reappraisal of gay people's place in society.

The new atmosphere is one of growth and development, a search for new values to replace those which have been recognized as damaging or inadequate. It is a rejection of social conformity, an insistence that each person must derive his or her own values and morals from his or her own experience. It is an exploration of the joyful and a rejection of the tragic. It is pride.

As gay people begin to reject the values and judgments imposed on them by straight society, they become increasingly doubtful that the straight life lives up to all the claims made for it. Told that homosexuals are tragic figures, unable to form satisfactory lasting relationships with one another, the gay person today looks at the reality of heterosexual relationships and wonders on what grounds they have been presented as superior. It becomes increasingly difficult to view heterosexuality as any sort of ideal.

For some gay people, heterosexual society becomes virtually unintelligible. The denial and disguise of actual sexuality, its distorted and sometimes grotesque presentation in the advertising and the entertainment media, are astonishing, almost freakish. The gap between public morality and private behavior is often so vast that there seems to be no healthy reason for continuing the charade. In contrast, the openness and honesty about sex which characterize the gay world seem far more sane.

Some gays begin to see heterosexuals in much the same light that heterosexuals have viewed homosexuals for years. A new "straight mystique" is arising in which the stereotypical heterosexual appears as a tragic, self-defeating, sexually inhibited individual, hiding his sexuality in the closet, while the media exploit his fascination with sex and his need to live up to society's roles.

Can heterosexuals ever really be happy?

A rising sentiment of gay separatism is growing in both the movement and the gay population at large.

A minority of gays see strict separatism as the ultimate answer. They seek the formation of self-governing gay communities, in which straight people would not be welcome. A constant influx of new gay people is expected as young homosexuals realize that they must sever their ties with the straight world if they are to have a chance for happiness.

Most gays, however, do not carry the notion of separatism so far. They are anxious to meet straight society on an equal footing, but do not feel that they can be expected to beg for their rights or make special allowances for prejudiced attitudes toward them. After seeing the meager results of years of attempts at education and legal reform within the political system, they are tired and sometimes angry: what's the big deal? Why is it so difficult to respect our rights, to treat us like human beings? What's the big delay? "We've waited too damn long for our rights."

There is a growing frustration, a feeling that perhaps straight society's inertia is too great to be overcome. It is here that the seeds of separatism are to be found.

Even so, the vast majority of gays still hope for a rapprochement. They know that not all heterosexuals are prejudiced against them, and they have no desire to adopt a stereotype view of nonhomosexuals. They feel that American society as a whole is undergoing a renaissance, a revolution in values, and they want to be part of it. As they have come to take pride in themselves and their way of life, many gays feel that they have a great deal to contribute to the reinvigoration and improvement of our society.

Some of these contributions are already explicit. Gay people feel that the straight world can benefit by learning from the acceptance of diversity, the frankness about sexuality, and the wider variety of sexual and emotional relationships that characterize the gay world. Other potential contributions remain indefinite: exciting ideas are taking shape in the gay community which have not yet reached maturity.

The gay population is in flux, and new myths are emerging to replace the old ones that gay people believed about themselves. It is these new myths that will shape gay people and their world in coming years, and it is here that many gays feel their most valuable contributions to society at large will develop.

Probably the most important of the new myths are those concerning gay identity and gay culture. The gay liberation movement is unlike many other minority movements in that so much of its thought is directed toward the future. It is not just a matter of looking to the future for equal status with heterosexuals, but a redefinition of homosexuality in terms of what it will be instead of what it is or has been.

Racial and ethnic minorities often turn to their earlier cultural traditions as they strive to define themselves and their role in the world. But gay people have no separate cultural history of their own—they have been present in all societies. In some cultures, such as that of early Greece, homosexuality was highly esteemed, but nothing in the past can serve as the basis for a distinct gay identity or gay culture. This foundation that homosexuals are seeking for themselves can only be developed in the future.

Is there something which homosexuals from all eras and all societies have in common? Who knows? Gay people have seldom had an opportunity until the present to be themselves, to develop free from the constraints of a larger society and its antihomosexual prejudices and pressures. Gay identity has always been shaped by the stereotypes of straight society. What would homosexuals be like if they were free to develop as themselves on their own terms?

Homosexuals today speak of an emerging gay identity. Nobody knows how it will take shape. We can only guess at the future by examining today's trends.

The new spirit that typifies the movement life is enormously appealing. There is a much greater aura of freedom, a much greater expression of uncomplicated affection and sexuality. The barriers that existed for so long among gay people of different types are rapidly falling.

Gay men and women are finding that they have much to share and much to learn from one another. Transvestites and leather and S&M people are no longer looked upon as the outcasts of the gay world—their insights into our society and its sexual roles are highly valued. Having rejected society's moral judgments about homosexuals in general, it becomes increasingly easy to question all sexual standards. What's wrong with liking to dress a certain way? What's wrong with different sexual tastes if nobody's rights are violated?

You can admire a person who enjoys the most impersonal sort of sex and does so without guilt or apology. You can admire a transvestite who achieves a rare beauty and grace because she is proud to be herself. My lover and I would have encountered hostility and snide remarks a few years ago had we come to a homophile organization wearing leather jackets. Today people seem to find our relationship beautiful.

In the future will sex be impersonal, casual, or will it involve a deeper commitment than is common today? Will there be transvestites, fetishists, sadomasochists? Will there even be homosexuals and heterosexuals? Who can say?

The spirit of liberation is not an attempt to determine the future, but to free it to develop as it will. It is by being ourselves, accepting ourselves as we are, that we create new alternatives. Nothing will do more to loosen narrow social roles and bring new life-styles into existence.

In the movement today the trend seems to be toward a rejection of exaggerated sexual roles. To a greater extent than the feminist movement, gay liberation is an inquiry into the basic roots of sexual identity. Gay people are questioning the very nature of gender, without refusing to acknowledge its existence as some of the more radical feminists do today. What does it mean to be a man? What does it mean to be a woman? Are there essential differences between the two? How can individuals of either sex best realize their full human potential?

If there is a basic identity that is becoming prevalent in the gay world today, it is one based on a radical freedom and individuality, a refusal to be defined by others, a deep commitment to self-determination. In itself, this example can serve as a valuable influence on straight society.

It is becoming clear that many aspects of the gay world past and present have been nothing more than a reflection of the dominant heterosexual culture and its antihomosexual values. Straight society often finds the gay world repellent and disturbing because it encounters its own essential values mirrored there in a blatant and undisguised form.

The gay subculture has been largely a product of the milieu in the gay bars. Nowhere else have gay people had any opportunity to come together in large numbers, exchange ideas, and pass on a tradition. Although many aspects of the bar scene are positive, others have distorted the nature of relationships and tended to mold the gay life into a parody of the straight life.

In a society which tried to disguise its preoccupation with sexuality, the gay bars became the ultimate sexual marketplace. In a society with rigid sexual roles, masculinity and femininity sometimes appeared in the form of caricatures in the gay subculture. In a materialistic society, sexuality and affection were often a matter of money: if you were old or unattractive it was expected that you would have to pay for love.

As gay liberation has made its impact felt, many gay people have begun to reexamine the whole bar scene. Some see the bars as unredeemable, forgetting the comparative sexual freedom to be found there. The bars are seen as exploitive, free to overcharge for watered-down drinks because gay people are forced to accept unattractive, uncomfortable, unsanitary, and often unsafe places to meet for lack of alternatives.

Others, recognizing that the bars are at least a mixed blessing, seek to eliminate their negative aspects or to bring about improvements. A growing sentiment is developing that the bars are there not as a favor but as a right, that they should exist as a service for gay people and not as an opportunity to make money off them. In several cities, the local gay community has begun to bring pressure to bear on the bar owners and has managed to improve the bars significantly. In New York and some other cities, however, this means bringing pressure to bear on the Mafia—a dangerous endeavor.

The alternatives to the bars are rapidly increasing. Various gay organizations in many major cities sponsor dances, discussion groups, outings, picnics, films, plays, cabarets, street fairs, lessons in art—and recently in self-defense—on a regular basis, as well as innumerable and seemingly interminable organizational and committee meetings. Today the homosexual has a much wider variety of other places to meet gay people. The new alternatives are particularly valuable for younger homosexuals who are first coming out into the gay world.

As the alternatives increase, a tendency is growing to promote the development of an indigenous gay *culture,* not merely a mirror image of straight society, but a new counterculture arising out of inherently gay experiences, needs, and values.

Straight culture grows out of heterosexual needs and experiences and is structured by the primary economic necessities involved in child rearing and marriage. Gay people have no need to shape their lives or their relationships on these economic foundations—as homosexuals, they are unlikely to have children to provide for. They need not emulate the comparatively restrictive patterns of straight life, but are free to develop their own characteristic lifestyles and form the relationships they choose. As overpopulation becomes an increasingly urgent problem, it seems likely that fewer heterosexual relationships will center upon child rearing and marriage.

All of us, heterosexuals and homosexuals alike, will be forced to adapt to the changing conditions of our world in the latter half of the twentieth century. It seems likely that the evolving gay world will have a greater and greater influence in society at large as the emerging implications of heterosexuality in a world racked by the inseparable population and ecological crises become more evident.

A new gay sensibility in the arts may also arise in the developing gay counterculture. No longer should there be any need to write or paint or act for the tastes of the straight majority, no longer should it be necessary for gay people to disguise—and sometimes diminish—their artistic experiences behind a façade of heterosexuality. For many gay people, straight culture has already become increasingly irrelevant—and boring.

An increasing divergence between straight and gay culture seems likely. This does not necessarily mean that gay separatism will become the dominant theme in the movement or the gay population at large in coming years.

The cherished myth of the great American melting pot has become increasingly hard to sustain. Racial and ethnic minorities have not been subsumed within a generalized American culture as was expected and hoped. Instead of increasing tolerance and a blurring of differences, we have seen an increase in the tensions between different minority groups and a failure of our society to realize the democratic ideals of equality and solidarity.

In recent years, there has been a growing tendency toward a new and more far-reaching American pluralism. Many people have come to believe that there is much to be gained by maintaining distinct cultural traditions within society at large. Minority groups maintain more self-respect and are more highly valued when they seek to maintain a group identity and tradition. Many gay people today see no more point in attempting to become "heterosexual" homosexuals than most blacks see in becoming "white" Negroes.

Our attention is focused on specific movements today: third-world liberation, women's liberation, gay liberation. The social unrest underlying these distinct movements reflects a growing concern with human liberation in our society as a whole. There is no social group in our nation that enjoys an ideal life today. Some are more privileged than others, but we all suffer the limitation of our potentials, the denial of the full scope of our humanity, and the minor but constant indignities and frustrations of a fast-paced, over-burdened industrial society confronted by more problems than seem capable of solution.

Like our society as a whole, the gay world is changing at an ever faster rate. There is no reason to assume that gay is better than straight—the very nature of homosexuality and heterosexuality is evolving to match the times.

In a changing world, many people in the older generation feel a certain envy for the young, who will live to see a new, perhaps more decent society. Much the same feeling is common in the gay world today, even among those most deeply involved in the movement.

When I came out into the gay world, I faced many problems. It was difficult to accept myself, it was difficult to withstand the hostility of straight society, and it was difficult to know how to find happiness in the gay life. Many of my friends and I have speculated somewhat wistfully on the good fortune of young men and women today who are discovering for the first time that they are gay. These are truly the "new" homosexuals.

The new homosexual today knows that there are other gay people and where they are to be found: he or she reads about them in the paper, sees them on TV, notices them on the street. Young gays may still have difficulty in accepting themselves at first, and they may be discouraged by public hostility toward homosexuals, but a new message reaches them which has never been voiced before: *Gay is good, gay is proud.* What would it have meant to me and my life to have heard these words ten years ago?

Even the gays who are coming out now face problems that no one should have to face. Regardless of how many changes there are in the laws, it will be many years before gay people are really treated with dignity, respect, and equality in our society. We can all wonder what life will be like for the homosexuals of the future—what they themselves will be like—but all gay people today must seek what happiness they hope to find within the gay world as it exists in the present.

What chance does a homosexual have for happiness in the gay world today?

# Is the Gay Life
# Really Gay?

Straights often find it ironic that homosexuals refer to themselves as gay. Aren't homosexuals lonely, frustrated people, trapped in a web of their own neuroses? Why do they call themselves gay?

The derogatory terms used for homosexuals—queer, fairy, faggot, pansy, nelly, queen, and others—could fill a dictionary of venom. Even people who are basically sympathetic speak with clinical detachment of "homosexuals and inverts," and often lower their voices with a tinge of embarrassment when they do so. Until recently, few straights ever referred to homosexuals as gay people.

"Gay" was a word we had for ourselves. It meant that we were different —but it didn't have a nasty ring to it and it didn't sound like something out of a medical text. Many of us first heard the word when we met other gay people. We'd heard the other words for years, and it was good to have one to describe ourselves and those we loved which did not remind us of others' insults.

Long before the liberation movement appeared on the scene, homosexuals referred to themselves and their way of life as gay. The word meant more than "homosexual." Gay meant vivacious, warm, lively, witty. Sometimes it meant dancing while the ship went down. Sometimes it meant picking up the pieces and making the best of things. It meant that even if the affair was over, you'd meet someone new the next night.

It was a comfortable old shoe of a word, worn with use but better for that, a word you would leave in the closet when straight people came to call. Homosexuals did not refer to themselves as gay in front of straights; they did not even refer to themselves as homosexuals in front of straights back then.

Today, more and more homosexuals identify themselves as gay—with pride, sometimes with anger. The word has become an assertion of identity and legitimacy. It is a word of confrontation: it says, I define myself—you do not define me. "Gay" is to "homosexual" as "black" is to "Negro."

Many gay people consider society's distinction between "heterosexual" and "homosexual" essentially meaningless. They do not view sexuality as a reasonable basis for defining or categorizing human beings. But because society makes an issue of the matter and discriminates against homosexuals, they call themselves "gay" as a matter of principle.

The change in the way homosexuals speak about themselves reflects a change in the way they see themselves. But most homosexuals still hold back from identifying themselves publicly, and some have not experienced the changes that others consider so valuable. The gay world is still in flux, the old coexists with the new, and there is tension between them. The gay world is many things to many people, but it is not gay for all homosexuals.

## SELF-ACCEPTANCE

I had never been to Fire Island, although I had heard a great deal about it. I knew that during the summer months New York gays went out to the island in droves every weekend and that it was a notoriously wild scene. At the beginning of the summer of '71, a friend invited Marc and me out to the island to spend the weekend at the home of his lover, and we accepted.

As we took the ferry out from the mainland, Marc told me a little about Fire Island. There were two primarily gay communities: the Pines, with a population about 60 percent gay, and Cherry Grove, which was more than 90 percent gay. The Pines was the wealthier and more elegant of the two. The summer homes there were incredibly beautiful and obviously expensive. The homes in Cherry Grove were more modest, but still a far cry from the average living conditions in the city's gay ghettos. Many of them were available for summer rental, and some gays would scrimp and save all year just to be able to rent a house on the island for a month or two.

There were several good gay bars and restaurants, but the most elaborate social affairs were the wild parties held in the best homes. The beach was beautiful and a good deal of cruising went on there, but the Meat Rack, the prime cruising area, was even more heavily traveled. People would deck themselves out in the latest, sexiest outfits and stroll, until they met someone. Few other places could boast a busier sex life, and the weekly influx of New York City gays brought many attractive people to choose from.

The turnover in relationships tended to be high. There was so much sex available that most people found it difficult not to take advantage of it. If two lovers had a mutual understanding about going out on the side, they might see very little of one another during their stay. The atmosphere of sexual abandon could place strains on even the most stable relationships. There was something in the air that favored brief but intense summer affairs, regardless of one's commitments during the rest of the year.

We arrived in Cherry Grove after dark and joined our hosts at their home. Early the next morning we got up to go exploring.

I was enormously impressed. There were no streets or cars. The houses that lined the boardwalks became more and more luxurious as we walked along from Cherry Grove to the Pines. They were hardly summer cottages. Many of the houses were daringly designed, modern architecture at its best; some were better described as estates, complete with entrance gates, private boardwalks, and swimming pools.

By the time we started back to the Grove, it was already midmorning. People were sitting out on their patios giving the eye to people passing by: the simplest form of cruising—you didn't even have to leave home. If you saw somebody interesting, you invited him in for a drink, and that was that.

We had been exhausting ourselves with movement activities in the city, and I began to wonder whether it was really worth it. Fire Island was certainly the ultimate gay community. If it could exist, maybe homosexuals did not have it so bad. True, you had to be quite wealthy to build a home on Fire Island, but perhaps this was just the start. Maybe there would soon be many more openly gay communities, less expensive to live in. Few gays on the island had any interest in the movement, and many were actually hostile to it. All this demonstrating and shouting in the streets was embarrassingly bourgeois.

On the other hand, the atmosphere seemed remarkably unliberated. We saw no display of open affection, although some people camped outrageously, as though they were trying to go one better than straight society's stereotype of the homosexual. Marc explained that many of the gays who had homes there lived a totally closeted existence back in the city. Many of them were highly successful and guarded their reputations carefully, letting their hair down only during the summer on the island. There was even a small squad of police from the mainland who marched around lording it over the local gay people as though the gay life was tolerated only as a favor.

Many of the businesses were run by straights. At the local supermarket, David Reuben's viciously antihomosexual book was prominently on sale—the equivalent, in my eyes, of selling Ku Klux Klan manuals in Harlem. We heard that several straight entrepreneurs were organizing tourist excursions from the mainland to come out and see this "unique" community of homosexuals—rather as if the island were a game preserve or a zoo. We found it difficult to understand how gay people could tolerate these things in a community in which, for a change, they constituted an overwhelming majority.

That evening, when we mentioned some of these sentiments to our host, we received a very heated reply. The Pines and Cherry Grove were not homosexual communities, they were communities of men. Actually, when the population of Fire Island as a whole was taken into account, there were not nearly as many homosexuals as detractors liked to suggest. The homo-

sexuals from the city who poured into Cherry Grove and the Pines on week-
ends were troublemakers. The property owners would soon be taking steps
to bring this problem under control. Our friend, who had invited us, averted
his eyes while his lover went on, and we felt that it would be rude to argue
the matter.

Privately, I was shocked. I could not believe anyone would pretend that
the Pines and Cherry Grove were anything but gay. Why were the property
owners throwing all-male parties and cruising the boardwalks at all hours?
What was this business about sitting on one's patio, Tom Collins in hand,
ogling the attractive young gays from the city? Did he really think that gay
people detracted from the island—why, they made it what it was, one of the
most colorful spots on the Eastern seaboard, a tourist attraction even.

Perhaps my earlier doubts about the movement had been unfounded.
It was enough that the only place in the country where homosexuals could
build houses and live together openly was on the tip of an island several miles
off the mainland of the continental United States. But that they should be
policed by straight cops who swaggered around flaunting their authority,
that they should be concerned not to be taken for homosexuals in spite of
the incredibly open gay life—this was really too much.

The tendency for movement gays to be critical or condescending toward
those who have not left the closet is something I have always felt guilty about
when I observed it in myself. When I first became involved in the movement
I had been impressed by something one of its early leaders had said: "Straights
ask what we mean about oppression. I'll tell you what I mean. Gay people
are ten percent of the population, and they're almost invisible. Many straight
people don't know they've ever even seen a homosexual. Why not? Gay
people are scared—that's oppression."

Most homosexuals are afraid to come out in the open. Unlike many
other minority groups, gay people can remain invisible and most still choose
to do so. Many have pragmatic reasons for staying in the closet: employment,
family, reputation, safety. Some hide because they feel that they should be
hidden, that society is right in saying that it is wrong to be homosexual.

Accepting oneself is not a problem just for homosexuals. They are just
as subject as others to nagging self-criticism and dissatisfaction, but they must
also deal with their homosexuality. Society says it is wrong to be homosexual, and many gay people feel guilty as a consequence. Society says that
one can be a heterosexual if one tries, and some gay people are ashamed
because they have not found it within themselves to change. For them, the
gay life is anything but gay.

Many homosexuals find it impossible to reconcile their sexual orientation with their religious beliefs. Some who view homosexuality as a sin feel
guilty after each sexual experience, are unable to enter into any sort of loving

relationship with another homosexual, and despise themselves for lacking the "moral fortitude" to be something other than what they are. Others abandon religion. Some are able to work out a personal religious solution without explicitly rejecting the doctrine that declares them sinners.

Most of the major denominations today are reexamining their views on homosexuality, but it often seems to be a matter of too little too late. Considering the effects religious intolerance of homosexuality has had on millions of lives for centuries, the theological caution with which some churches approach the subject today seems callous.

The establishment of gay churches has helped some homosexuals retain religion as an important part of their lives. But many who cannot bring themselves to abandon their original faith continue to confess their "sin" while church fathers debate the issue.

Parents' reaction to their homosexuality makes it difficult for many gays to accept themselves.

Few families go so far as to disown their homosexual child. They may simply become cool toward him, less friendly and affectionate, or they may criticize him for not making a sufficient effort to change. They may treat his homosexuality as a skeleton in the family closet, or accuse him of tarnishing the family name. Some harp on the idea that he should seek psychiatric "treatment"; others try to arrange dates with women for him in the hope that he will develop heterosexual interests. Some parents maintain apparently cordial relations with their homosexual son, but have little to do with him in fact and discourage him from visiting them. If a homosexual has a lover, some parents refuse to allow them to visit together.

When a friend of mine revealed her homosexuality to her parents, she was told, "We still love you, but of course we won't be able to see you any more. Drop us a line every now and then so we'll know you're still alive."

Parents do not behave this way maliciously—they are as much the victims of society's antipathy toward homosexuality as is the homosexual himself.

My own parents have had trouble accepting me in spite of their real efforts to do so. They do not mention me to some of their friends because they have heard them express dislike or distaste for homosexuals and fear that they will lose valued friendships. A few of their friends have remarked that if they had a homosexual son they would disown him—how will these people react to my parents' attempt to understand me? It is a sad commentary that my writing this book in an attempt to explain some of the problems gay people face in our society will probably cause my parents and other relatives to face some problems themselves.

Many gay people, worried that the news might be so shocking as to be fatal, continue to hide their homosexuality to "protect" their parents. I doubt that most parents would wish their children to go on living in secrecy for years simply to spare them discomfort, but there are probably some who would not consider this selfish. A few parents even use their child's homosexuality as a weapon against him: how can you do this to us, how can you make us suffer so?

Family problems can be a major block to self-acceptance, and in recent years many gay people have formed consciousness-raising groups especially to discuss the problems they encounter with their families, how to tell them about their homosexuality, etc. Considering the difficulties involved in having a homosexual child, some parents might do well to imitate this example.

Accepting the psychiatric establishment's view of homosexuality as sick precludes self-acceptance for many gays. Too many accept the analysts' assumption that homosexuals are unhappy individuals, unable to enter into meaningful and successful relationships with others. Rather than devoting their energies to testing the validity of these notions, some gay people expend all their efforts trying to deny their homosexuality. When it turns out that this has brought them little happiness or love, the "experts' " analysis becomes a self-fulfilling prophecy.

Some people are not bothered by their homosexuality, but are unable to accept themselves because of the hostility they are likely to encounter from others. It would be easier, more comfortable—smarter—to be heterosexual.

Considering the barriers to self-acceptance, it may seem surprising that so many gay people do accept themselves. For many, self-acceptance is simply a process of maturing. Things that seemed enormously important during adolescence tend to fade and many people naturally grow more comfortable with themselves as they grow older. They have come to realize that few moral issues are as sharply defined as they once seemed. They are willing to give themselves the benefit of the doubt.

Some gay people find that it is enough simply to know that there are others like them. They become involved in the gay world and begin to pay less attention to straight society's attitudes. Finding acceptance among gay friends, they begin to develop some self-esteem. They find that they can live quite comfortably as homosexuals if they exercise some discretion. They stop feeling guilty for being different.

When this happens, some homosexuals reject the values or relationships which hindered them in accepting themselves. Some turn away from their earlier religious beliefs, some from their families. Some become cynical about straight morality when they see how seldom behavior matches ideals; a few come to view heterosexuals as sick.

Others accept the belief that homosexuality is neurotic but don't feel that it makes much difference one way or the other—everybody's neurotic these days, they say.

There are many paths to self-acceptance, and the majority of gay people come to accept themselves with greater or lesser difficulty. But self-acceptance is no guarantee of happiness in the gay world or anyplace else. Certain facets of the gay world are not designed to make happiness easy to find.

## THE GAY LIFE

You have to find your own place in order to be happy. This is as true in the gay world as in the straight world, and most people spend some time finding out about themselves, make a few false starts, a few poor decisions, before they find happiness.

The greatest danger lies in giving up too soon. Some people become embittered or cynical; others compromise on a life that is neither happy nor unhappy, fall into a regular pattern of behavior, a life-style, which they do not find really satisfying, but which is at least bearable and makes few demands even if it offers few rewards.

Whether or not a homosexual finds happiness in the gay world is often influenced by his first contact with it. If he lives in a small town he may never realize the extent of the gay world. His sexual contacts may be impersonal, and he may assume that these are the only kind available. If he enjoys them, he may be perfectly happy, but if he needs a deeper sort of involvement, he may be unaware that this is possible and live a very lonely and unhappy life.

It is not just those who come out far from the heart of the gay world who may not realize what it has to offer. Many homosexuals in New York and other major cities have never been to a gay bar. Sometimes these are people who simply don't like bars, but often they are struggling to deny their homosexuality. Other times they are people who have never questioned society's stereotypes about homosexuals. They see themselves as rare exceptions and want to avoid anything more than a peripheral involvement with the gay world and the "undesirables" who inhabit it.

Even those who have accepted themselves often fail to find happiness because they create situations for themselves in which there is little possibility for it. Unhappily married homosexuals would often do themselves and their families a great favor by seeking a more realistic arrangement. Homosexuals whose fear of discovery limits them to sexual contacts which do not fulfill their emotional needs often sacrifice happiness for financial security that is less likely to be jeopardized than they imagine. Some gay people need enlightened psychiatric help, not with their homosexuality, but with emotional problems which keep them from finding fulfillment as homosexuals.

Often gay people find themselves repeating self-destructive patterns of behavior that seem related to their homosexuality but are not. Some are compulsive in their search for sex, in spite of the fact that they do not really need this much sex or even enjoy it. Others may look for sex partners in situations that are extremely dangerous or in which they are likely to come to the attention of the police. People often put their sexuality to other than purely sexual purposes; in such cases, the problem is not the sexual orientation, but the self-destructive way in which it is being expressed. Some homosexuals who have not accepted themselves act out their self-hatred through their sexuality and would benefit from professional help.

Many gay people are lonely and unhappy until they enter the gay world. Their lives may change so radically when they do that there is a tendency to feel the millennium has arrived.

The opportunity to be oneself for the first time may have an enormous impact. After years of never daring to speak the truth about oneself, of having to maintain a constant façade, there can be a profound relief in encountering the openness of the gay set. Even if one remains closeted in all other areas of life, knowing that one can let one's hair down and speak positively about things that are otherwise taboo can make it bearable.

The joy of finding other people who do not consider one's feelings peculiar, one's sexual interests abnormal, can be so great that many young gays embrace the gay life unselectively. They may affect interests, opinions, and mannerisms that do not reflect their own personality, but those of the individuals they find most impressive. It sometimes takes a while to get one's bearings.

Primarily a social milieu, the gay world opens up a whole new range of potential acquaintances and opportunities for entertainment. If one is reasonably attractive and outgoing, one can rapidly develop a busy social life.

Although some bars cater to an exclusive type of clientele, the gay world is characterized by a degree of social mobility among different races and social classes not common elsewhere. One has the chance to meet and have sexual relations with wealthy and important people. A certain glamour and prestige derives from being courted by those whom one would not be likely to meet in everyday life.

A whole new world opens up for the especially good-looking young homosexual. The transition from social outcast to social lion can be so flattering that some young gays forge their identities around their desirability, developing rather swelled egos in the process. The gay life may be a social whirl for them, but as looks fade, these individuals often arrive at a more realistic and balanced self-appraisal that may make them feel a good deal less gay.

The easy availability of sex is another attractive feature of the gay world for some. Casual gay sex is readily available, comes in all varieties, and involves few responsibilities.

Straight people seldom take such a positive view of the sexual scene in the gay world; many speak disapprovingly about "homosexual promiscuity." It may be true that gay people are more promiscuous than straights, but by and large they have a greater opportunity to be so. In straight society, sex often involves responsibilities that simply do not apply to homosexuals. Many straight men and women would give a great deal for the chance to be a bit more promiscuous.

Many people encounter only frustration in their sex lives because they are trying to apply inappropriate standards to themselves. The person who is temperamentally suited to impersonal sex, for example, is likely to feel trapped and resentful if he forces himself to become involved in lasting relationships. The person who needs a great deal of affection along with sex will be miserable if he restricts himself to impersonal encounters.

Most of the sex that arises out of encounters at the gay bars or cruising areas can be characterized as casual sex. A person may strike up a conversation with a stranger or with a previous acquaintance. If they find they are mutually interested, they may go home together for a drink, a smoke, a chat, and then sex.

The average pickup is not impersonal. People tell each other a little about themselves. The visitor may leave after having had sex, or he may end up spending the night. What starts out as a one-night stand may easily turn into a brief affair without either partner making any claim upon the other. One can carry on several minor affairs at one time without much difficulty. Occasionally a lasting love will develop—every romance has to begin somewhere. Often, in the gay world, casual encounters lead to deep and lasting friendships, long after any sexual interest has faded away.

For some, the seeds of unhappiness are to be found in the very aspects of the gay world which other gay people find so enjoyable. A wild social life and readily available sex are not a real possibility for all homosexuals.

All too often, good looks serve as the primary mark of value in the gay world. The person who is unattractive may have some difficulty finding sex partners. The same goes for the straight world. But several factors modify the importance of good looks.

For one thing, unlike in the straight world, sex *is* very casual. No long-lasting commitments are entailed in an evening's sex, so few people choose their sex partners as though they might have to spend the rest of their lives with them. For this reason, while good looks are preferred, they are anything but essential.

Youth is said to be at a premium in the gay world. Aging can create problems for anyone. As one begins to look older, there is often a strongly felt need to prove that one is still desirable and sexually attractive. The older homosexual must often make rather drastic adjustments.

Readjustment is particularly painful for those who have relied principally on good looks in earlier years. As good looks fade into less glamorous maturity, some gay people suddenly find that they are no longer the center of attention. Some adapt gracefully; a few strive desperately to recapture or preserve the past, turning to cosmetic aids to hide the passage of time.

The mythology of the gay world emphasizes the plight of the older homosexual, claiming that if he cannot afford to pay for affection he will be desperately lonely. While some older homosexuals who can afford it do turn to hustlers and callboys, this picture of tragedy in later life is far overdrawn.

Like heterosexuals in the same position, most older homosexuals find that sex is a less important part of their lives than it was when they were younger. If they have no lasting relationship with someone else, they are still likely to have acquired a circle of friends with whom to share their later years, especially since they have continued to meet new people rather than having been somewhat tied down by a marriage.

Life is not usually dominated by sex for homosexuals, any more than it is for heterosexuals. Many straights and gays find their major emotional fulfillment in their jobs, political activities, hobbies, or creative talents in later years and—in some cases—throughout life.

Appearance and age are factors over which one has limited control. Personality and emotional makeup also tend to set certain limits on most individuals. In the gay bars, shyness can be a handicap. Unless you're a real knockout, you have to be somewhat aggressive in order to make out. You can't just stand in the corner and expect admirers to come in droves.

Those who are shy often have to develop a line of patter and enough self-confidence to approach others if they hope to find sexual partners with any regularity. It can be just as difficult to summon up the nerve to approach an attractive man as to approach an attractive woman.

For those who find it difficult to overcome their shyness or fear of rejection when they first enter the gay world, the gay life may be anything but gay, and the bar scene may seem like a compulsory nightmare.

The bars and cruising areas can appear as a necessity even for those homosexuals who are least able to function in such a milieu. Needing sex or simple companionship, they may be drawn to the bars night after night and, once there, find it impossible to make any sort of contact with other people. Some, unable to adapt, become regulars who never speak to anyone, always remain on the outside looking in, and occasionally drink themselves to an early grave out of sheer loneliness. Others are fortunate enough to find a lover as shy as themselves and are never seen in the bars again.

Is the gay life really gay? If we are asking whether it is frivolous, carefree, or effortless, the answer is no. If we are asking whether all homosexuals find happiness, the answer again is no. These things are not true of the straight life, and there is no reason to believe that gay people have it any easier than others. But if we are asking whether most gay people manage to find happiness, lead productive lives, and cope with the inevitable problems that everybody encounters in life—yes, the gay life is a good life.

## SELF-RESPECT

Should a homosexual come out of the closet?

For a few gay people, the secrecy of the gay world is an added attraction. In our fragmented society, many people feel a strong need to find some .nore specific focus of identification, something special to belong to or be a part of. Some homosexuals find that the gay world fulfills this need. They see it as a sort of secret society to which they belong, something that lends glamour and excitement—mystery—to their lives.

Those who enjoy the secrecy of the gay world are comfortable with the status quo in which homosexuality is illegal and mostly underground. If it were out in the open, they feel, it wouldn't be all that much fun. The whole business of maintaining a façade, so tedious and unpleasant for most, is an adventure for them. They may experience a thrill in seeing how closely they can flirt with the chance of discovery, how much they can get away with saying or doing without attracting real suspicion.

Most gay people, however, find little enjoyment in the need to hide and pretend. If they like the gay world, it is because it is gay, not because it is hidden.

It is not impossible to be happy living in the closet. The majority of homosexuals avoid drawing attention to their homosexuality, many take great pains to avoid its discovery, and yet most of them lead reasonably happy lives. There are occasionally irritations and inconveniences, but usually after a few years it becomes second nature.

The homosexual who leaves the closet, on the other hand, often encounters major problems. If he is unlucky, he may lose his job. Straight friends may no longer wish to associate with him. His relationship with his parents and other relatives may suffer. It is possible that he may be physically attacked if he makes his homosexuality quite evident in public.

Then what motivates gay people to leave the closet?

As might be expected, the motivations are diverse. Younger homosexuals are coming out in the greatest numbers. Many of them have tasted confrontation elsewhere: the black civil rights movement, the peace movement, radical campus politics. The gay movement is part of the larger youth movement, and the young in America today seem to have a particular sensitivity to principle, a streak of idealism that verges on the messianic.

Many gay people finally leave the closet because they want to integrate

their lives. Tired of maintaining a façade that has become increasingly
burdensome through the years, uncomfortable pretending to be something
they are not, they don't want to have to watch what they say or to whom.
No longer willing to hide their happiness or unhappiness and the reasons for
it, they want to start living as complete human beings and feel they have
that right.

No one motivation can explain the phenomenon of gay liberation. Just
as one's homosexuality is a very personal thing while one remains in the
closet, the reasons for coming out are ultimately personal.

I did not come out because I saw it as a matter of personal integrity.
It was really a rather accidental process.

I had a hard time accepting myself as a homosexual. I was anything
but happy during adolescence and the first years of adulthood. I struggled
with my homosexuality and attempted, if not to change it, at least to suppress
it. This got me nowhere, and I found myself stymied. I took a leave of
absence from college, got a job, and lived at home for a year until the
pressure became too great and I fled into the military. In the service, one
bad experience followed the next until I thought I could stand no more. In
a sudden surge of dazed relief one night, I attempted suicide.

There was no way to go on living as I had been. I began to realize that
I had not so much wanted to be heterosexual as I had wanted to be happy.
The two were not necessarily the same for me. I no longer cared whether or
not I was homosexual—all I cared about was learning to live with myself
happily. Everything else was secondary.

This was a start. Things didn't change overnight. Coming to a new
understanding of myself was not easy, and I was fortunate enough to find
support when I needed it most. So many things I had taken for granted
about myself and the world had to be rejected, so many new things had to be
learned. It was a full year before I really saw myself in a new light.

I accepted myself as a homosexual and realized that there had never
been any question for me of being anything else. It was not a grudging or
reluctant acceptance. For the first time in years, I really liked myself. I found
it hard to believe that I had spent so many years struggling and growing
steadily unhappier when the solution was so simple: all I had to do was be
myself.

I had accepted myself, but this didn't mean that I had left the closet.
I saw no reason to. With my family and close friends I was perfectly open
about being gay, but I avoided advertising the fact elsewhere. I was happy
and was finding life more rewarding than I had ever imagined it could be.

A few years later things were still going well. I heard about the Stonewall riot and took an academic interest in the appearance and growth of

the liberation movement in the months following it, but it never occurred to me to become personally involved. I had never been a joiner.

The following spring, however, in the aftermath of a love affair, I needed something to draw me out of myself. I wanted to start meeting new people. A friend and I decided to go to a few meetings of the different gay organizations in the city and see what they were like.

We happened to choose the Gay Activists Alliance first, and I never went anywhere else. At first I was even embarrassed to be there. I felt as though I were dropping in on a revival meeting of some sort. This feeling was soon transformed into an enormous respect for some of the people in the organization. I had never seen homosexuals carry themselves quite so proudly or speak so frankly and with such assurance.

Within a month I was thoroughly addicted to GAA, not so much on principle, but because of the changes it was working in me. I went to demonstration after demonstration. At first I would march quietly in the picket line and join the chants in a low voice, somewhat embarrassed about being so visible in public. Soon, however, I was leading the chants myself. It got to the point where I knew I would have laryngitis for a day or two after each major action.

I underwent enormous changes, saw myself and the world in a whole new light. Where I had once been resigned, it now made me angry to be treated as a second-class citizen, insulted and slandered, treated like dirt. I was impressed by one of my friends in the organization who would immediately escalate to indignant outrage during any confrontation. I saw him shake his fist in the faces of police and public officials and wondered whether I would ever become sufficiently uninhibited to express my anger so openly.

I found out that I could at the Fidelifacts zap. I discovered for the first time that there were years of anger bottled up inside me and that I could tap it whenever I chose. It was one of the most valuable discoveries of my life.

Letting the years of anger out was a purifying process which left me more free to enjoy life. The tensions and aggravations I had carried within me had only diminished my own happiness and self-respect. I had grown up feeling that rigid self-control was essential for survival, that anger was too dangerous an emotion to express. I suddenly learned that anger was healthy rather than dangerous. To express it was to direct some very appropriate emotions where they belonged, rather than inflict them upon myself. It was like removing a heavy burden from my shoulders: I felt really free for the first time in my life.

Invisibility is a seductive prison. Silence is a comfortable cell.

I had no reason to anticipate the feelings that were unleashed in me. I had not minded the small ways in which I denied myself in order to remain hidden. It took very little effort to hide—fear made it easy. I had felt no urgent need to stand up for myself, no burning urge to resist. I was willing to make the necessary compromises and avoid drawing attention to myself.

When I accepted myself as a homosexual, I also accepted certain limitations and restrictions. I saw these as facts of life, like skin color, height, age, and gender: constants. Part of being homosexual was the need to exercise greater discretion, to dissemble, to bow to the demands of society. These things were unavoidable, just as having black skin meant you would inevitably encounter some prejudice. Perhaps these things did not always have to be so, but for the present they were facts of life.

Inch by inch I had given in for years, stifling a feeling here, holding back a word there. I expected less, but that did not mean that life could not be happy. If you did not expect too much, I thought, you were not disappointed when you did not get too much. I never expected to be able to live the same life that heterosexuals led, so I felt no real anger or pain when day after day I held myself back from doing things they were entitled to do, hid the feelings they were entitled to express. Slowly, effortlessly, comfortably, I sacrificed a little part of myself each day, never realizing how much I had lost.

If I had had to make these sacrifices all at once, I might have rebelled. If someone had told me that I would have no right to love, to feel, to take pleasure in my own body, it would have seemed monstrous. If someone had told me that I would have to hide, lie, and dissemble for the rest of my life, I might have resisted. If someone had told me that if I broke the rules which *they* had set I could be locked up, beaten, brainwashed, spit on, called names, and subjected to indignities for the rest of my life, I might have fought to the death to defend myself.

But nobody told me.

It is easy to remain in the closet. You become your own jailor, your own cop. The better you get at hiding, the less you feel your restrictions. At the beginning, society knocks you down for breaking the rules. Soon you learn not to break them, and life becomes easy in comparison.

This is not an experience restricted to homosexuals. To a greater or lesser extent, every person in our society—perhaps in all societies—comes to accept limitations without ever realizing their magnitude. Life is easier if we can avoid becoming aware of how much has been done to us, how much has been taken away, for if the realization breaks through, the injustice of it is terrifying. How can you survive the struggle to regain all that has been lost? How can you avoid the struggle and still maintain your self-respect?

This is the rumbling in America today: the closet doors are opening for everyone.

Today most gay people are still in the closet. They are accustomed to their lives and never dream that they could live another way. Many find reasons to justify the restrictions they place on themselves. Others do not even think about it.

Leaving the closet is easier for some than it is for others. Those who stand to lose the most often find it most difficult. But the fears most homosexuals have about the consequences of revealing themselves are often magnified completely out of proportion. Partly this is because they serve a purpose. They help to justify remaining in the closet and take the sting out of the need to hide. Partly this is because until recently they had never been tested. Homosexuals have always assumed that straight society's expression of antihomosexual sentiments implied a readiness to act upon them. This is not necessarily true.

What happens when a homosexual leaves the closet? Usually he finds that his fears were unrealistic.

His parents do not succumb to the news that he is gay. They may ignore it, pretend they never heard it, or simply fail to grasp its importance. Some become upset or angry, some grow distant and cold. More often than not, relations slowly return to normal and may improve in the long run because of the greater honesty that is now possible. A few completely reject or disown their child when he reveals his homosexuality, but the value of their love in the first place is called into question by their response. Perhaps it is better for all concerned that the truth has come out.

Some gay people do lose their jobs when they come out, but many retain them. In any large city, there is seldom a problem in finding other employment, although some financial sacrifice is usually involved. In the last few years, large companies concerned about their corporate image have become increasingly reluctant to fire homosexual employees.

The danger of physical assault is not much greater out of the closet than in it. Unless one is easily identifiable as a homosexual by the way he dresses or behaves, nobody on the street is likely to take any more notice of him than in the past. It remains true that some neighborhoods are safe and others are not.

When they leave the closet, many homosexuals do begin to call attention to their homosexuality in public by wearing gay lib buttons, holding hands, or changing their mode of dress. Some consider this an essential part of coming out: they *want* to be identified as homosexuals—they have been mistaken for heterosexuals all their lives. They no longer want to be invisible, even unintentionally. It is a matter of principle and pride.

Several of my friends have been beaten up in public or harassed by the police for holding hands. Several people I know have been refused service at restaurants or otherwise mistreated when their gay lib buttons were spotted. But beatings are likely only in the rougher parts of town or when there are few people on the streets. Even the most militant gays usually show some discretion about where they make their homosexuality obvious.

Few homosexuals in any large city today need to fear that their lives will change drastically for the worse if they decide to leave the closet. It is the homosexual who lives in a small city or town who must still exercise a great deal of courage in coming out. It is here that beatings by hostile straight gangs or the police have become increasingly common. Often the formation of a fledgling gay organization triggers off a vicious backlash, and in a few small cities gays are already talking about organizing to defend themselves against such attacks.

Some homosexuals remain in the closet because they are uncertain whether they really are homosexual. Perhaps they have had numerous experiences with both sexes, consider themselves bisexual, or believe they may eventually adopt a heterosexual orientation. They believe that to come out as homosexuals will define them for once and for all in society's eyes, if not in their own. Often they have not accepted their homosexuality in the present and will not be able to accept it as part of their past should they become heterosexual. The heterosexual who feels he must deny having had homosexual experiences is just as much in the closet as the homosexual who hides his homosexuality, although it may be even easier for him to maintain his secret.

Some homosexuals are held in the closet only by the fear of what others will think of them when their homosexuality becomes known. They accept themselves, but they know that many straight people will look upon them as perverted, disgusting, or sick. They are sensitive, and it is important to them that others think well of them. It is true that straight people often do change their estimation of a person when they learn that he is homosexual, but fewer than might be expected consider homosexuality a matter of major importance. The homosexual who comes out in public may lose a number of straight friends, but those he valued most will usually stand by him.

Coming out would pose no major difficulties for many more homosexuals than have actually done so. Many stay in the closet, not so much out of concern over the consequences of revealing themselves, but primarily because they see nothing to be gained.

The gay person who comes out in straight society stands to gain a great deal more than just the freedom to be himself. There is the relief of not having to hide any longer and the pleasure of being able to speak frankly about himself, his feelings, and his way of life. But even these things cannot account for the increasing numbers of gay people who are deciding to come out.

The real value in coming out is emotional. Hiding usually requires so little effort that it is rarely felt as a strain, yet every time a homosexual denies the validity of his feelings or restrains himself from expressing them, he does a small hurt to himself. He turns his energies inward and suppresses his own vitality. The effects may be scarcely noticeable: joy may be a little less keen, happiness slightly subdued, he may simply feel a little run-down, stand a little less tall. Over the years, these tiny denials have a cumulative effect. Every feeling that was ever restrained, every word that was never spoken, every spark of anger that was quickly suppressed, leaves a lasting mark and seeks another outlet. Many of them do find an outlet, often in self-defeating ways.

When a person comes out, the dam is burst. He can get in touch with all his emotions. He feels his loves more deeply, his pleasures more keenly, and his anger in a clean and honest form—he is no longer fighting himself. It feels good. It is a precious discovery. It shows. Look at the faces of liberated gay people. Look at their eyes, their smiles.

But there is more to be gained than this. Every time a homosexual holds himself back, denies the validity of his emotions, accepts the need to hide, he silently agrees that straight society is right to force such a life upon him. He may accept himself, he may even respect himself, but that self-respect is never complete. There are always unacknowledged reservations.

Coming out is always a gradual process—you cannot change your life overnight. But most gay people who have left the closet recall a particular moment or experience that was especially important, the point at which they really knew they were free and would never hide again. For me, this moment occurred at the end of June in 1970 when the first march was held in New York to commemorate the Stonewall riot.

There had never been a gay march in the city before and nobody was sure how the police and the straight public would react. A good deal of contingency planning went on behind the scenes in case of violence. The crowd swelled and swelled, surpassing the wildest expectations. Suddenly we were off.

I doubt if the spirit of that first march will ever be recaptured. The crowd was defiantly beautiful. I had never seen so many different gay people, so many smiles, such radiance—where were the unhappy homosexuals I had heard about all my life?

Feelings ran high. We moved uptown past police lines, blue uniforms, billy clubs, patrol cars, flashing lights: I could smell the confrontation. Before we reached Central Park we were a tide flooding Sixth Avenue from sidewalk to sidewalk for blocks and blocks. We were strong, our voices rocked the buildings as we passed. OUT OF THE CLOSETS AND INTO THE STREETS! We were gentle: "I am a lesbian and I am beautiful," read a sign. We were a tapestry, a riot of color, a madcap dance, the last American revolution.

I reeled in the glory of it, walked as I had never walked before, soared. I looked up at the walls of glass and stone, at the tiny faces looking down, and laughed and shouted: *I'm gay and I'm proud.* I hadn't shouted since I was a child. When had I really felt proud before? The years of hiding and hating myself and putting up with things and hurting and lying and wanting to scream ripped through me and exploded.

There's no going back after that. You can't feel those feelings and take them back to the closet and nurse them. When you know what it really means to be free, you know that freedom is life. Do you know how it tastes to be alive for the first time?

Oppression in any form requires the complicity of the oppressed. To come out is to refuse to oppress oneself, refuse to play the game. To come out is to assert one's validity and equality and to declare that one will defend them. It is the only real form of self-respect.

There is no moral obligation to come out of the closet—or if there is, it is not one which any one homosexual can determine for another. We would never have been in the closet in the first place if we had not allowed others to make our moral decisions for us.

Freedom must be chosen.

# Appendix:
## Incidence of Homosexuality

Estimates for the number of homosexuals in our society varies widely. Some people will claim that everyone is homosexual to some extent. Others claim that only a tiny minority of people are homosexuals. Because a combination of heterosexual and homosexual experience is far more common than exclusive homosexual experience, there is no real way to draw a line between homosexuality and heterosexuality.

Kinsey and his coworkers approached the problem by concentrating on the balance between homosexual and heterosexual experience in any individual's life. They devised a rating scale which reflected the actual amount of homosexual experience far more accurately than the simple labels "homosexual" and "heterosexual."

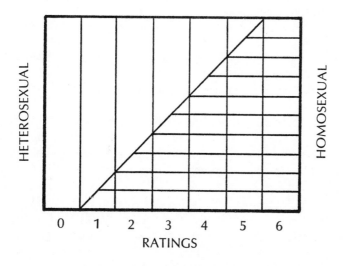

Fig. 1.   Heterosexual-homosexual
continuum

251

On the heterosexual-homosexual continuum (Fig. 1), a person rates 0 if he or she has no homosexual experience whatsoever. This includes "psychic" as well as physical responses.

The person who rates 1 on the scale has had predominantly heterosexual experiences, and only incidental homosexual experiences, not necessarily physical. These might include an occasional experiment with homosexuality out of curiosity, occasional feelings of attraction for members of the same sex, or homosexual experiences under extenuating circumstances, such as drunkenness.

The person who rates 2 has had more than incidental homosexual experience and has definite homosexual interests, whether or not he or she acts upon them.

Those who rate 3 on the scale have about the same amount of homosexual and heterosexual experience, physical or psychic. They feel no strong preference for either heterosexual or homosexual activities.

Those who rate 4 have more homosexual than heterosexual experience, but continue to have strong interest in heterosexual activities.

Those who rate 5 are almost entirely homosexual in their interests, but do have occasional incidental heterosexual experiences, psychic or physical.

A person who rates 6 on the scale is considered to be exclusively homosexual, and has no heterosexual experiences of any sort.

The heterosexual-homosexual continuum does not solve all the problems involved in determining the number of "homosexuals" in our society. A person's rating may change several times throughout life. Someone who rates a 6 may later rate a 4 or even become predominantly heterosexual. Similarly, an exclusive heterosexual, rating a 0, may later acquire a taste or even a preference for homosexual activities. There is no clear-cut way to determine whether a particular individual is heterosexual or homosexual and will remain so.

Kinsey attempted to clarify the situation by focusing on the percentage of adults—age sixteen and over—who had a particular rating for at least three years. Some of these would retain this rating throughout their lives; others would be classified differently during another period in life. The findings are shown in Fig. 2.

These are the figures that are usually cited when estimates of the incidence of homosexuality are made. Thus, it has often been claimed that one out of every six men is homosexual because 18 percent of the adult male population has at least as much homosexual as heterosexual experience for at least three years. But is this an adequate way of defining homosexuality? What about the man who has the same amount of homosexual as heterosexual experience for three years and then adopts an exclusively heterosexual life style—is he a homosexual?

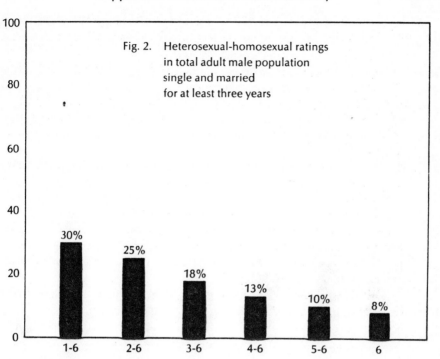

Fig. 2.   Heterosexual-homosexual ratings
in total adult male population
single and married
for at least three years

Those who say that 18 percent of the population is homosexual seem to be inflating the figures unrealistically. By the same token, those who wish to minimize the incidence of homosexuality often cite Kinsey's finding that 4 percent of the adult male population is exclusively homosexual throughout their lives. This means that they have no experience with heterosexuality whatsoever. This is an unrealistically low estimate—it would exclude most of the people I know who consider themselves to be homosexuals.

A far more accurate estimate of the number of homosexuals in the United States can be found when the number of people with each rating *at a particular time* is considered (see Fig. 3).

Close to 14 percent of the adult male population at any time is having at least as much homosexual as heterosexual experience, but certainly not all of these should be considered homosexuals or would consider themselves to be so. Something more than 10 percent but less than 14 percent have a distinct homosexual preference, but it seems safer to take the lower figure. Even so, not all of these people will consider themselves homosexuals.

Ten percent of the male population has enough ongoing homosexual experience so that they are likely to believe that society would consider them homosexual, even if they themselves are uncertain about their sexual

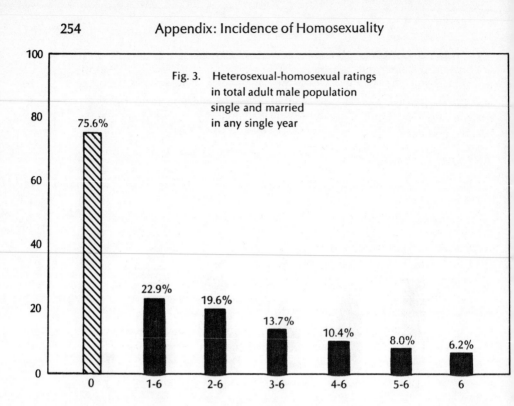

Fig. 3.   Heterosexual-homosexual ratings
in total adult male population
single and married
in any single year

orientation. It therefore seems reasonable to take 10 percent as the figure for the incidence of homosexuality among men.

What about women? If we want to know the part of the total U.S. population that is to be considered homosexual, we must take women into account as well. Kinsey's data on female homosexuality were less specific than those for male homosexuality. He found that the incidence of female homosexuality was approximately one half to two thirds that of male homosexuality. Thus, for the adult population as a whole, the incidence of homosexuality should be roughly 8 percent.

Percentages can be confusing and often misleading. The figure of 8 percent makes homosexual experience seem a great deal less common than it actually is, for this is the percentage of the population we would consider "homosexual," not that which has had some sort of homosexual experience.

Kinsey found that 37 percent of the adult male population had at least some homosexual experience to the point of orgasm. Fifty percent of those who remain single to age thirty-five have had an orgasm in a homosexual experience. Approximately 50 percent of all males have had at least some psychic response of a homosexual nature. Homosexual experience is anything but uncommon.

How accurate are Kinsey's data?

Kinsey himself suggested that the figures may be low. Those interviewed may have been reluctant to admit to homosexual experiences—some people may have refused to be interviewed due to fear of discovery of their homosexual experiences. The data on women may be inaccurate for a number of reasons. Physical intimacy between females is not so readily judged to be homosexual in our society as that between males. Furthermore, sexual relations to the point of orgasm in female homosexual relations are less common than among males, although the psychic responses may be definitely homosexual. There is reason to believe that gay women are more invisible in our society than gay men.

Forgetting—intentional or unintentional—of homosexual experiences must be taken into account as well. Many people would prefer not to remember their earlier homosexual experiences and seem to be quite successful in suppressing their memory of them. When Kinsey asked adult males about preadolescent homosexual experiences, only 48 percent could recall having had any, while 60 percent of the preadolescent boys interviewed admitted that they had had homosexual experiences. Considering the negative views our society holds about homosexuality and the reluctance to admit homosexual experiences they encourage, it seems reasonable to suspect that two thirds of the male population and one half of the female population have had at least some minor brush with homosexuality at some point in their lives.

Naturally, Kinsey's percentages are projections based on a sample of the total population, and specifically on white males and females. The incidence of homosexuality may vary somewhat in minority racial and ethnic groups. Some people, uncomfortable with Kinsey's findings, have suggested that his sampling techniques exaggerated the actual incidence of homosexuality in the U.S. population. Dr. Kinsey had this to say:

We ourselves were totally unprepared to find such incidence data when this research was originally undertaken. Over a period of several years we were repeatedly assailed with doubts as to whether we were getting a fair cross section of the population or whether a selection of cases was biasing the results. It has been our experience, however, that each new group into which we have gone has provided substantially the same data. Whether the histories were taken in one large city or another, whether they were taken in large cities, small towns, or rural areas, whether they came from one college or another, a church school or a state university or some private institution, whether they came from one part of the country or another, the incidence data on homosexuality have been more or less the same.*

*Sexual Behavior in the Human Male, Kinsey, Pomeroy, and Martin, p. 625.

The Institute for Sex Research at Indiana University, founded by Dr. Kinsey, undertook a major new study of homosexuality in 1968, which is expected to be ready for publication sometime in 1972. This study should update Kinsey's findings, and the interested reader would do well to remain alert for its appearance.

Until further data become available, the original Kinsey study remains the most comprehensive and accurate sexual survey to date and must be taken as the basis for any realistic estimate of the incidence of homosexuality in our society. Following these data, I have used the figure 10 percent for adult male homosexuality and 8 percent for adult male and female homosexuality.

There is bound to be some disagreement. The reader will have to come to a personal decision on the basis of the available evidence.

# Selected Bibliography

The following are not the only books that deal with homosexuality, but they are among the few I have seen that do so in an unbiased manner. As general reference works, they would be of value to both straight and gay readers. The lack of adequate scientific studies of female homosexuality testifies to the invisibility of lesbianism in our society.

HOMOSEXUAL BEHAVIOR AMONG MALES: *A Cross-cultural and Cross-species Investigation,* Wainwright Churchill, Hawthorn Books, Inc., New York, 1967. Absolutely *the* best book ever written on the subject.

PATTERNS OF SEXUAL BEHAVIOR, Clellan S. Ford and Frank A. Beach, Harper & Row Publishers, Inc., New York, 1951. A cross-cultural and cross-species examination of all human sexual behavior.

SEX OFFENDERS, Paul H. Gebhard, John H. Gagnon, Wardell B. Pomeroy, and Cornelia V. Christenson, Harper & Row Publishers, Inc., New York, 1965. A study of those arrested for sex offenses of all types.

THE GAY WORLD: *Male Homosexuality and the Social Creation of Evil,* Martin Hoffman, Basic Books, Inc., New York, 1968. A good overview of the gay world from a cautious sociological viewpoint.

SEXUAL BEHAVIOR IN THE HUMAN FEMALE, Alfred C. Kinsey, Wardell B. Pomeroy, Clyde E. Martin, and Paul H. Gebhard, W. B. Saunders Co., Philadelphia and London, 1953.

SEXUAL BEHAVIOR IN THE HUMAN MALE, Alfred C. Kinsey, Wardell B. Pomeroy, Clyde E. Martin, W. S. Saunders Co., Philadelphia and London, 1948. *The classic.* American discomfort over male sexuality may be reflected by the fact that Kinsey's original study is now out of print and difficult to come by.

THE GAY MILITANTS, Donn Teal, Stein and Day, 1971. A useful history of the background and the first year of the gay liberation movement.

SAPPHO WAS A RIGHT-ON WOMAN: *A Liberated View of Lesbianism,* Sidney
    Abbott and Barbara Love, Stein and Day, 1972.

For those in search of the gay world . . .

*Periodicals*

THE ADVOCATE, P.O. Box 74695, Los Angeles, California 90004. For good
    political coverage of the movement.

GAY, Four Swords, Inc., P.O. Box 431, Old Chelsea Station, New York City,
    New York 10011.

*Guides*

THE ADDRESS BOOK, 2166 Market St., San Francisco 94114. Guide to the
    U.S. and Canada for gay men and women.

For further information on available guides, and periodicals, write: Oscar
    Wilde Memorial Bookshop, 291 Mercer St., New York, N.Y.
    10003.

*The Movement*

A listing of gay organizations across the United States is available through
the Institute of Social Ethics, Central Station, Box 3417, Hartford, Connecticut 06103.

For information on gay organizations in individual cities—or advice on how
to organize one—contact: National Gay Movement Committee, Gay Activists Alliance, P.O. Box 2, Village Station, New York, N.Y. 10014.

λ The *lambda,* first used by GAA-New York, has spread across the
country and is rapidly becoming a national symbol for gay liberation.